**PERTH AND KINROSS COUNCIL
LEISURE & CULTURAL SERVICES
LIBRARIES & ARCHIVES DIVISION**

This book is due for return on or before the last date indicated
on label. Renewals may be obtained on application.

TO THE POLES
(Without a Beard)

TO THE POLES (Without a Beard)

The Polar Adventures of a World Record-Breaking Woman

CATHARINE HARTLEY

with Ying Chang

ISIS
LARGE PRINT
Oxford

919.8 (LP)

First published in Great Britain 2002
by Simon & Schuster UK Ltd.

Published in Large Print 2003 by ISIS Publishing Ltd,
7 Centremead, Osney Mead, Oxford OX2 0ES
by arrangement with Simon & Schuster UK Ltd.

British Library Cataloguing in Publication Data
Hartley, Catharine
   To the poles without a beard: the polar adventures
of a world record-breaking woman. – Large print ed.
   1. Hartley, Catharine – Journeys – Polar regions
   2. Large type books
   3. Polar regions – Discovery and exploration
   I. Title
   919.8'04

ISBN 0–7531–9894–0 (hb)
ISBN 0–7531–9895–9 (pb)

Printed and bound by Antony Rowe, Chippenham

For my family and for Geoff Somers

Acknowledgements

Mary Hartley — my wonderful, adventurous and extraordinarily understanding mother
Oliver & Louise Hartley
Gargy
Gilly Yeatman and Geoffrey Cotton

David Keys — my Guru who has shaped my life and without whom I would have achieved nothing

Jane Edden — who inspired me all those years ago to be brave and who continues to be such a loyal rock

Claire Messenger — without you I would have undoubtedly tipped over the edge!

My flat mates Nikki Ashley and Jo Finnie who tirelessly saw me through both journeys with humour, positive encouragement and unconditional support, managing base camp London superbly

Geoff Somers
Victor Serov
Veijo Meriläinen
Grahame Murphy
Steve Peyton
Justin Speake

Fiona and Mike Thornewill
All without whom . . .

Paul Landry and Matty McNair. Thank you for hospitality and encouragement and for never doubting I could succeed

Pen Hadow
Anne Kershaw

Liza Helps for mind-blowing selfless generosity

Trevor Gardiner, Chié Nakagawa and Brent Escott of Club Direct Travel Insurance
Simon Gilfford of Manugistics
Georgina Meddows Smith
Tina Price
Thank you all for taking the gamble and giving me the opportunity

Jane Fleury for providing me with such incredible support and nurturing me on my journey from a terrified floor assistant

Ying Chang
Natasha Fairweather
Helen Gummer
Victoria Hobbs
Thank you for giving me this wonderful book writing opportunity. It's undoubtedly been my most enjoyable journey to date

Maggie Millman and The Fresh Horizons Team at The City Literary Institute

Shane Winser at the Royal Geographic Society
Rebecca Stephens

The Marylebone Mountaineering Club for providing a haven of sanity where I felt normal

John Bradshaw — thank you for not giving up

Finally my Father, who was with me every step of the way and would be so proud of this book

Catharine Hartley

My greatest thanks are to Catharine herself, for allowing me to participate in the making of this book. Her story is so singular, her character so distinctive, and her friendship always so true that my part in the writing has been pure enjoyment. Natasha Fairweather guided the project impeccably. I feel very privileged that this book has brought me into contact with her intellectual discrimination and emotional refinement. Helen Gummer and her colleagues, Cassandra Campbell in particular, were always encouraging, kind and amenable, despite an exigent production schedule. Hilary Foakes gave wise advice to us regarding the possibility of this book from years before it came into existence. Finally, for their warmly given assistance to me in the early, tentative stages, I should like to thank Sarah Castleton, Jill Crossland, David Dees, Rita Petrilli and Anne Taylor.

Ying Chang

Contents

The South Pole

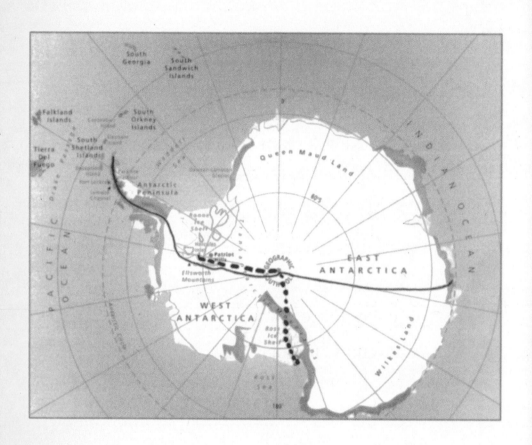

Key:

- - - Our route — "Plebs to the Pole"
•••• Captain Scott's route
——— Geoff Somers' 1989 Trans-Antarctic route

The North Pole

Key:

- - - Our route — "The North Pole in Style"
• • • • Alternative route from Russia

"Just as you are about to give up, take one step forward and then another . . ."

Mandi Upward

PROLOGUE

At the Top of the World

There is nothing at all at the North Pole. It is exactly the same as every other patch of ice around it. So there would be no visible culminating point, no gigantic scientific base as there is at the South Pole, no grand finale. Only the reading on our satellite navigation instruments would tell us when we reached our goal — 90 degrees North, 0 minutes, 0 seconds, or as close to it as the global positioning system (GPS) machine would record — 89°59′59″. Paul, our guide, paid close attention as the figures slowly climbed, and the three of us followed his tracks, as he weaved to and fro making the necessary corrections to our direction.

Suddenly, he stopped and shouted. We had arrived. It had been a journey of fifty-six days, and over 480 icy miles, arduous, but almost enjoyable, with stunning scenery. At first, we simply laughed and giggled from elation and sheer relief. We could not take it seriously;

we just skied about, bumping into each other. Then, in a moment of seriousness, Paul took a ski pole and planted it into the ice. We each put a gloved hand on the stick and announced that on Saturday, 5 May 2001, we had arrived at the North Pole.

Fiona and I were not only the first British women to walk all the way to the South Pole and now the North Pole, we were also the first women in the world to man-haul to both — no machinery, no dogs. I could not take in what we had achieved. Now Paul burst into tears, and without thinking I gave him a hug, a grateful, elated hug. I had never imagined I would succeed; for the next hour I was light-headed with happiness.

We had decided it would be the last day, but the Arctic Ocean had tried to disagree. Instead of smooth, flat pans over which to pull our sleds, we faced one big ridge of ice rubble after another. As we pushed, lifted and hauled our loads over each obstacle, it had seemed endless.

After about twelve hours Mike pointed out what must be a Russian icebreaker on the horizon. We could not believe it. How could a Russian ice-breaking ship have come this far? We became very excited. We started planning to go on board for tea. Maybe they would give us vodka, whisky even. Wow! How exciting to be able to talk to other people after all this time! Fiona even wondered if they would have shampoo and a hairdryer that she might borrow. I wondered about the sailor boys. It kept us going for the next two hours, and all our irritation disappeared.

At the next break we asked Paul if he thought the ship was near enough for us to visit. Yes, he said, but we would not get inside. Because, of course, it was not a ship. It was actually an ice formation that looked like one. We did not believe him until we looked through Mike's telephoto lens and sure enough, it was just ice. So we kept going, concentrating on just putting one foot in front of the other, trying to keep up our enthusiasm. In sixteen hours, I had eaten thirteen bars of chocolate. In the last hour Paul took charge of the GPS. At around 89°58′ with just one mile to go, we stopped to take out our cameras and attach our Union Jack to Fiona's sled.

It was not simply the last hour of two months or the last mile of 400 for me. It was the culminating point of an eighteen-year journey, both physical and mental, to become my own person. The patch of nothingness I stood on that day had a significance for me that reached back into the whole of my adult life.

CHAPTER
ONE

An Ugly Duckling

When I decided to walk to the South Pole I was neither a hardened explorer nor an expert in fundraising and public relations, but a dreamy London stage manager. I was looking for a new direction in my life and when I realized that no British woman had ever yet walked to the South Pole it became my new goal to visit this little-explored wilderness and have that adventure. In the end I made two very long, very cold journeys that were voyages of self-discovery and comedy too. But when my adventures began, I was completely ordinary, literally, the girl on the Clapham omnibus.

I cannot hope to convey the repetitiveness of walking all day, day after day, pulling my sled. And if I could, you would not want to read it. On the whole, the terrain was completely constant, a flat or flattish plateau. Only two things could successfully fight the boredom of the days, the infinite, beautiful landscape in front of our eyes, and a constant fantasy life inside my head. So I will spare you the drudgery of putting one ski in front of the other and instead tell you a more human story of how this all came to be and how it took place as much in frantic urban preparations as in the solitude of the Polar wastes.

Although inspired by the great Polar explorers, my journey was undertaken in a very different spirit to theirs. So my story is different too. I have never dedicated my life to daily doses of pain, suffering and puritanical redemption. I was, I am, a thirty-something city girl who left behind a life of failure, too many cigarettes and much too much alcohol, in search of self-respect, in search of myself.

I was born in Withington Hospital in Manchester and spent the first six months of my life on the fourth floor of a block of flats. As I sat in my pram, I had women above and below and either side of me, cooing and giving me attention. Perhaps as a result, I became an extremely quiet and contented child, kind, and more gentle than self-assertive.

My mother was an artist specializing in calligraphy and stained glass, my father a careers adviser and true English eccentric, with a gloriously dry sense of humour. After my father died, my mother took up travelling herself. Her solo journeys included going to Papua New Guinea and indeed to Antarctica on a Russian icebreaker. It was all the more admirable because she was diabetic and dependent on injections of insulin twice a day. So I can say that adventure ran in the family.

When I was four, we moved to the south coast. This was where I really grew up, above all in Chidham, in a farmhouse which my mother bravely bought derelict and restored.

My mother, and her mother before her, used to go on holiday to Sark, one of the smallest Channel Islands. I first went myself when I was seven, and I loved it immediately. It was only three miles by two, it had no cars, and was a place of utter tranquillity. There was nothing to do except eat, read, and go for short walks. As a place that never changed, it had an impression of comforting familiarity about it and became my second home.

Even as a child, I liked challenges. Each year in Sark, I would walk right to the north end of the island. At low enough tide, I could balance on a rock just big enough to hold my two feet. Had I lost my footing on the rock, which was always slippery from the waves breaking over it, I would have fallen to certain death. This seemed terribly exciting; I do it to this day. To get to the end or top of things was always somehow important to me.

My brother, younger than me by three years, turned out wild. I loved him completely. He was mischievous, always getting into trouble and always in detention. He grew up to be charismatic and a great raconteur. Everyone wanted to be his friend. My brother's wildness was thought suitable for boarding school, while I was keen to stay at home, so he went to Wellington College and I to the local comprehensive. I know my mother always felt guilty about this, but I never remember feeling hard done by. I just remember, even at that early age, being intrigued to see how we would both turn out.

I was not very good at my lessons, so I found school difficult. It was made even harder because I was hopeless at sport. In those days we had to suffer being picked for teams. I was always the last to be chosen. I couldn't catch or hit a ball, and when playing rounders I was always deep fielder. I would walk miles away from the pitch and sit making daisy chains. Being so bad at sport was demoralizing — it meant bullying and few friends and stripped me of confidence. To this day, I loathe and despise any form of competitive sport and I still cannot play rounders on the beach, not even with friends. Later, I was to find that many people who went expeditioning or climbing were laying the ghosts of being failures at this kind of sport, though I cannot say how consciously this influenced me.

My religious education teacher, a wonderful woman called Mrs Lancaster, was the person responsible for what would be a turning point in my schooling and a signpost to my future. She liked me. She found my awkwardness endearing and asked me if I would like to form a drama club with her. Surprised and intrigued, I agreed. In improvization classes I put my own persona into imaginary characters and exaggerated it. People were hugely entertained by this. They loved it and even laughed. In my fourth year at school, Mrs Lancaster offered me a leading role in the first-ever school play and I played a dotty aunt in *The Italian Straw Hat*. The role came easily to me. The whole school was required to attend and, suddenly, I found that attitudes changed. The bullies decided I was quite "cool" to know, I made friends, and although my sporting skills had not improved I stopped being the last to be chosen. In rounders, extraordinarily, I began to manage to hit the ball and soon afterwards I even caught one.

I duly left school with O (ordinary) levels in religious education, music, English and dressmaking, but I failed my two A levels. I did not really have any academic options. I suppose it was predictable that, instead, my chosen career would be in the theatre. I decided to go to drama school. But during my first amateur dramatic production, when I was backstage, not acting, I saw an actor burst into tears from the anxiety of having to learn and remember lines. So on impulse, I changed my application form to apply to be a stage manager. I had, however, chosen a profession that required methodical organization, something I had yet to learn.

My career, if that is the word, was unorthodox. I worked for various opera, ballet and repertory theatre companies. There were few permanent jobs in stage management, so my contracts invariably lasted anything from two weeks to five months. It was an industry largely for young people. In many ways, it was a wonderful and special time for me, in particular my time at the Nuffield Theatre in Southampton.

We were all in our early twenties, energetic and enthusiastic, although we often played to houses half-empty or worse. Our hours were long, usually 10a.m. to 11p.m., Monday to Saturday. We would spend most of our nights smoking bongs the size of lampposts, and chewing the cud about life, the concept of infinity and, most importantly, boys. The combination of these open theatrical people and the artificial aids allowed me to lose my inhibitions and taught me how to express myself. Moreover, we had an excellent boss who allowed us to be ourselves, however extreme that might be, so long as we did the work.

Whether it was then my real character or just a pose I had adopted from self-defence, my manner had its problems. One day, we were transferring a controversial Russian play to the West End. Much of the action took place around a television. On the morning we opened, the one on stage broke. I was sent off round Southampton to find a new one — a new, working 1970s TV, that is, although it was ten years later. It took me till 3p.m. but I succeeded, to everyone's relief. I had saved the day. But just as I left Southampton to drive the TV to London, there was an enormous bang. Sure enough, I had not shut the doors properly. The television had fallen out of the back of the van and smashed all over the motorway.

I took a deep breath, and walked back into the office. "Hi chaps! Bad news about the TV. Fell out of the back of the van." My boss turned red and left the room without a word. I noticed my stage manager in tears of hysterical laughter. He took me to see an Eddie Murphy film to cheer me up. Of course, the next day, the entire theatre knew.

At the end of each contract I would pack all my worldly goods in the back of my 2CV, say goodbye to everyone that I had become so involved with and drive off to a new town, a new life with new people, but the same old plays. And frustratingly, the same old me. In retrospect, it was a very unsettling way to conduct my life. I had no base and no one group of friends — they were all scattered over the country. My life was the theatre, largely from the unsociable hours I worked. I knew no one outside and had no hobbies. But I was happy in my own simple way. I was cocooned in this fluffy thespian world and it felt very safe and very comfortable. I wanted nothing else.

For several years, I had a boyfriend called Julian who did similar work and had the same contentment. Very early on, I invited him to go sailing; growing up by the sea, this was the one sport I was reasonable at. He was terrified of water since being caught under a wave as a child, but I reassured him that my captaincy would be flawless. As we set up the sails, I noticed that the bung (the stopper for the drainage hole in the back of the boat) had been stolen. Annoyed that I might have to cancel and lose my chance to impress, I ignored this. It is a trait of mine to press on to my goal and ignore any obstacles and if this was an advantage in my polar odyssey, it was not so here.

Off we went. We had packed the boat with a picnic and we planned to sail to an island for a romantic swim. It was a beautiful afternoon; maybe he would tell me he loved me. Alas, the wind rose. Water seeped into the boat through the unstopped hole. Before I knew it, the boat had filled with water, and Julian was panicking. I told him we would simply go back, but as the boat was now completely submerged, this was wishful thinking. I made a half-hearted attempt to row before seeing it was hopeless. Julian and I began to tread water while I looked for escape.

Help came — a yacht hove to. Julian was near to tears and I struggled to give a rational explanation to the three couples and their children on board. The yacht was skippered by a formidable businessman, who did not hide his contempt at my incompetence, but suggested he collect my boat, which had drifted ashore, using the yacht's own dinghy. Unfortunately, his dinghy's motor failed after he set off, and he too was stranded in the mud.

The tide now fell too low to allow the yacht back into harbour. The children were whimpering for their home comforts, the adults muttering about being late for work on Monday. We decided we should look for the poor skipper and accepted a lift from a boat small enough to enter harbour. But for the others the price of their kindness was the next seven hours (until 3a.m.) spent afloat till next high tide.

We quartered the area for hours without success, but next day I found the yacht in the harbour — with the skipper. I could say nothing, other than brandish two bottles of malt whisky at him as an apology. Silently, he took them, but handed me a brush and soap so I could remove the mud accumulated when the boat had run aground. Five hours' scrubbing later, he let me go. The next day my own boat mysteriously turned up on my parents' drive, but Julian himself promptly disappeared for a fortnight.

These anecdotes of buffoonery are not here to amuse you, or not just to. They give a picture of me as a young woman. I felt lovable and popular only because I was so scatty. I entertained people; they found me endearing. I was shy, so I hung on to any personality trait that made me popular and I played up to it. I wanted to be taken seriously, to be respected, to be good at something other than making mistakes. But I was so shy that I could not even say anything in a group of a few friends, so I would remain silent. I would then feel inadequate for being boring, so I would stand up and trip over just to get a laugh.

I had always longed to travel, ever since I was a child. I wanted to go to places that were undiscovered. I spent hours poring over my mother's atlas of the world. I was curious about other cultures, especially those which were rarely visited. As early as thirteen, I remember planning a trip to Papua New Guinea as I thought it the last place on earth still untouched by Western civilization. At the age of fourteen I had had a weekend job as a chambermaid in a grand hotel in Chichester. I used my wages to open a travel fund. I graduated to selling ice creams at the festival theatre, then I was working for my living, and all this time my travel pot grew. At the age of twenty-three, I set off to Thailand with my friend Rachel for six weeks' "real" backpacking. On my return I would marry Julian.

I was immediately disappointed. I thought I might find the wild travel and unspoilt locations I had dreamed of. Instead I found myself hanging in hammocks and eating mushroom omelettes. In an attempt to get away, we headed up to Mae Hong Son and trekked among the northern hill tribes. Two days we walked and two we rafted, ending up in a village high in the mountains. At last I was hopeful that

I might be somewhere unused to tourists. Perhaps the children would find us amusing, even frightening. Instead, we were greeted by a villager who spoke perfect English and took us to his makeshift bar to sell us Coca-Cola. Then we were ushered into a house where we were given tea, but asked for money. The children, far from being timid or curious, were pushy and direct, demanding sweets and presents. Later, we were given an obligatory pipe of opium for ten baht. It had absolutely no effect.

"It's *your* day today, Cath, we'll do what you want, and then go back to the coast."

Rachel was now drained by my constant desire to get out of civilized society. I had felt the village to be a sham. It had reminded me of those events in London where tourists are served fish and chips and serenaded by women in Victorian costume. But we were close to the Laotian border, and the guidebook said the last town was quite "Wild West", difficult to reach and best avoided. This was all the encouragement I needed. We went by truck, then motorcycle. When we arrived in the town I persuaded another truck to take us further. My aim was to cross the border itself, knowing full well it was closed.

Eventually we reached the Mekong, the river separating Thailand from Laos. I was desperate to cross. Over the other side I could see women bathing topless and carrying children on their backs in cloths. It was a new culture, a forbidden land. But before long we were stopped by an hysterical farmer making throat-slitting signs and firing an imaginary gun. He led us into a field, put us on a truck with his daughter, and told the driver to take us away. Later, his daughter explained that had we crossed, the Laotians would have executed us as American spies. Rachel was extremely frightened, and vowed never to let me have a day of my choice again, but for me the experience was phenomenally exciting; I wanted to go back and find a way across that river. Or another one.

When I returned, Julian was there to meet me with open arms. Mine were closed. For the first time in my life I had been taken away from my creature comforts, my eyes opened and every other sense made alive. I had only scratched the surface, but I could see there was so much more to life than theatre and marriage. By the end of the week, Julian and I had parted company and I began planning a trip to Papua New Guinea. I knew that this country was the home of indigenous tribes that really remained undiscovered by Westerners.

My next job was at the Glyndebourne opera as assistant stage manager. My tasks were simple — to set props in the right place, make tea and sit in on rehearsals poised with a handkerchief or a glass of water. We also had to memorize each movement made by the actors and re-enact them for the lighting director to put effects in the right places.

The scenery was built by twenty crew, all men, who lived in the so-called "Huts", a den of every imaginable vice. It was the ultimate honour for any girl to be invited in to play, and just to gain kudos in the company, even if only from my choice of boyfriend, I became involved with one of them. He was a bad man, nicknamed the Axe Murderer by my mother. The "Huts" were an eye-opener, and my new home.

One day there was a dress rehearsal. I had an easy job — I always had the easy ones, because I was not thought capable of managing anything complicated. During a scene change one wall of the set collapsed, destroying the props and furniture. The damage was repaired before the performance, and was not in any way my fault, but to my horror I overheard the director and the stage manager talking.

"I suppose all this happened because Catharine was head ASM."

"You've got a point there."

I did not cry, I got through the show, went to my room and took a long hard look in the mirror. Nobody took me seriously. My boyfriend was an alcoholic moron who showed me no respect. I thought very seriously and realized I had arrived at a decisive moment. I had to change my life. That night I sat and wrote a list of all the character traits I hated in myself and also those I liked.

The good side? Kind. Full stop. A good start, maybe, better than being a mean old cow. But the "hates" column went on and on. "Unable to hold a conversation, terrified of social situations, inability to succeed, thick, simple." I had another vice — drinking. At most social functions I would get blind drunk. I preferred gulping to sipping. My favourite was tequila. Sometimes I would end up in a gutter and, recently, I had become so drunk I woke up in a strange bed, naked, alone and unaware of how I had got there. "Alcoholic mess," I wrote.

Then I thought back to Thailand. I remembered how much I loved travelling and how little I feared. The best plan, then, would be to set out with my list, but alone. This would mean I would have to introduce myself to and converse with strangers. I would have to be organized and to survive on my own abroad. A week later, I turned down another Glyndebourne contract and planned my character-forming travels instead. To my family's horror, the Axe Murderer decided he wanted to go travelling with me, and out of lust I agreed.

We did not travel well together. Not long into the trip I ran away to Alice Springs, a small town right in the middle of Australia. Few stayed for long, for most it was just a stop on the way to Ayers Rock. Here I managed to be given a job in a travel agency. My boss was vile, so no resident would work for him. Instead, he employed young, vulnerable, female travellers like myself and tried to seduce them, harassing them if they refused. Fortunately for me, he had just opened up a new shop in a hotel, which I ran by myself, and he had two pretty, very young blondes to work beside him in the office.

I took lodgings in the local YWCA, where I shared with a group of extraordinary people. We were all on the run — one woman from a mental institution, another from her husband, an armed robber from the law, and I from my own broken heart. Alice was that sort of place. White wine spritzers became a thing of the past and I quickly learned to drink beer and Bundy rum.

One day, I overheard the armed robber saying: "I think that Pom is a tart." I was furious and banged on his door. I took two steps inside until my face was next to his and shouted at the top of my voice: "If you want to get on in this dump, don't you ever call me a tart! Do you understand me?"

He apologized profusely and became a perfect gentleman. I couldn't believe what I had done. It was the first time I really remember standing up for myself.

Alice felt claustrophobic, which was odd as it was in the middle of such a huge continent. Then I understood. The nearest towns were over a thousand miles away, Darwin to the north and Adelaide, south. There were no means of getting away for the weekend. Instead, for seven months, I was part of the mad local community. With time, my heart healed and I was ready to move on.

I spent an extraordinary year living among indigenous tribes in the Solomon Islands and Borneo. My life was simple — getting up in the morning, bathing in the river or the sea, eating, going into the jungle with the women to collect berries and vegetables, then endless evenings attempting to communicate and drinking copious amounts of rice wine. The natives must have thought me very strange, but they never showed it. Perhaps it was just that we had no real common language for them to quiz me, but all I experienced was unfailing kindness.

In Borneo it took many days to reach these remote villages. I would take a boat as far as I could into the jungle and then sit and drink tea in an "urban" village. I might have to wait days, in which case there would usually be someone willing to put me up in the village, although occasionally I would have to camp. Sooner or later I would meet jungle dwellers who had come to buy provisions, and eventually, through these chance meetings, I would always be invited to stay with a family. Then I would stock up on rice and fish as a form of payment for the hospitality I was about to enjoy, and be taken even deeper into the jungle by canoe. It never occurred to me that absolutely nobody knew where I was and how much trust I was putting in my host family.

I was blissfully happy. I had time to stretch myself in other ways, meeting new people, jumping out of aeroplanes, climbing on glaciers. All the time I was shortening my list of character flaws. Each day I gave myself a new challenge, however small, introducing myself to a new person, or organizing the next journey with perfect efficiency. It became addictive, and I became reckless. Towards the end I was so sure of myself that I took risks, such as hitchhiking alone in Brunei. And then I moved on to risking the lives of those around me . . .

CHAPTER
TWO

Looking for Directions

The heat of the afternoon sun was overpowering, the tree was barely four feet high, its shade minimal. I tried climbing it to see if I could see anything, a fruitless gesture. I joined Ina, my German companion, under the tree. We were completely lost. What if we waited here? Maybe someone would come and find us. No, no one knew we were here except the hut warden, who was clearly a crazy hermit. And how on earth would one find anyone in this massive wasteland? I thought about waiting until nightfall and then lighting a fire to attract attention. But then I realized that in this searing heat it would only start a bush fire. I had absolutely no options and Ina had fallen into a fitful sleep.

We had been travelling in Java, where I wanted to climb a mountain in the remote Baluran National Park. A truck, then a motorcycle had taken us there and we stayed at a tiny hostel with a watchtower. The motorbike would return for us next day. The solitary warden gestured towards the mountain. If we started early and just followed a stony path for two hours before climbing up, we could be there and back by noon.

At six we set off. After two hours and nowhere near the foot of the mountain, the path ended. Of course, I decided we should continue. Ina accepted my bullish confidence. After another hour, the foot of the mountain was still far away. Now the heat began. We had not brought lunch, imagining we would be back by midday. Our water supply was dwindling rapidly and I noticed Ina was tiring and light-headed — sure signs of dehydration. Even I realized we had to turn back. But we had no compass either.

I looked around me. The terrain was very flat, dry savannah desert with just a few trees. It now struck me that if we did not retrace our footsteps exactly we would miss the stony path and therefore the hut. It was, after all, in the middle of a massive expanse of scrubland. And if we missed it, we could be walking for ever. Without food, and in temperatures of 40°C and with only half a litre of water left, we would die in a day. I decided not to confide in Ina.

We turned round on what I hoped was an accurate 180° and set off back. Two hours later it was clear we were completely lost. Ina was becoming dangerously dehydrated, utterly exhausted, slightly tearful and unable to think straight. It was now unbearably hot and I was completely responsible for getting us out alive. I put Ina under a dry, leafless tree. Then I looked about. There was nothing but empty scrubland.

I had almost resigned myself to death. That sounds melodramatic at this distance, but, then, it seemed very real. From my bush-walking experience in Alice Springs I knew that we could not survive long in this kind of heat without water. And we already had barely any left. I decided the best thing would be to make us both as comfortable as possible and just wait. I wrote to my mother and in my diary.

After a while, I stood up and thought how ridiculous it was just to sit under a tree waiting to die. I looked around and saw hundreds of pawprints in the sand — the tracks of deer or civets. These animals have to drink, I thought, these tracks might lead us to water and at least give us more time. Although I don't believe in Fate, I asked the gods above to help me choose. My eyes fixed on one set of tracks. I gently woke Ina up and helped her to stand.

"Where are we, where are we going?"

"We're just walking a little further."

Grimly, I followed the track my guardian angel had chosen for me, certain it would lead to help. An hour passed — nothing. A second hour — we were exhausted again. My trust in Fate was starting to diminish. Suddenly, there in front of me was the watchtower.

Our mood turned from desperation to euphoria in an instant. We ran indoors, hugging the bewildered Indonesian warden and ordering Coca-Cola. After a while I began to question why I seemed to have this need to press on in situations regardless of the consequences or dangers, what it might be that drove me in this way. I resolved to control it — next time I might not be so lucky. But it has actually stayed with me to this day and without this streak of obsession I would not have had the impetus to reach the Poles.

22

I met David in a hotel lobby in Auckland, New Zealand. I was coming to the end of my travels and he was on business. At the time I was suspicious — I thought he was trying to pick me up. We spent the evening together and had breakfast the next day, but didn't exchange numbers. But I woke up the next morning with an inexplicable desire to see him again.

I had absolutely no contact details, but the hotel told me his home town, and directory inquiries his number. When I called, I had to prompt him before he remembered who I was, but he told me I was welcome to stay when I "returned to Sydney". I threw away my ticket from New Zealand to Cairns (and the bus ticket for Darwin) and instead purchased two new ones — New Zealand to Sydney and Sydney to Darwin. This cost me £300, money I could not really spare at the end of my trip. I knew absolutely nothing about him; he might have been married, a rapist, or a psychotic, but I had to see him, whatever the cost.

When I arrived, David instructed me to get a train to a disreputable outback town where he was working. There we went for a drink in an Aussie bar. It was rough and it was full of ockers intently undressing me with their glazed, drunken eyes. David told me he lived in the country, about an hour away, so after a few too many beers we set off, weaving along dirt tracks deep into the New South Wales outback. It was dark and nobody knew I was here. I must be completely out of my tiny mind again, I remember thinking.

David later became the most important man in my life, the only one I ever seriously considered marrying. I asked him to live with me in London and for two years he patiently put up with my madness and lack of confidence. He tirelessly strove to bring out the best in me, and taught me to make decisions, to take control of my life. He believed it was up to each person to make what he wanted of himself, that we were all in charge of our own destinies. His lessons were intoxicating; I held on to them firmly.

Coming back from travelling is always hard. I had intended to stay away for six months; it had been two years before I returned. On the plane home, I consulted my list of personality defects to see how much I could tick off. The list was clearly shrinking. I wondered how I would fare back in the real world.

The first thing I established was I could no longer endure a nomadic lifestyle. I had had enough of travelling, of any kind. I needed money and my friends. So I lived in London and went back to the theatre. At the end of a year's contract, I had drunk all my money and David had come to England. I landed a job at the BBC as a runner.

Starting this was all the tougher because I was thirty, but essentially still a dogsbody, even if it had taken four interviews and a panel grilling to be accepted. My job description read: "Collect celebrity guest or presenter from reception, escort them into make-up, ask if their clothes need pressing. Give them tea (this I would buy out of my own meagre wages because the production never gave runners a float). Take guest on to set." This last required careful timing not to keep the artist waiting for the production crew nor the crew waiting for the artist. It was impossible to get right, of course, and I was always yelled at down my headset. I had no microphone, only a listening device, so I could not argue back. Runners suffered in silence.

On my first day on *Top of the Pops*, I was given a rock singer. Three minutes before he was due on set I knocked on his door. This would give us two minutes to walk into the studio and a minute's leeway. There was a grunt from inside, which I took to mean "Come in". I opened the door to find a blonde head stuck firmly into the star's crotch. Politely, I was told to fuck off. I shut the door, mortified, and ran down to the studio floor. By now the director was shouting in my headset, "What the hell are you doing? We're waiting." I hastily explained to the floor manager that oral sex was delaying the artist. "I don't care if he's having an orgy with every single Teletubby, I want him on set NOW!" he screamed back. So I ran back and called out that I was terribly sorry, but could he hurry up. The director was waiting. Then I paced up and down impatiently, until eventually the door opened and the singer staggered out, dishevelled. But it was I that received a serious reprimand.

I tried terribly hard, but although the work was so easy I often seemed to get it quite wrong. One of my first series was working on the *Steve Wright Show*, a lavish Saturday night light entertainment programme with many celebrities. Each day I had to type the cards for the dressing rooms. My first list was Spike Milligan, Wet Wet Wet and a Mr Niger Benn. Strange name, I thought, I wonder who he is. I diligently checked the spelling three times over — spelling had always been a weak point for me at school, but it was a terrible sin for a runner to misspell an artiste's name. An hour into the show I was hauled into my ex-boss's office. She was purple with rage. "You idiot," she snarled. "How could you misspell *Nigel* Benn's name?" The horrible truth dawned. Of course, Nige-l Benn, the leading black boxer, whose nickname was "The Dark Destroyer". At the end of the day I was told I was incompetent as well as racist and sacked from the show.

The next day I had to see my boss again. She had calmed down, but worse, she was now playing psychologist. She put on a voice she imagined was soothing. I had to sort myself out. I looked like a frightened rabbit most of the time, I gave the impression of scattiness; I needed to toughen up.

"Oh, and Catharine, you really must stop blushing all the time, it gives a poor impression and makes you look pathetic."

Blushing had always been an enormous issue for me ever since I was a teenager. A blusher endures crippling agony. I could never speak up in class, I always found it difficult to tell a story in a group and I avoided the promotion to stage manager in my theatre days because I was so terrified of blushing when I had to make announcements to the team. Worst of all, when I began to blush, somebody would always point it out. The horrible colour crawled down my face and neck and finished in ghastly blotches on my chest. Eventually it became so bad that I wrote to Virginia Ironside, the agony aunt for *Woman's Own* magazine. My letter was published with a very kind reply advising me that there existed a "blushing support group". But the idea of ten people sitting in a circle all with beetroot faces filled me with absolute horror. Now I took her comments really badly. It was as if all that hard work of independent travelling had been for nothing; my list of personality defects was suddenly growing again.

In the past it was all too easy for me to become lazy, to neglect to do things because I was relying on "Fate". So often I would hear myself saying that Fate would bring me a career, a husband, or happiness. Accepting responsibility for myself was terrifying, not having a god or a superstition to turn to when things went wrong. It made me panic, but I found the panic was so horrible it would actually motivate me to do what had to be done. So I guess I always had this philosophy in me somewhere, but was just too scared to believe in it.

Like most Australians, David loved sport. I loathed it because of my schooldays, so he gently suggested trying something non-competitive. He took me to North Wales and in a shop window I noticed an advertisement for a rock climbing course for beginners. I had watched climbers for many years hanging from ropes on the sea cliffs near where I lived. I admired them, but never entertained the idea that I could ever do anything like that myself.

To David's delight, I loved it. The exhilaration of feeling afraid but working through it and getting to the top was very powerful. After two days I had learned to climb a rock face. A virtually horizontal one, perhaps, but a rock face nevertheless. I felt extremely pleased with myself.

In December 1995 David's visa ran out and he left. We had talked of marriage but I would have had to move to Australia and this was something I was not ready for. I found being single again at thirty tough. I imagined I was never going to meet anyone ever again, the world seemed utterly void of single people and full of couples. I was pursuing new interests just when all my friends seemed to be settling down for life.

Many friends refused to see me without their new partners, so invariably I would be the gooseberry trying to make conversation while they caressed each other or stole kisses at every turn. Girlie gossip was now becoming a thing of the past. Instead I was expected to reveal any gossip I had to both girlfriend and partner, because they were now one. At Chidham, since my brother had married, I moved up into his old room. The walls were red and covered in his old Ozzy Osbourne posters, and the carpet stained with the evidence of many nights of over-indulgence. It became most fondly known from then on as the spinster's attic.

"I will *not* be a sad, dried-up old spinster," my New Year's resolutions for 1996 began. "I will survive as a singleton. I will do something towards finding a new boyfriend. I will live out what I have learned from David. I will improve my life at the BBC." It was a year when I made every effort to put into practice independently what being with David had brought out in me.

Many of us in the entertainment industry do reach a point where we question our jobs. We yearn to do something humanitarian. In my early days, I defended our industry with a passion. I always used this story. I was working on a pantomime. My duties consisted of throwing glitter, understudying the back end of the cow and mixing and clearing up gunge. One evening, a small boy who had just lost both parents in a car crash came backstage with his aunt. He wanted to meet the princess, and she, sympathetic, took out her prop handkerchief, and gave it to him with a big lipstick kiss on it. "Whenever you're sad, hold this hanky to your face and you'll feel better." A year later, I was there again when the boy returned. This time the aunt told me, "You know, he *has* kept that hanky with him at all times, and whenever he felt sad — which of course was quite often — he *did* hold it. I swear it got him through this last year." After the Niger Benn incident, I kept this story in mind, but it didn't seem to help any longer. I needed a way out.

CHAPTER
THREE

New Life, New Dream

Once again I registered Corporal Fraser's look of glee. "Hartley! You're a fucking imbecile. You're not leaving this camp until you find them!" We were all lined up to return our guns but when I put my hands in my pockets at the end of the weekend, my cartridges had gone. In the army, there is no worse sin than losing a weapon or ammunition. For an hour I ran about looking under trees, in fields, everywhere. Finally, the cartridges were found in my wardrobe. By now, the whole company was lined up ready to fall out. They looked on sympathetically as I was given a roasting. Was I about to fail yet again?

I was having the "save the world" syndrome. Increasingly upset by the situation in former Yugoslavia, I wondered if I could help there. As I had no suitable qualifications I was advised to apply for the Territorial Army Medical Corps. I was also attracted by the challenge of the other activities on offer, climbing and so on, if I could become a corporal.

A month later I set off on an induction weekend. We had vigorous physical exercises, intelligence tests, and were told to speak for five minutes in front of the other candidates. Terrified I might blush, I smuggled in a small pot of foundation and applied it liberally before my turn. To my delight, I was accepted and told I would attend three weekend camps and a fortnight's training in the summer.

The tone was already different at the first of these weekends. We were issued with uniforms, and taught about weapons and biological warfare. The physical workouts were demanding, the trainers harsh. I began to feel like a fish out of water, a fluffy lovey who had spent all her life surrounded in theatrical cotton wool suddenly plunged into boot camp. Nor had I thought through the real implications of "joining up". I had not considered that I might have to use a gun. I had not realized all new recruits train to be soldiers first. Only then, as corporals, could they learn a trade, such as to be a medic. I was interested to see why others had joined up. For many it was just a means of pursuing their love of the outdoors, for some it was a game, few really wanted to serve Queen and Country and even fewer had imagined the possibility of being called up for a war.

The next "camp" was even tougher. We were deprived of sleep and I was addressed as Hartley, No. 45, or Fuckwit rather than Cathy Sweetheart or Darling as I was used to. Classroom work was frightening. After an hour's lesson on chemical warfare or first aid, questions would be asked of us randomly. Invariably I could not remember the names of all these horrid gases that were going to kill us. More practically, we were taught how to don suits and gas masks in the case of a biological attack and spent much of our time learning about the gun, as I called it, or weapon, as I was constantly being corrected.

The weapons instructor was called Fraser. An accountant in civilian life, he thought me a namby-pamby media bimbo and took enormous pleasure in humiliating me publicly. Our first exercise was to take the gun, sorry, weapon, apart and put it back together again, while memorizing every component. I just could not do it. The more he shouted at me, the more terrified I became. I shook so much that I could not name the parts, let alone reassemble them. The class was supervised by an officer, and though officers were generally privately educated and all had degrees, they were less experienced and much younger than their corporals. My officer, clearly intimidated, just laughed nervously at Fraser's behaviour and did nothing.

Before we were fallen out, the names of those miscreants who had to see the company captain were called out. Of course I heard my own name. I was escorted to see Captain Hobbs. "At ease, Hartley," he said wearily. "Now, how do you think you did this weekend? Did you enjoy yourself? I do hope so. But I have to tell you your marks this camp have not been terribly good. In fact, your weapons report is well below average. Do you think this is fair?" Captain Hobbs was younger than me and looked quite humane. He spoke gently — it was the first time that weekend anyone had been kind to me. I cracked. "Sir, I don't know what I'm doing here. I'm a member of Greenpeace and a pacifist.

All I want to do is help people, and all I'm doing is being taught how to shoot gu— I mean weapons."

Captain Hobbs's jaw dropped. He paused a moment, then as if he were addressing someone mentally unstable, he said, "I do understand your feelings, Hartley, but you have to realize we are just teaching you to defend yourself, not to be a killer. Now, we don't want to lose you, but why don't you have a jolly good think about whether you want to continue, eh? Dismissed."

I felt all my gains from travelling had been wiped out. I had regressed back to my twenties. My initial feeling was to run away and never return, but after a week regaling my incredulous theatrical friends with my sufferings, I decided not to be beaten. If I chose to leave the army it would be on my terms. I especially wanted to prove myself to the ghastly Corporal Fraser.

So continue I did. I was advised to start again from weekend one. Determined to make a success of it this time, I spent hours pressing my uniform into razor-sharp creases, and dubbining my boots until I could see my reflection. I worked, listened and concentrated hard. And it was easier second time round; I knew what to expect and had a certain confidence from guiding the new recruits.

"Ah, Hartley, back, I see. Would you be so kind as to show the new recruits how *not* to put your weapon together?" Fraser was sniggering with anticipation. It was Saturday afternoon. Weapons instruction. But I had swotted up for hours at home. I fitted the weapon together without hesitation, naming each component correctly. Fraser was stupefied. The weekend went like clockwork. My physical performance was superb from nightly training at home and my academic work faultless through many hours of swotting. Captain Hobbs was impressed, he admitted he had not thought to see me again.

However, I thought about a soldier's duty very seriously, and asked myself if I would ever be able to shoot anybody if called up. I would not. So I resigned. Never one to do things by halves, my next plan was to join climbing, scuba-diving and water-skiing clubs, turning myself into an outdoor junkie. It was through the climbing club that I became friends with Ying, who was always to encourage me in my mad ideas, but as much because the resulting stories amused him as from any real concern for my character development or well-being.

At the BBC, I found the way we were assigned to shows hard. Each show would request its staff, and the unrequested would work on the unpopular shows. It was back to being picked for teams at school. Because I was quiet and did not drink with producers in the bar, I was rarely requested. But there was an unofficial competition between all the stage managers as to who was asked most and it seemed the winners were loud, sociable and loquacious. However, one day I was picked to be a floor assistant for the prestigious BAFTA Awards. It was to be held at the Royal Albert Hall, awash with stars; it would be a real honour to work that night.

We arrived in the morning and were briefed about our duties. We would each be given five celebrities to collect from their dining tables and take to make-up, before escorting them backstage to be handed an award to present. I looked down my list. Diana Ross. "My God," I thought, "she's one of my heroines." At our briefing, we were told to collect each celebrity two awards before the one they were presenting.

I was summoned to see Diana Ross's PR manager. Diana would need to be collected earlier because she wanted to change and reapply make-up. So we decided that she should be collected five awards in advance. The ceremony began. It was splendidly lavish and I was quite overawed. Eventually the time came. I approached her table and followed her as she swept out in her chiffon. Only when she was changing did I realize my terrible mistake. Incomprehensibly, I had forgotten to collect her early. I had done it two awards ahead, just as with all the others. We had just five minutes before she was due on. I felt sick.

I confessed to the PR, who looked at me as if I was an imbecile and said coldly, "Diana rushes for nobody, you'll just have to wait." Then I ran backstage and explained to the floor manager. "She can't be late," he gasped. "We can't possibly stop the whole BAFTAs." So the assistant producer banged on the dressing-room door, apologizing but asking her to hurry. The PR lady was puce with anger and I was close to tears.

Suddenly the door flung open and out stepped Diana. I spluttered my apologies for such an inexcusable mistake. She looked at me: "I never ever miss a cue, but you must make sure this never happens to anyone again."

I nodded frantically, but worse was to come for me: "I am terribly sorry, Diana, but I am going to have to ask you to run with me."

We made it backstage just in time. After the event there was a huge party, but I was too depressed to go. The other floor assistants tried to cheer me up, but I was inconsolable. All I had had to do was deliver someone on stage on time and I had failed even to do that.

At such times one turns to what one is good at and comfortable with. I had seen advertised a charity cycle ride round Jordan. I had left it too late to apply, but as I needed to get away, why should I not go independently? On impulse as always, I hired an old mountain bike, stuffed the panniers with a few clothes and a puncture repair kit, put it in the plane and set off. Flights direct to Jordan were expensive but, luckily, the border with Israel had just opened. I therefore managed to get a seat on a charter to Eilat with Club 18–30 holidaymakers off for their sun and sex. When I landed in Eilat, I had a lift into town on the Club 18–30 transfer bus, and then I asked a local to direct me to Jordan. "Go straight along that road for a few miles and then turn right," he replied, as if giving directions to the post office. Off I pedalled. Within five minutes, both my tyres had blown. It had not occurred to me that tyres must be deflated before going on a pressurized plane. Now I realized I had absolutely no knowledge of cycle maintenance. Perhaps it was unwise to be crossing a

Middle Eastern country alone, one with very many miles between each town. As always I never think about these things until I have to.

I wheeled the bike back into Eilat and found a friendly mechanic. He looked extremely grave when I announced my plans to cycle north all the way up to Petra, then back down again before going into the Wadi Rum Desert. He clicked his tongue.

"I think you not well in head, lady."

"I am quite aware of that, thank you."

He fixed my tyres and gave me a much more substantial maintenance kit. My own tube of glue and three tyre levers were put to shame. "I pray for you," were his parting words as I wobbled off into the desert.

Cycling proved to be a wonderful way to travel. I had no problems at all with the bicycle. And I felt utterly safe, as the Jordanians looked after me so well. After visiting Petra, which proved as enchanting as I had heard, I cycled back. I chose a route where after fifty miles I needed to turn left into the Wadi Rum Desert. Further on, I was to turn right into the village of Wadi Rum itself. If I missed this right turn, I would stay on the road, which eventually would become a track leading into Saudi Arabia. It was, therefore, imperative that I arrived before nightfall. I calculated that if I set off early enough I could make the journey in a day. I would, however, keep a check on the time and find somewhere to sleep en route if I was late.

My watch had been given to me by my brother and was most expensive and reliable. I made good progress, and as I turned left towards Wadi Rum my watch read

3p.m. That gave me plenty of time to cycle the twenty miles to the village before nightfall at 7p.m. Soon after, however, the sun began to set. How odd, I thought, how can it be sunset already? I checked my watch; it had stopped.

But as I looked up again, my breath was taken away by the astonishing beauty of the desert. I stepped off the bicycle and watched as the sun set over the mountains. The rocks were deep shades of pink and red. I had never seen anything so moving in my life. I was completely alone. I had rarely been touched by the beauty of nature, but now I just sat down and sobbed. This is what it is all about, I thought. It is not about getting Diana Ross out of her dressing room in time, it is about this, this raw, sublime, emotional experience. And again it was connected to finding my own path. I had cycled round Jordan alone, despite everyone's scepticism that I would probably end up hanging out in a bar in Eilat with the 18–30s.

Soon after it went dark, really dark. I could barely see my hand in front of my nose. How on earth was I going to find the turning? Luckily, I was learning and had had the sense to inform the police in Wadi Rum that I would be arriving. After just half an hour, I saw the headlights of a jeep. It pulled over and two bemused but laughing policemen stepped out. They took me to the village where I spent hours trying to explain to them why an Englishwoman should end up cycling round Jordan by herself.

I came home with new confidence, elated. My colleagues, clearly surprised that I was unscathed, praised my bravery. But I was not brave, these sort of experiences really did not frighten me. They served as a wonderful enrichment of my life. I loved the challenge. After lunch I had to go and meet the producer of a new show I was going to be working on. That was what real fear was. I paced up and down the corridor, smoking for ten minutes before I finally plucked up the courage to knock on the door.

It was the trip to Jordan that finally made my mind up. I desperately needed to succeed, at something, anything really. My school results had been poor, my career in stage management was one I had stumbled into, not chosen, and I did not seem much good at that either. Now I began to see the field in which I was going to succeed one day. I was going to become an adventurer. But how? And where could I go? These days there are few unexplored places, nowhere left to discover. Journeys not yet made, peaks not yet climbed — these are rare. It is hard enough to find somewhere unspoilt, let alone unvisited. Except the polar regions, of course.

My first idea was to cycle round the Canadian part of the Arctic Circle. I would fly to Vancouver and then cycle north, circumnavigate my way round the Arctic Circle east, using planes when the road stopped, then boat to Greenland, sailing down the west coast, up the east coast, over to Iceland and then cycle back to London via the Shetland and Orkney Islands. I planned the entire trip, but with the boat and plane fees it seemed totally unaffordable. So then I thought of Antarctica.

Antarctica is one of the most remote and extreme places on earth. Its gigantic icebergs and ice shelves are unparalleled on this planet. Its vast mountain ranges and the enormous emptiness of the polar plateau defy comprehension. The wind speeds there can rise above 200 miles per hour and the temperatures in winter can fall as low as −89°C. Antarctica certainly remained one of the last unexplored wildernesses. It was also a place that was said to be beautiful beyond description.

Although I had never read about them systematically, the polar regions had always fascinated me. It was not so much the beauty and spirituality of the place that seized my imagination, but the idea that people rarely chose to go there. I did not try to explain it, but I was tremendously excited by that. Undoubtedly it was the same feeling that had driven explorers. Those historic figures, Robert Falcon Scott, that most English of all examples of endurance and fortitude, and Ernest Shackleton, famous for not losing a single man on his expedition, became and have remained folk heroes. And then I also found out no British woman had yet walked all the way to the South Pole. When I discovered this, the gauntlet was down. I was going to be that woman.

With hindsight, my ambition was of course utterly ridiculous, as I did not have a grain of experience. Indeed, Scotland was the coldest place I had ever been to before. The only experience I had had of snow and ice was a couple of package ski holidays to Bulgaria. But what I did now have was a compelling dream and I refused to let this one slip away as another of my mad ideas that had never quite materialized. For over a year,

I infiltrated the polar world, turning up at talks at the Royal Geographical Society and reading every book I could find on the subject.

I read more present-day books than historical accounts. Everything seemed very intimidating. I never had a minute's doubt that I could do it, but that is because nothing I read or looked at could ever have prepared me for what it was really like. The books were largely set out as day-by-day diaries of the men's misery. Not a morsel of pain was left out and each wretched, frost-bitten and life-threatening moment was embellished in horrifying detail on every page. It was, of course, alarming, yet not until I experienced it did I understand how terrible it really was.

One day I was having lunch with a friend and noticed in her newspaper an article about a selection course for a relay walk to the North Pole. A film financier called Caroline Hamilton was looking for twenty "ordinary women". The plan was to divide the women into five groups, and for each team, suitably trained, to travel for around ten days before being airlifted out and replaced by the next. I was desperate to apply. After some frenzied detective work I found the right number to ring. But I was too late. The selection had been made the day before. It took me weeks to get over the disappointment.

Then, in September 1997, I met a polar explorer called Pen Hadow of the Polar Travel Company, who had been logistics manager for — and inspiration behind — the British Women's Polar Relay. He now had a vision of leading the first guided expedition to the

South Pole. It would arrive there for the Millennium. The idea was that anyone could apply, irrespective of experience. My usually reticent, polite manner evaporated; I badgered him endlessly for a place. When I made my New Year resolutions for 1998 in the company of my dear friends and ex-colleagues from the Nuffield Theatre, these were to give up smoking and not get so drunk that I became undignified and ended up in gutters. Oh yes, and to walk to the South Pole. There was a roar of laughter. "OK Cath, we won't hold our breath."

Pen invited me to attend a four-day selection course on Dartmoor in June. Not all the participants were competing for a place on this particular expedition. Somehow I was convinced Pen had told me the first test would be running a whole marathon — it sounded a pretty tough way to select the team. So I trained ruthlessly every day. As it turned out I had misheard him completely and the furthest we were expected to run at one stretch was only three miles. But the misunderstanding meant that I arrived very well prepared.

We spent the entire four days hacking over the moors with little sleep. We were given many challenges, such as abseiling in the middle of the night or wading through freezing water. Every attempt was made to wear us down physically and mentally. I enjoyed this immensely: I have a Puritan, even masochistic streak in me. I liked less the excruciating moment when we had to sit down in a group and reveal what we thought were the positive and negative aspects of one another's personalities. It was all very Oprah Winfrey. I enjoyed even less those unbearable lateral thinking problems when you have to work out how to fit together a series of squares and circles using only an earlobe and a chamber pot. I did, however, make two friends: Madelaine Mason, who was fifty, was hoping to walk the very last part of the journey to the South Pole, and Liza Helps — well, she has a heroic part to play later on in my tale.

At the end of the course I smoked three cigarettes in succession while waiting to see if I had been accepted. And I was. There would be four of us and Pen. I was the only woman. I was euphoric. I could not believe that I was being given the opportunity to fulfil my dream. My mood soon changed, however, as the prospect of raising the necessary £30,000 began to sink in.

I liked the others in our team of four. Jez was a charming geography student from Cheltenham, Ben was a high-powered businessman and Ian was a Welshman with an abundance of energy and enthusiasm. Ian already had good experience of the cold — he worked as a fork-lift truck driver in huge warehouse freezers. As we understood it, we were a team and Pen instructed us to reassemble in November. But he told us to raise the money separately. I had fifteen months to find it.

CHAPTER
FOUR

Fundraising for Beginners

"When I get to the Pole you can fly in a shopping order that I made at the start of the journey — the ultimate delivery service — it's brilliant," I screamed maniacally down the phone at the supermarket chain marketing manager. "Yes, Miss Hartley, I appreciate it is a terrific idea," the voice replied soothingly, with the unnatural calm used for the deranged. "But can I point out it is less than three weeks before you depart and as a company we usually require a period of two or three *years* to decide on forthcoming sponsorship opportunities. Anyway, I don't mean to be rude, but it does interest me rather how you expect to succeed without any experience, isn't it a bit foolhardy? *I mean, Scott died out there you know*." Yes, I knew Scott died out there. How many times had I heard that one already?

Sponsorship, I learned, was all about branding. What I was about to do must somehow enhance the image the sponsoring company wanted its brand to have. I would agree to wear a label bearing the company's brand name on my clothing, sled, sleeping bag and food wrappers. Moreover, because I would be breaking a record in being the first British woman to walk to the South Pole, I supposed that I would receive publicity, so the potential sponsor would hope the brand name would be widely seen, on television and in newspapers and magazine articles. This is where the company made their money back — free advertising if you like. An advertisement in a newspaper or magazine, a commercial on television cost thousands of pounds. Instead, the company would gamble that I would get publicity. In return for this simple task it would give me thirty grand. It was pretty straightforward, I thought.

Of course, I had totally underestimated the real difficulties of raising sponsorship. In reality, I was about to embark on what would be all but unendurable, an exhausting effort that would involve me in a string of catastrophic situations. I was even advised that if I succeeded in the gruelling task of finding the funds, the walk to the Pole would be child's play.

I had never fundraised a penny before and was completely clueless as to how to go about it. I began my campaign by tentatively writing nice begging letters to companies whose names I had obtained from Sainsbury's food labels. I tried to think of firms who would benefit from being associated with a woman. There seemed to be numerous opportunities. Among many others I contacted Starbucks, my favourite coffee house, saying I could be photographed drinking a double tall latte at the Pole.

As a smoker I wrote to numerous tobacco companies saying I would happily smoke their cigarettes all the way to the Pole. It was ludicrously unhealthy, as well as unethical, but seemed worth a shot. I had what I fondly thought were inspired ideas. Surely it would be a simple job for me to persuade Tampax to sponsor me in return for proving that tampons could be used at −30°C. My mother even suggested I write to Durex and hint their products might come in useful — I would be the lone woman on a team with four men. I could not fault my own choices and naively expected companies to think the same and for the money to come flooding in.

Straightaway the rejections started coming through the post. From what I understood, the days when company directors would throw ten grand at a mad adventure had long passed. Although companies sometimes had huge sponsorship budgets, everything was strictly controlled. The money now tended to go to charities or community projects. How could I argue with that? The others who benefited were already famous. Footballers like David Beckham, Formula One racing drivers, any personalities who were glamorous could guarantee companies huge amounts of media coverage and were, therefore, good value for money.

My rejection letters always kindly acknowledged that my dream was inspired. But nobody was prepared to gamble their valuable sponsorship budget on a flaky media bunny without an ounce of experience, who blithely imagined she would be the first British woman to walk to the South Pole. In retrospect, I know this was fair enough. There had been generations of accounts about Scott and Shackleton. The enormous tragedy and pain that their expeditions had endured was always painful to read. It seemed ludicrously unlikely that Catharine Hartley from Clapham, who could not even boast she had walked the Pennine Way, would succeed where they had failed. And no company wanted to be associated with a failure.

I now discovered that Caroline Hamilton, who had organized the British Women's Polar Relay two years previously, was assembling her own expedition and hoped to be the first British woman to walk to the South Pole. I heard her interviewed on radio and discovered that she was going to lead it herself. Her companions were four other women. I thought it would be more challenging and fun to go with an all-female team and gave her a call. She was very pleasant, but politely refused me, saying the team was already chosen. I could not complain, but was pleased I had found the courage to ask her anyway.

By February, all four of us were still struggling to raise the money for our expedition. And we were all a little uneasy. In trying to find individual sponsorship, we had all hit brick walls. We were halfway in time between selection and supposed departure. Pen decided to organize a team meeting in London to put us all through a crash course in raising funds. We went to a wine bar in Earls Court. Although we were all worried about the fact that we had no money, I suppose we hoped Pen would set us right. We had come to look on him as a sort of god-like figure.

I knew immediately something was wrong. Pen looked very anxious and was pressing his fingertips together in an extremely unnerving manner. He came straight to the point explaining that a company called Adventure Network International (ANI) provided the only commercial transportation into Antarctica. They had decided to organize their own expedition to the South Pole. Extraordinarily, they had no fewer than five teams set up to go, so there would be no seats available on their planes for us. The only other transportation was for the scientists that worked out there, and this would certainly not be available for us. And there were just no other aircraft. The expedition was not going to happen after all.

The table fell silent. I had been on the wagon for a month in an attempt to become a dignified thirty-something, but now I fell off instantly. I downed a glass of red wine and snatched a Marlboro Light from a neighbouring table. None of us knew what to say, so we just stayed dumb. Poor Pen was beside himself with disappointment, too; he could see no way out as a team with him leading. He offered to introduce us all to ANI and urged us to join individually one of their expeditions instead. Dismayed, but desperate to go, I arranged to meet the head of ANI, Anne Kershaw.

Anne had a formidable reputation as a business-woman, but was utterly charming, too. Far from being an archetypal "beard", she was petite, blonde and beautiful. To my delight, she was only too happy to offer all of us a place on the fifth of her expeditions. Apparently, the first four were now full, but there were places on the last. Clearly there was a crazed international rush to be at the South Pole for the Millennium.

"What difference does it make to us if we are on the last trip?" I ventured cautiously.

"It just means that you will be the last group to leave."

"Are there any other British women booked to go?"

There was just one, a Fiona Thornewill who would be coming with her husband, Mike. They were already paid up and they would be on the first expedition.

"OK, Catharine, I will accept all four of you, but I need a £7000 deposit in two weeks, otherwise I will have to let the places go."

Two worries hit me immediately. How in God's name would any of us come up with seven grand in two weeks? But, just as bad, if this Fiona woman was already booked on the first trip, how could I possibly bill myself the first British woman about to walk to the South Pole? It had all turned into a circus. From what had been just five people walking to the Pole for the Millennium, there would now be an entire parade, it seemed, and this made a mockery of my own proposal. It also became very apparent that it was every man for himself. Anne was merely there to provide the logistical support, but any PR campaigns, training and actual fundraising were our responsibility.

The need for action left me no time for doubt. I telephoned the rest of the team and told them the situation. Without exception the "seven grand in two weeks" deadline left them gasping. Two days later, Anne called to say that someone had dropped out of the second expedition. Would I like that place? She felt it might help my publicity campaign by giving me more of a chance to be the first British woman. I accepted and in doing so realized I was leaving my companions to their own devices.

It felt odd, bad in fact. I felt I had let them down, but for once I was not going to be polite. I had been given an opportunity and I was going to grab it with both hands. In doing this, I realized that I was now totally alone. It was down to me and only me to fund the expedition. I no longer had either Pen or the others to help me. That security had been a complete illusion in any case. But how could I find £7000 in two weeks?

I was working on *Blue Peter* at the time. Desperate to meet my first payment deadline I decided to send a global e-mail to every member of the BBC, home and abroad. I hoped to secure either money, or interest in filming a documentary. Let me stress I had permission. An anonymous voice at the IT help desk explained how to do everything. Off it went. Seconds later my phone rang.

"Miss Hartley, this is Julian, head of IT. It appears you've sent a global e-mail to everyone at the BBC. This is terrible. It should never have happened. What in God's name were you thinking of?"

"But I had permission!"

"OK. Well, don't panic yet, we do have ways of controlling situations like this."

A pause on the line, as if it were him doing the panicking.

"Just please, please don't send any more."

It was only moments before the chaos began. Someone from Features and Documentaries decided to send me a sarcastic reply, on the lines of "Me and my friends want to go to the Bahamas. Please give us £10,000 to have a good time". What was lethally unfortunate was that he pressed "reply to all" rather than "reply to sender". So this e-mail too went to everybody in the BBC, home and abroad. Minutes later, BBC Sports responded: "Dear Catharine, we think your expedition to the South Pole is a wonderful idea. Ignore that stupid guy in Features; he is just jealous. Go for it and consider £20 pledged from us." It was very kind but, intentionally or not, they too had pressed "reply to all", so the entire Corporation was witness to this e-mail, too.

Now I had a premonition of doom. I somehow knew I was in deep trouble. I left the office, went to the newsagent's and bought my first packet of cigarettes in a month, after I thought I had successfully given up again. As I smoked an entire cigarette in one draw, I overheard two girls chatting outside the office.

"You won't believe it, Dawn! Some silly cow has put out a global e-mail asking for dosh for some stupid expedition, and she's crashed the whole system."

With an unnatural, cold calmness I went back upstairs to my office. The whole room just turned and looked at me. "Are you OK, Cath? Julian from IT phoned. Can you call him back immediately?"

No one was laughing. Far from giving me a storm of abuse, Julian just said simply, "I just want to confirm for your own information that the BBC e-mail system has in fact crashed." There was a short pause and then he finished the call with: "Catharine, I would just like to say that I feel really sorry for you right now."

In the time that I had been out having my fag fourteen more people had sent e-mails, facetious or supportive, and each had pressed "reply to all". My manager gently put her hand on my shoulder. "Take the afternoon off if you like."

"Yes. Please."

Just before I left the man from Features and Documentaries telephoned me, apologizing profusely. He had meant his e-mail as a joke, but it had backfired with terrible consequences; he, too, and the fifteen others who had pressed the evil "reply to all" button were in big trouble. I spent the weekend in drunken oblivion telling my hideous tale to anyone who would listen and shuddering at the thought of all the foreign correspondents unable to e-mail back their reports from Sierra Leone, Bosnia, Outer Mongolia . . .

I hoped that Monday morning would never arrive but, of course, it did. Although I found it hard to get out of bed, I knew I had to go in and face the music. The first thing I did was sit down with my new manager, Jane. Apparently the Corporation had been thrown into total chaos. Teams of IT staff had been brought in over the entire weekend to rectify the situation. The story had appeared on the local television news and a full article was printed in the internal newspaper. An investigation was launched and, of course, I was responsible. As Monday was my last day on *Blue Peter* it was decided that I should take the next two weeks off. It was a kind way of suspending me pending an inquiry.

As I wandered into the tea bar and then back into my office, all I could hear anyone talk about was the "silly cow who crashed the system". It was a monstrous scandal; everyone was revelling in it. I winced as I heard people describe various consequences of my howler with patronizing glee and then marvel at my stupidity. Nobody realized I had had permission. By great good fortune, however, no one recognized me. Nervously I turned on my computer.

I had hundreds of e-mails. Some were very nice, offering me £20 donations, but many left me appalled. "Because of you, I lost many of my documents and had to spend the entire weekend in the office sorting out the mess you caused," said one. "I suggest you ask for forgiveness not money," was another. There were many crushing messages. I felt as if I had been branded across the front page of the *Sun*. I was utterly humiliated and in complete shock. But most of all, I worried about the other sixteen people. I felt unbearably guilty that I might be the cause of destroying other people's careers.

I went home and spent the two weeks with my mother. I literally took to my bed and fell into a huge depression. It looked inevitable that I would be sacked. After the two weeks I returned to work and was called up to face an official investigation panel. After telling my side of the story, I was told that IT was claiming they had not given me permission, that I had rung and asked, but they had refused. This was a lie, but I had no proof. Two days later an inquiry was launched by the Director-General, Sir John Birt. Again, I had to go through the same painful questions. Eventually, only the support of Jane, my boss, and the decision of the Director-General allowed my reinstatement.

Even now, I can barely raise a smile at my mortification, although I will no doubt dine out on the story for the rest of my life. Only the other day I was stage-managing a show for Dale Winton. One of the producers said: "Catharine Hartley? Hmmm, why do I know that name?"

"Well, I have just walked to the South and North Poles and the expeditions received quite a lot of publicity."

"No, it's not that. I know! Weren't you the woman that crashed the BBC e-mail system three years ago?"

So the whole of the BBC thought I was a complete fuckwit, and I had to agree.

Meanwhile, what about the expedition deposit? I had £6000 salted away. They were my life savings; they were to be a deposit on a house. I drew everything out of the bank and sold my car — a beloved MGB — to raise another £800. Then I sent the money to Anne Kershaw knowing that I would never see it again. If I failed to raise the full £30,000 then I would forfeit the £7000 as well as my place. I was past the point of no return.

After running away to see David in Australia for convalescence and sympathy, I did go back to work. Luckily, I was offered my first job as a location manager. This meant that I was out filming in various parts of London, and did not have to operate from

Television Centre at all. No one there was BBC staff, so my terrible secret was safe, I could continue with my new job as if nothing had ever happened.

Whoever said filming was a glamorous industry, well I would like to kill them. My job was to find locations, and loads of them in a very short space of time. I would be asked to find anything from a sixties disused pumping station to an Edwardian stately home. I would then persuade the owners that the presence of a film crew would not cause any disruption. One director even wanted to knock down an interior wall so he could open up the room. My powers of persuasion must have been outstanding, because the owner agreed. Frequently I could not find the location required. Panic would set in as I tore around London and the suburbs desperately searching for a medieval castle within the M25, because the production did not have enough money to put people up in hotels.

"Oh, and Catharine, could it have one of those cute Rapunzel type towers, and we'll need to land a helicopter in their maze, too?"

"Medieval castles don't have mazes, Rory," I'd desperately venture.

"Oh, you'll find one sweetheart, just keep looking."

But my favourite moment came when we were filming near an airfield, so the soundtrack was affected. Over my radio the director barked, "Catharine, will you please call air traffic control and ask them to divert the planes. I can't possibly work with all this noise." I did telephone, if only out of interest to see in what way they would tell me to clear off. I was greeted with a snort of laughter and a "Roger, Houston".

I still had to pick myself up and return to the unrelenting task of raising the money. On one particularly bad day when I was about to overdose on St John's Wort and vitamin B12, my mum sat me down and said, "Cath, if you walk away from fear it just gets bigger and bigger, but if you move towards it you will find it actually shrinks. Go back to work and start fighting again for this sponsorship. You can do it, I know you can." It was absolutely invaluable having this kind of support from her. I never needed to explain myself. She just accepted this was something I needed to do. No doubt her own love of travelling contributed to how she always understood me.

I was worn down by the continual effort of writing hundreds of fruitless letters. But a student friend, Nigel, helped me target companies in Chichester, where, after all, I had grown up. Using the local business directory, he wrote as many letters as he could, and a week after, I had my first bite, from a Trevor Gardiner, the PR director for Club Direct Travel Insurance. They were launching a new package for adventurers, called Extreme, and needed a way of marketing it. It sounded perfect, but, unfortunately, they had very little money themselves. So we agreed I should keep looking for other sponsors as well. It was the first positive reaction I had had in months, but this one little development completely renewed my energy.

I was realizing that just writing letters with my sponsorship proposal was not enough. Rather than companies I now tried the hopefully philanthropic rich and wrote without success to everyone on *The Times* Rich List. Then I tried advertising. I placed a slot in *Private Eye*'s "I need" section, which prints requests for money — say, to pay for a PhD or develop an invention. A very nice voice left an answerphone message offering me £20,000, but his mobile cut out before he could give me all his phone number. I could not trace him. Later I realized it must have been his idea of a joke.

A week later I had a call at 11p.m. from what sounded like a young, well-spoken man. He had always wanted to visit Antarctica, he said, but for certain unspecified reasons he could not do so. But he had just inherited an apple orchard worth £1,000,000, and he would very much like to offer me £20,000. Then he paused. "Here comes the catch," I thought. "All I require, Catharine, is that you and I go to bed together, just one night, *it's that simple*."

In a second, my mind was scrambled. It *was* that simple; it was just one night and then I would have all the money. No more stress, no more rejections, no more exhausting, laborious fundraising. "Fine, Tom," I heard myself saying. "Would you like to give me your name and telephone number and we can make an arrangement?" As he was giving out his address I suddenly saw sense. Stop, Catharine, stop right there!

"I'm sorry, but actually I think this is not a good idea," I said, I hope with more composure than I felt. "Thank you very much for calling me and for this kind offer, but I think it best if I turn you down."

Tom was disappointed, and insistent, tempting me with all the wonderful things he was going to do to me. I became frosty.

"Thank you, I'm quite sure it would be spectacular and if I change my mind, be assured I will, of course, give you a call."

The phone went dead. I began to shake violently, more because I knew I had nearly agreed. Jo, my flatmate who worked in PR, advised me the next day that I had done the right thing. It did, indeed, emerge that this had probably been a tabloid reporter trying to set me up. Had I eventually reached the Pole, my indiscretion would have been exposed. "*Blue Peter* Stage Manager Shags Way to Pole." It was a headline that might have induced me to emigrate to Australia.

"I think you should try Geri Halliwell, Cath. I mean, she's into Girl Power and she's got loads of dough." It was my flatmate. It was a good point, but the problem was always to get the proposal past the PR minder who might chuck it in the bin. Then my friend Jane Edden, an artist of great imagination, helped me brainstorm. We decided the best idea would be to enclose a very striking photograph, something at least to make her look for a second. Then she might choose actually to read the letter. Various mad ideas came to mind, as one bottle of wine slipped into another. Dressing up all the Spice Girl dolls as polar explorers, with Geri's dog Harry disguised as a penguin, was my favourite. Then we could freeze them all in a block of ice and deliver the parcel to the recording studio.

58

This transposed into our final idea. Next day, I braved my hangover and staggered to the stationer's to buy clear plastic, as used for overheads. On it we printed: "Geri Halliwell, please sponsor the First British Woman to walk to the South Pole." We then placed it in an enormous baking tray of water and stuck it in the freezer, clearing out all of Jane's groceries in the process. Two days later I returned to find that it had worked perfectly. I put on make-up and posed in her garden, holding the new block of ice with enormous gardening gloves. The photograph came out brilliantly, the pleading words showing clearly behind the ice. "She has to bite, she can't fail to be intrigued by that," I exclaimed.

Well, I did not hear from her, but I had found a brilliant marketing tool. I had one photo session with Jane every week for the next few months. Each time I would type up a new plea on a new piece of plastic replacing Geri Halliwell's name with Richard Branson, Jilly Cooper, Chris Evans, anyone I could think of. By the end I was finding out the managing directors of companies I was writing to and inserting their names. So it would read: "Joe Bloggs from Company Blah. Please sponsor the First British Woman to walk to the South Pole." It worked insofar as every person or company contacted me, often by phone, and all remarked on how impressed they were with the marketing idea. Every letter without exception was read. Not one went straight into the bin.

Even if I got only one bite in a hundred letters it was enough to keep me positive, and justified my keeping going. But I found I was never trying to persuade just one person. I got four bites from the "ice technique", all from marketing directors who were very interested, but the proposal always had to go to a board of some kind, and that was where it failed.

I discovered, however, that what I found the most difficult to deal with was negative thinking. I was all too aware that few people thought I could succeed, and as time passed I found myself being subjected to "a quiet word". "Cath, I know you want this really badly, but don't you think it is time to let go now . . . I mean you are stressed, you are smoking fifteen a day, you're — well — not Cath any more . . . Let's go and have a nice holiday instead, maybe cycle round Holland or something." The chats were normally accompanied with a nice crisp glass of white wine and gentle, "therapy" voices that one might use on a mentally unstable person.

I did appreciate their concern, but I felt brainwashed. What I actually needed was 100 per cent support from everyone around me — I did not want a single person to doubt me. But few, justifiably, believed in me and, besides, everyone who cared about me was worried about my mental state if I ended up not raising the money and having to forgo the expedition. No one realized that, in my own mind, not succeeding was unthinkable. It was going to happen. With hindsight, I realize now that it is always absolutely essential to have this very attitude. Everyone will doubt you anyway; if you succumb to doubt yourself you will fail. I do believe it is that simple. I, therefore, clung on to those that supported me and avoided those that were cynical. My family and friends' support was constant and invaluable, and has remained there unconditionally to this day, whatever messes I get myself into.

By now I realized I was not offering potential sponsors enough. I must guarantee them media coverage. This was a tricky one for me. I was shy and very unassuming; the thought of being in the newspapers unnerved me. Publicity did not excite me in any way, and the thought of being the centre of attention was quite horrifying. To this day I doubt if I could ever have a conventional wedding, because I know I could never walk up that aisle and be the focus of people's attention even for a day.

However, no press coverage, no expedition. I stayed late at work one night, faxing every newspaper I had ever heard of. The *Daily Mirror* came back to me the next day. I am not, I hope, a tabloid snob, I read the 3a.m. Girls with the best of them, but I definitely did not want to appear in a tabloid myself. The reporter's name was Jane, and she was very insistent. Although I had made the call in the first place, I then beat around the bushes like an idiot, protesting I was not what she wanted. Finally, I agreed to meet for coffee. She assured me that we would not do an interview, but instead just talk through the possibilities of what one might involve.

So we met. I was allowed to choose my favourite café. I was plied with coffee and muffins. She was lovely. I really warmed to her and before I knew it I was talking — talking too much. Just as if she were a therapist. Three hours later the tapes contained intricate details of my past, plans, dreams and, of course, yuk, romances. How had she done it? Four years previously I had easily managed to talk my way out of joining a powerful religious cult. Now a mere journalist had ambushed me. I scuttled home nervously, jittery on caffeine, to consult Jo.

"Did she have a Dictaphone, Cath? If she didn't you're fine. Everything will be off the record. Can't print it."

"She *had* a Dictaphone, and she wrote everything down, *everything*. Even about me being in love with John downstairs."

"Look you can't mess around with journalists. Now you're in the media machine you've got to learn how to protect yourself. Otherwise you'll humiliate yourself completely, and God knows who else."

Although she obviously saw what vulnerable prey I was, Jane treated me impeccably. She let me have complete copy approval and removed anything I didn't like. I did have to do a particularly gruesome photo shoot, in implausibly and perfectly pressed outdoor gear with layers of make-up, but the article itself turned out to be painless. She later became a wonderful ally and is to this day the only journalist I completely trust.

My first radio interview was with GLR, the BBC's own London station. Jez, who was still trying to find the money too, came along. We were naively hoping that even in mid-afternoon a rich person would be listening in and leap to a phone. As it turned out, a scraggy, trendy and surly researcher met us. Without saying hallo or shaking my hand he said straightaway in a bored voice: "Yeah, I know you! You're the one who crashed the e-mail system, you gave us loads of hassle." He showed us into a side room, not giving us coffee, but telling us we could help ourselves, before leaving us without any briefing. I was totally thrown off guard.

We were introduced to the presenter, a wild, bubbly woman, only a couple of minutes before going live. "We'll talk for around three minutes and if it goes well we'll continue after the news . . . people phone in to ask questions as well," she gushed, all in one breath. But "it" did not go well, nobody phoned in, we did not continue after the news and we saw ourselves out. Nor did Scraggy Trendy deign to thank us or say goodbye. Over a restorative brandy in a nearby pub, Jez told me he was having absolutely no luck fundraising and would now give up. He said Ian was in the same boat, while Ben had been given a contract offer that he could not refuse, as a bribe to abandon his polar ambitions.

"Looks like you're on your own, Cath. I wish you all the luck in the world. I really hope you get the money and get to the Pole. Crappy old GLR will be begging you to come on then."

My working day generally began at 5.30a.m., when the caterers arrived, as breakfast had to be ready by seven. At 7.30a.m., the rest of the crew would arrive and I would let them into the location. The majority of my stress occurred before 8.30a.m., a depressingly early start, but filming did not finish till 7p.m. I would then have to wait around until the location was cleared of equipment, and then move the unit to the next day's location. I would not reach home till ten. So the job did not lend itself well to a harsh training regime and finding £30,000 of sponsorship. As time wore on I took to lying. I would tell the production manager that I had to go off and check out the next day's location, or find some other suitably plausible excuse. What I would do then was drive the car half a mile down the road and just sit there for a few hours, telephoning marketing directors on my mobile.

Anne Kershaw had now given me another deadline of four weeks for the next £10,000. I had no personal money left, the pot was absolutely empty; I simply had to find a sponsor. Anne also told me that many participants had dropped out, mainly for financial reasons, so there were now only two teams left. Yes, Mike and Fiona were still on the first team and, yes, they had paid up, she replied to my transparently unsubtle questioning. That night, I dreamed that Anne had been made into a Barbie doll, rather like the Spice Girl dolls. I realized that I must see Anne as a Supreme Being, but that I was probably going mad myself.

I was soon going to be embarking on one of the most physically challenging expeditions known to man, let alone woman, so training was extremely important. Unfortunately, apart from running around Clapham Common, and the odd weekend away with my climbing club, my time was completely taken up by failing to raise my sponsorship and holding down that extremely full-time job.

The *Daily Mail* called me to ask if they could do an article about my training. The fact that I hadn't actually started became apparent reasonably quickly as I bumbled my way through her intensive questioning on my non-existent training regime. The reporter paused, puzzled, then said, "How would you like the *Daily Mail* to organise this for you? We could get you a nutritionist and a personal trainer, and then follow your story." It sounded wonderful.

My first day at the gym was with Phil, a very pleasant instructor doing a master's in sports science. Of course, I made straight for the Jacuzzi and fluffy towels but, instead, he deposited me on a computerized machine into which he programmed a workout. It was a shock and I realized I had to focus more on the physical side of this challenge, not just the financial.

The problem was there was still no money. It was now September and we were due to leave in October. I had just six weeks to go. After fourteen months of one rejection after another, I had changed, from necessity more than choice, into a formidable and demanding woman. Demanding, of course, money. Gone were the polite begging letters inviting companies to donate. Now I would find a way of getting past the receptionist and going straight to the marketing director. Before he could speak, I would give him a fifteen-second pitch — who I was, what I was intending to do, and what a great opportunity it was for his company. I would then send a proposal and follow up the call two days later. After this, I would badger him on the phone until he finally said no. It was all horrible, but what else could I do?

And then I got a call out of the blue from Trevor Gardiner of Club Direct. All this time, he had not lost interest. Now he had been in touch with Anne to offer insurance for her two teams and she had invited him to the ANI seminar, to be held at the Royal Geographical Society. He asked me if I would mind accompanying him and Brent Escott, his managing director. Would I mind?!

"This is it!" I screamed at my flatmates. "Calm down, put on some nice clothes. Knock 'em dead, and grovel like you've never grovelled before," they advised. "Oh, and Cath, don't for Christ's sake get pissed. And your fags! Leave your fags at home. You're supposed to be inhumanly fit, not some booze and nicotine addict."

The evening was set up as a marketing event for Adventure Network International. Around 200 people attended to hear stories of Antarctica and one of the speakers was the Englishman Robert Swan, one of the great modern-day polar explorers, the first person to walk to both Poles. I admired him enormously. He spoke about an expedition to the South Pole where he had retraced the steps of Captain Scott. It was stunning and inspirational. Everybody in the hall left that evening ready to conquer the world.

More importantly, Club Direct were now ready to sponsor me. Trevor and Brent had been overwhelmed by the evening and chatted away enthusiastically while we mingled with the adventurers. Next day Trevor rang to say that Club Direct wanted to make me an offer, but they could not give me the full amount. It was four weeks before I was due to depart and I still needed another £10,000 to enable me to go. Trevor understood this and agreed that I could continue to look either for a co-sponsor or for a sponsor who could pay the full amount. I had to believe that I would get the other £10,000 from somewhere.

Soon it was my last day at the BBC. I had handed in my notice a month before. This was an enormous gamble, as I had no job to return to. I was giving up on five years of security, but I had no choice, I would be away for too long. I left quietly and with little ceremony. I told few people why I was leaving as I was too afraid I would have to go back in a month's time, tail between my legs. On my way home I popped into the off-licence for more wine and cigarettes. I ended up explaining everything to the assistant as by now I was talking at anyone who would listen. "Try First Quench," he said. "They're a new drinks company. I bet they'd be up for giving you ten grand." By now anything anyone suggested became something I would follow up.

Time was so tight, indeed, that, like a woman possessed, I would take the name of every large business I drove past and call up the marketing director. Computers, sweets, toothpaste, vacuum cleaners, anything, you name it, I could find a reason for them to sponsor me. I even tried the new on-line supermarkets. I became completely accustomed to negative replies and mercifully immune to them.

OK, here we go again. Let's try First Quench. For the first time in perhaps the last hundred calls I didn't get the "Can I just stop you there, Miss Hartley?" She let me finish. I almost forgot my words as I was so used to being cut off before the end. "Sounds great, Catharine! I can tell you now that I am very, very interested. I understand there is a time issue here, so I will get back to you as soon as I can. Thank you very much for your call."

There were only three weeks to go; I had bought my plane ticket to Chile and was in the process of finding someone to rent out my room. Anne Kershaw was, understandably, pressing me heavily. She had given me four more days to come up with the money. If not, she said, she would, with sadness, have to take away my place.

I had become so stressed that my sleep patterns were totally disrupted. I would wake up at four every morning in complete panic. I would be able to hear my heart madly thumping. So I would generally smoke two cigarettes and sometimes have a glass of brandy in order to go back to sleep. Then at seven I would wake up again, and need another cigarette before getting up.

This ridiculous state seriously concerned Jo and Nikki, my endlessly supportive flatmates, who were doing their best to keep me from going over the edge, while increasingly astonished that I seemed determined not to give up. But this was one time I had to succeed. To everyone else, this was just another of Cath's mad ideas that would come to nothing, but to me it was my one big chance to prove to myself and others that I could win, that I was no longer a failure.

Ten grand. That was all I needed. A measly ten grand. In the last few weeks, my plans had grown ever more absurd. I had everyone I knew buying lottery tickets. I even applied for life assurance. Not because I wanted any, but because if I filled in the form and set up a standing order I would be put in a prize draw with the possibility of winning, not just ten grand, but half a million. The letter assured me that I was already a winner, and would find out how much I had won just as soon as they received the completed form. When the cheque came, it was, alas, only for £5. The *Chris Evans Breakfast Show* was giving away £10,000 every morning that week, a friend told me. All I had to do was ring up and leave my phone number. The lucky contestant would be phoned back and then, live on air, would have to answer a simple question. One right answer would win the money.

I tried ringing for several minutes. Finally I got through and, optimistic as ever, I left my details. Ten minutes later my own phone rang. I picked it up on the first ring, crazed with excitement. But it was First Quench. They were terribly sorry but they would not be able to sponsor me on this occasion, although everyone thought it was a wonderful idea.

I had four days now to pay up. What could I do, what the hell could I do? It would be so unlikely that another company might come up with the money in the next four days. That would be a crazy thought. I had no property to remortgage. I paced around the flat smoking one cigarette after another and eating chocolate. All this time, I had been desperately trying to put on three stone for the expedition. The intense cold would make us all burn so much fat that it was essential to start off heavily overweight. I had been assigned a special diet from my nutritionist. Unfortunately the stress I was under and the number of cigarettes I was smoking meant I had only gained half a stone. It was, however, the least of my worries.

CHAPTER
FIVE

"I'm Really Going to the Pole"

"Ten grand, that is all I need, Mrs Harris, just ten grand," I pleaded. As a last resort, I had realized a loan would be the only way. I rang my bank and was put through to the manager's assistant, Anita Harris. I blurted out my story, barely able to hold back hysteria. Mrs Harris was calm, kind and, amazingly, she seemed to understand my psychosis. She agreed to talk to her manager.

That afternoon the phone rang. I did not recognize the voice; it was a Mr Hugh Perkins and he was from Barclays in Chichester. I had never met him in my years of banking there, but he was my branch manager. "I am not supposed to do this, Catharine, but I have just had the most wonderful holiday walking in the Himalayas and your story has really touched me. I would like to offer you a £10,000 interest-free loan. I'm just about to retire so I can do this." I was absolutely overjoyed. I thanked him about a hundred times over. Three days before Anne's deadline and three weeks before I was supposed to leave, he had come up with the remaining

71

money and been my unlikely salvation. Fifteen months of increasingly surreal attempts at fundraising had ended in this. I was going to walk to the South Pole!

I rang Trevor Gardiner straightaway, and so began the formidable — but necessarily brief — task for us to gain as much publicity for him as we possibly could. I think he was concerned I might not make it all the way to the Pole and therefore wanted to maximize publicity while he could. At last, out went the press release. Every day requests came in. Very quickly, I had to learn to talk, smile and just be in front of the camera, both photographic and TV. I did not enjoy it. Of course, I was far from being a natural. But there was one programme that I felt privileged and honoured to feature in. *Blue Peter* invited me back, but to be in front of the camera this time, not behind.

It was a mad day. Rather than my normal cycle ride to work, a car came to fetch me and I arrived in style with my clothes, equipment and sled. It was very strange, as I knew all the crew and cameramen. Caroline, the stage manager who had taken over from me, was even my closest BBC friend. Nothing prepared me, however, for the terror of being interviewed with five cameras on me. After a rehearsal, I was then wheeled into make-up. Knowing me very well and having worked with me for three years, the make-up artist, Karen, took delight in making me up beautifully and piling my hair on top of my head into a beautiful chignon. We then did the dress rehearsal.

I was appalling. I stumbled over my words and I was absolutely red in the face. Fortunately, I had warned

Karen about my blushing problem and she had kindly applied a green base. I rambled on far too long. I knew it myself. After the dress rehearsal, I received notes from the editor to cut everything by half. It was also made clear to make-up that I looked like Krystal Carrington from *Dynasty* rather than a "ruffty-tuffty" polar explorer, so I was whisked back into the chair, where the make-up was toned down and my hair released from the chignon. The main show was equally shocking and, in my panic to cut down the number of words, I almost failed to speak coherently. Thankfully, it was not a live show, and I overheard the director in the gallery saying, "Look, don't panic, we can work wonders in the edit suite."

I watched the finished product with my flatmates Nikki and Jo the next night and the result was absolutely excruciating. As I was introduced, you could see me swallow with fear and my face contort in horror. Clearly I had been irremediably bad, because much of my interview was hidden by library footage of Antarctica. Apparently, in parts, I had been better — or less bad — in the dress rehearsal, which had also been recorded, so they decided to use clips from both this and the real show. In some shots, therefore, my hair was up and my lips glossed in true Krystal fashion, and in others my gloss and eyelashes had miraculously disappeared and my hair had fallen down into an "abandoned" look. My flatmates loved it, of course, roaring with laughter at the incongruity of my hair. I was extremely embarrassed. It was the first and last time that I have ever watched myself on television.

At the weekend, I finally managed to take the train up to the Lake District to meet our guide, Geoff Somers. He had been in continual contact over the past few months but because I did not yet have the money it was very difficult to speak to him seriously about the logistics of and equipment for the trip. Now I was really sure I was going, but, true to form, there were no more than two weeks before departure. When I met Geoff he was in his kitchen going through his mushroom book identifying a pile of fungi on his kitchen table. I offered him a tangerine from my train picnic and I always remember that, strangely, he warmed it up on the cooker before eating it. This struck me as rather odd for a polar explorer. We spent a couple of days going over equipment, clothing, the journey, the pace, anything and everything was covered, including a potted history of his extraordinary life achievements, which read like an adventure story book.

Geoff had been born in Khartoum in the Sudan, but he had been mainly brought up in Britain. He had always had a keen interest in the outdoors, and became an instructor in Outward Bound Schools all over the world; for two years he was deputy director of the new school in Sabah, Malaysia. Then, for thirty-three months without a break, he worked as a guide for the British Antarctic Survey. After a second tour there, he joined an international team that, with the aid of husky dogs, traversed the longest diameter of Antarctica — nearly 4000 miles in 220 days. In 1993, with a companion and three camels, he journeyed from the Pacific Ocean across the Australian deserts, walking for ninety-seven days to reach Uluru (formerly Ayers Rock) at the centre of the continent. On 12 December 1995, he co-piloted the first manned hot air balloon flight over Antarctica. For outstanding services to Antarctic exploration and outdoor education, Geoff was given the rare award of the Polar Medal, and the MBE.

I found Geoff very shy and humble. I noticed early on that he loathed any kind of attention and resented those who used their expeditions to gain publicity. I was utterly in awe of him, too. He was the most fascinating and exciting man I had ever met in my life. I respected him totally and would have jumped off a cliff had he asked me to. He thought I was just a silly girl, but over the two months of the expedition I am pleased to say I genuinely won his respect.

Geoff told me that there were still two groups walking to the Pole, but four people had not yet managed to raise the funds. In a day or so they would be withdrawn and the two groups would contract to one. I wondered how Fiona, the other British woman, would feel about this. When I telephoned her, she was naturally taken aback to hear she would no longer be the only woman on the first expedition, but she was very gracious about it. It also now seemed absurd that we were conducting separate publicity campaigns. Should we not pool our resources and do things together? It was very odd finally speaking together after I had read so much about her. I had been asked to do a photo shoot in a freezer and asked her if she would like to join me. She in turn invited me to a press call at the

National Maritime Museum. The next day it was confirmed that the group was now indeed one and consisted of nine of us, including two guides.

Originally, I must admit, I had not really thought about raising money for a charity. It was hard enough finding £30,000, let alone more for others. Then, one person in particular out of whom I was trying to prise money said, "What you are attempting, Catharine, is great, but to be honest I think it's all rather self-indulgent. I mean, if you do succeed you will come home and achieve recognition but what does that do for anyone else?" I decided he was absolutely right.

A couple of charities that I approached were nervous about being associated with a possible failure, even disaster, and had therefore been reluctant to become involved. But Sense, a charity for those who are both deaf and blind, was different. I had discovered them in the course of researching what I might do with my life after the polar expedition.

I was already familiar with the feelings one has on returning from travelling. It is often very hard to adjust and I always found it important to find a new challenge immediately on my return. I was very aware that even if I did succeed in my polar journey, life would not suddenly open up other opportunities to me; it was up to me to find them. Perhaps I would be able to use the expedition as a proof of determination, irrespective of its outcome.

I eventually hoped to go to university as a mature student to retrain, because there was a profession I had wanted to enter since I had left school — Speech

Therapy. Because I had not done well in my exams this career had not been open to me. In addition, I had known that, as a person, I needed ten years or so of being wild and of travelling before I would be able to settle down to a "steady" job. As soon as I was accepted on Pen's original expedition, I had already envisaged that when I left for the Pole it would also be a good moment to move from the BBC. So before the fundraising had taken over completely, I had attended work experience sessions to help with future career choices, and this was how I had come to know of Sense.

This particular charity touched me. It struck me just how lucky I was to be able to go on this expedition and be able to actually see and appreciate everything around me. I suddenly felt a fraud that if I did succeed I might receive press coverage and recognition. But for what? It was not enough to do it just for myself. When I rang Sense, I spoke to a man called James. Wow! How wonderful it was to hear a voice that sounded overjoyed to be a part of my project. By return of post I received sponsorship forms that even had penguins on the top. His enthusiasm made all the difference. I was determined to raise huge amounts of money. We decided that I should take a Beanie Bear to accompany me. Christopher, as I named him after the founder of Sense, would become the first teddy bear to walk to the South Pole.

The publicity requests kept coming. Trevor had done an extremely good job in making the press aware of our departure and they also seemed to be very interested.

Although I knew this was how I was earning my sponsorship money I did find it all unnerving. The more coverage I got, the more dramatic and notorious my possible failure would be, even though I remained determined that failure was simply not an option. Each reporter tried to find a more quirky angle. I did a lunchtime television programme for Channel 4 on Clapham Common, which contained a wonderfully bizarre clip of me pulling car tyres around the common, pursued by four dogs and a ferret. Car tyres were the established way of simulating a sled. But, sad to say, although I pulled them enthusiastically for the camera, I had not really trained with them at any other time, let alone with stray dogs or pet ferrets . . .

The frozen food company Iceland now kindly let me sit in their freezer for an hour or so just to get a feel of how cold I might be. At −19°C I was absolutely freezing. We used the freezer a couple of other times to do publicity shots, but in both cases the camera started to shut down. I knew I would be facing temperatures of −35°C and now I started to feel very nervous. I used to go to pieces in the cold and it was the first time I had had to come to terms with this. In fact, I hated the cold. I have terrible circulation, and was one of those girls that would hibernate under a duvet in the winter. So often, one thinks one can handle things and it is not until one is actually in that situation, in the cold and wind, that one realizes one cannot.

A couple of nights later I had a party, partly to celebrate my going away and partly to raise money for Sense. Jo and Nikki decorated the flat with paper doilies to look like snowflakes, and I stole a mannequin from the prop store at work. We dressed him up as me in polar clothing and painted his nose and fingers black, to look like frostbite. I thought it was absolutely hilarious, but Jane Edden, whom I had known from childhood and was my oldest friend, could not see the funny side. She was quiet that evening and later revealed that she was concerned how light-hearted I was about the expedition and how little I seemed really to understand the dangers I was about to experience. In retrospect she was absolutely right, but at the time I was too excited, naive and drunk to notice. The frostbitten mannequin was to become a huge lesson in irony.

I rang Pen a week or so before I was due to depart. We had not been in contact for a while after his trip fell through, but when I finally got the money I telephoned him to say that I was on my way. To his credit, he was ecstatic. He lent me skis, boots and a wonderfully warm polar jacket, saving me hundreds of pounds. Just before I left he sent me a postcard on which was written, "There will be times when you think you will not be able to go on, there will be times when you will think you can't take another step, but you will succeed, just persevere, persevere, persevere." I took the postcard with me and kept it in my knickers bag all the way to the Pole. The mantra stayed with me also; I was to chant it religiously.

I had arranged to meet up with Mike and Fiona at their National Maritime Museum press call. But before this, on the same morning, Fiona and I were asked to appear on the BBC show *Breakfast*, our first big TV appearance apart from a brief slot on Sky News and my disgraceful performance on *Blue Peter*. As I had not been allowed to display the Club Direct logo on my clothing at the latter, *Breakfast* was especially important for Trevor.

I was suffering from acute stress at this point. Nothing was ready. I was still waiting for much of my clothing to arrive, and I had not moved out of my flat. Any spare minute I had was taken up with generating publicity, and wonderful though it was to be going, I was having to think through that I was actually going to be walking to the South Pole. I had my usual disturbed night. This morning was no different, except that I also had to get out of bed and into a cab for the interview.

We arrived at Television Centre with twenty minutes to spare. So we had time to have a cup of coffee and put on our expedition clothing. But it became apparent that my Club Direct logo was not on my clothing as planned. It had only been stuck on with tape and must have come off when I was hurriedly preparing that morning. I was absolutely horrified. I phoned my flatmates at home who were poised eagerly at the TV set awaiting my second appearance, and sure enough the label was on the floor. It was too late now to have it couriered over, so I had to be interviewed without it. This was to have been Trevor's big marketing moment and I was about to destroy it. Shortly after the interview, my mobile rang. I blurted out a stream of apologies, but there was nothing I could really say to placate him.

From the BBC we drove straight to the Maritime Museum. This was where I met Mike for the first time. He had a dreadful cold, and I could see that, like me, he was mentally and physically exhausted and close to breaking point. Already that morning, his car had been towed away. It had taken him two hours and £175 to retrieve it. After the press call, he and Fiona rushed back home to Nottingham to pack.

Just as they left, Mike shouted, "Catharine, just to check, you have got your visa for South America, haven't you?" I went white and felt sick. I had no idea we needed a visa to get into South America. I was stuffed. I thought, how was I going to get a visa in a day and a half? "Only joking!" he guffawed with laughter. "Right . . . OK . . . thanks . . . that's good then . . . a joke . . . of course!" I tried and failed to be flippant back. "See you in Chile, then. Bye." Then I noticed that my nails had sunk so far into my palms I had actually drawn blood.

The flat was in absolute chaos. Jane and my mother came to be with me full time. My mother was frantically sewing Club Direct logos on my clothing and Jane was clearing out my bedroom so another tenant could move in while I was away. I sorted out the equipment, skis, clothing, thermal underwear and general clutter that littered my sitting room, smoking cigarettes at every opportunity.

The night before I was due to leave, Jo, Nikki, my mother and Jane cooked me a sumptuous dinner. I was unable to speak. I finally had sponsorship, I had resigned from the BBC, I had nearly every national

81

newspaper interested in me, I was going to be walking to the South Pole! . . . I was petrified, like a rabbit caught in the headlights of publicity and of unknown terrors. My mother and my flatmates, too, were mentally and physically drained, they had lived through the last eighteen months with me; I could not have done it without their support.

At midnight they all retired to bed, but I stayed up half the night filling in my university application form. This was absolutely insane, but I realized if I did not send it in before I left, I would miss the deadline for the next academic year. I even found time to write a single page, scrawled book proposal for Ying to tidy up, though the idea I would either have a worthwhile story or something I could sell seemed very remote at the time.

My mother and I left for the airport the next morning. The previous day I had mislaid my goggles and face mask so Jane had a courier deliver a new set from Dunstable that morning. Something is always left undone in a rush, and in my case, it was, of all things, my gloves. It was quite obvious that the hands and feet were what succumbed first to frostbite, but all we had time to do was stop at the outdoor supplier "Snow and Rock" on Kensington High Street. While my mum waited on a double yellow line, I dashed in and tried to explain in the calmest voice I could muster that I was about to go to Antarctica for a very long journey. I needed the warmest and best gloves known to man. The assistant looked alarmed and suggested the mountaineering section. I grabbed the most expensive gloves I could find, threw the money at him and fled.

We were, predictably, stuck in traffic, our clapped-out Mini Metro stalling at every junction. In panic, I left the car at Hammersmith to take the underground, while my mum drove my luggage. Somehow, we managed to meet up at the airport with minutes to spare, in time for me to have to pay £150 in excess baggage, before I had a photograph taken by the *Daily Mirror*, then literally ran to the gate and straight on to the plane. I think this was good for all of us — my aunt and sister-in-law's father were there, too — as I feel a long goodbye would have been difficult for all.

Just as I was boarding, my brother telephoned and said, "When you are having a bad day, remember that we'll all be thinking of you at that moment, and willing you to go on." This comment went over my head at the time but came back on the expedition. It was to help enormously to know that and I clung on to such thoughts in moments of difficulty. But for now, imagine me on the plane with a large gin and tonic, on my way to Punta Arenas in Chile and breathing a huge sigh of relief that what I thought would be the worst part of my expedition was well and truly over with.

CHAPTER
SIX

To the South

Of all the continents Antarctica is the most isolated and least forgiving. At times it is terrifying for those who venture there. The first obvious psychological effect is that life in the outside world becomes totally insignificant, and with little to distract the mind other than cold and extreme discomfort, that mind becomes one's entire focus. This can lead to mental purification, or uncover deep wells of pain. All return from Antarctica changed — sometimes for the better but often for the worse, unable to take up their lives in normal society.

Most expeditions to the South Pole start from a seasonal base camp called Patriot Hills, if only as a flying-off point. Antarctica is, of course, not an exact circle in shape, and walking from here allows the shortest journey from rim to centre, and also involves the fewest technical problems — there is no real mountain or glacier travel. Scott, who had walked from a completely different part of the continent, set himself a much more arduous task.

The airport from which we would fly to Patriot Hills was at Punta Arenas in Chile. When I arrived there on

23 October, the camp was still deserted, but as soon as the weather allowed, a Twin Otter aeroplane with skis attached to the wheels would fly in to start the season. This would have a skeleton crew, who would prepare an ice runway for a much larger Hercules aircraft to land. The first Hercules would in turn contain the staff who would prepare the camp itself for all the expeditioners following soon after. This service offered the only commercial flight into Antarctica. The only other flights in ferried scientists and base staff.

All kinds of people came to Antarctica on the Hercules. Some would be mountaineers, perhaps wanting to climb Mount Vinson, the highest mountain on the continent. Some would be coming in to make the whole journey to the South Pole, others just the last few miles. Many arrived to take trips to view penguins, and that year, 1999, others would then take the long flight all the way to the South Pole, just to be there at the Millennium. All had their own reasons and dreams for coming to this expanse of white wilderness, for choosing this over a holiday of comparable cost, say in the Bahamas.

The walking season is quite short in Antarctica, because, at 80° south, it does not get light until the beginning of October, and is always cold and windy. A couple of weeks are then used up each year setting up Patriot Hills as a camp. Aircraft do not like too much severe weather. Neither do pilots, snowmobiles, tractors or their drivers. The propane gas in the cooking tents and all the pipes freeze up, radio machinery does not always work and easily breaks, batteries are too cold to produce power. It really is still winter, whatever the time of year is supposed to be.

The season ends at the end of January because the weather closes in again. There are long periods of wind and whiteout; it becomes too cold to climb Vinson or do treks. The South Pole closes down about 20 February, as it becomes too cold to operate aircraft there. Soon after, the sun goes down, giving twenty-four hour darkness. At the coastal bases, the sea starts to freeze in March, the weather worsens, and for the tourist ships there is little wildlife to see as it has migrated elsewhere. Long before true winter begins it is important to be completely out, because it is important to leave several weeks as a safety margin in case of problems.

The scientists and support workers at the South Pole base do spend the winter there, and most of the Polar heroes of the past had that experience at least once. Sometimes, modern-day explorers do also. Robert Swan did so, for example, in order exactly to recreate Scott's journey.

It was not till I arrived at Punta Arenas that I met all the remainder of the team. Extraordinarily, it was the first time we were together. Normally a team would have trained and prepared for a trip like this in advance, maybe for years, getting to know the intricacies of one another's strengths and weaknesses. Scott, for example, wintered in the Antarctic before setting off for the Pole. So these issues were considered as long ago as 1912. Instead, here was another enormous gamble: would we actually work effectively together as a team under such extreme conditions?

There were nine in our expedition, including two guides. Geoff's assistant, Victor Serov, was an utterly indestructible man from St Petersburg. He had experienced the lowest ever temperature recorded on earth: −89°C. He came over as kind and jolly, but I think he did doubt my abilities. As for the others, Grahame Murphy was a Scottish marathon runner. Although the fittest of us by far, he was built like a greyhound, very slim and slight. Veijo Meriläinen was fifty years old, but very fit, a bespectacled Finn who just fancied a couple of months out of the office. Then there was Steve Peyton, a plumber from Cambridge. He was a ball of positive energy; he clearly relished physical hardships.

But the one who most interested me was Justin Speake. Although only thirty-six, he was already a wealthy businessman, so, incredible to me, he had avoided the long and agonizing search for sponsorship by simply writing a cheque. He had equally simply selected all his equipment from "Snow and Rock", the upmarket shop where I had bought my gloves at the last minute. "I just selected the best of everything they had," he said, blasé. At the time I was extremely envious, but in retrospect the agonizing fifteen months of raising sponsorship had given me the greatest feeling of achievement and success — as much as the journey itself. Justin had read nothing and knew nothing about Antarctica and her dangers, and was completely uninterested in the actual journey. His only goal was to be at the South Pole for the Millennium. He had no idea of the purgatory he had signed up for, although, to his credit, he was to deal with it admirably.

Justin still remembered the boredom of a New Year he had spent alone in a car park in John O'Groats, the very northern tip of Scotland. So his goal was quite simple, he wanted to spend the Millennium not at just another party but somewhere he would always remember. He had had extensive experience in mountaineering. Before signing up, he had been for fitness tests at Birmingham University and successfully run a mountain marathon on no training, but he had prepared very little for the expedition — some running and three weekends skiing. He was not nervous or apprehensive, however. He was confident that he could solve any problem, and he set his mind to solve any problems en route. Unfortunately, most of his clothing was lost in transit. So his week in Punta was actually spent scavenging replacements where he could. He was extremely direct and strong-minded, but very endearing, and unnervingly perceptive about people. I could not help admiring his unfailing confidence in entering into something he knew absolutely nothing about.

I already knew the Thornewills, of course. Mike was a police officer and Fiona a recruitment consultant. Mike's travelling background was similar to mine and he had wanted to walk to the South Pole since reading stories about Scott and Amundsen in his childhood. Fiona had led a much more conventional life — beach holidays in Ibiza rather than jungle treks. But she did have immense physical strength, which was an obvious asset. Soon after they were married, Mike asked Fiona if she would walk to the South Pole with him. Amazingly, she agreed, so long as he raised the money. In fact, I found out that only Mike, Fiona, Grahame and I had any sponsorship at all. I was especially impressed by Steve, who had clearly worked all hours to pay for the trip. Like me, he would be spending considerable time afterwards repaying his debts.

All my companions had had at least a taste of cold conditions. Grahame, for example, had recently sky-dived over the North Pole. As a Finn, Veijo was from near the Arctic Circle anyway. Even Justin had run mountain marathons at altitude. Mike and Fiona had spent time training in Spitzbergen in winter. To my concern, I quickly discovered I was the only person who had absolutely no previous experience of the polar regions at all.

On our second afternoon I had tea with Fiona. We decided to have a few moments alone to discuss the most intimate of the logistics, those of female hygiene. Were we going to choose to deal with periods in freezing conditions or were we going to take the Pill? How many pairs of knickers should we take? We decided on two and then bought sixty panty liners, one for each day. How were we going to keep clean? I had brought enough wetwipes, but only if I rationed myself to one every morning.

We also talked about training. Because all my time outside my job had gone towards raising money, I was still very ill-trained. The *Daily Mail* had only intervened a couple of months before my departure, too late to have much effect. Even then, I was only training twice a week on machines, with the odd aerobics class and run. For the past six months, Fiona had got up each morning at 4.30a.m., attached an enormous tractor tyre to a body harness and pulled it up and down a dirt track for two hours. *Two hours? Each morning?* I thought. In the evening she would work on her upper body. Once a week she would run to work and back — twelve miles each way.

Fiona was tall, strongly built and obviously fit. I was scrawny, wiry and I had little obvious muscle. I was still smoking and recovering from a hangover from our first night party. Now it struck me that I was completely physically unprepared. In panic, I made a desperate attempt to catch up; I went on a long run up a hill in Punta. Of course, it was completely hopeless. All sorts of apprehensions flooded into my mind that night.

Strangely, I had never really considered failure. It had not actually crossed my mind. Ignorance is bliss, after all. I suppose it is like having a baby. You read the books, you go to prenatal classes, you know it is going to be bad. Everyone has told you this, but nothing really prepares you for just how bad it turns out to be. I think this naivety was good in one sense because it actually gave me the courage to go ahead, rather than being too frightened to try. But equally, it meant that I had none of that healthy fear that would have driven me to prepare correctly. Only now did I become frightened I had bitten off more than I could chew. I suddenly realized it might have been very, very stupid, and catastrophic failure might result.

It now struck me, in my panic, that no British woman had ever even attempted the journey to the Pole, let alone succeeded. How on earth had I managed to get myself into this astonishing situation and how did I have the audacity to think that I would be the one to succeed?

In addition to my lack of training, I had another problem. I had not had sufficient time to research my clothing. In contrast, Mike and Fiona had been extremely efficient and thorough. They had spent a great deal of time talking to both clothing suppliers and polar explorers and come up with a perfect layering system, specially manufactured for them by the company Rab, out of a material called Pertex. Mike and Fiona were efficient in every way, well trained mentally and physically and had superb PR support. They had thought of everything, and put me to shame. But I had done everything completely alone, so I could not feel too inferior. In my own way, I was actually starting to feel rather proud.

We spent the first three days packing and checking all our food and fuel, weighing out bags of sugar, tea and dried fruit exactly to the ounce. It was vital that we kept the weight down to an absolute minimum. I know the weight issue becomes compulsive in most expeditions of this kind, but rightly so. We would be hauling this weight eight hours a day for sixty-one days in adverse conditions, it was imperative to keep everything to a minimum. Geoff spent an hour with each of us going through all our "luggage".

The first thing to go was my first aid kit. There was a group medical cache but we were also allowed to take a personal supply. Mine was an enormous carrier bag jammed full, designed to indulge hypochondriacs like myself. "This is an absurd amount of medication, Catharine," he exclaimed, brandishing a particularly large tub of Anusol. I went red. In contrast Geoff's own medical kit consisted of one dozen aspirins, a roll of sticking plaster, ten Elastoplasts, six squares of moleskin, sunscreen, lipsalve, a crepe bandage and a dozen Panadol. It was wrapped up neatly into a piece of cloth the size of a playing card.

The next thing to go were my cigarettes. I had bought a box of 200 Marlboro Lights at duty free with the intention of smoking my way to the Pole. Steve had grassed me up and my new companions were justifiably horrified. They forbade me to smoke, rightly claiming that not only would it be ridiculously detrimental to my fitness, but also totally unethical in such a clean environment. We were forbidden to leave any waste on the continent, so I would be carting my fag ends all the way to the Pole. It was finally agreed that I could have a packet flown in to the South Pole to smoke if I got there. Taking away my cigarettes made me extremely nervy. In the chemist that afternoon, I stocked up on Nicorette chewing gum, justifying this as my personal luxury, rather than the special chocolate, perfume or hip flask of alcohol, the chosen treats of other team members.

At dinner that night, we met two Australians, Peter Tresseder and Tim Jarvis. They were attempting to cross the entire continent from Berkner Island down to McMurdo Sound. They wanted to be the first people to achieve this 1650-mile journey completely unassisted. This meant that when they got to the South Pole they would not have the luxury of being flown home at the end of the expedition like us. Instead, they would have a further 850 miles to go. I felt humble in their presence. They had been waiting to set off for two weeks, but bad weather had prevented them. So they were extremely anxious, as it was imperative they had as much time as possible to achieve their goal.

We also met a Frenchwoman called Laurence de la Ferrière, who in 1996 had become the first Frenchwoman to walk to the South Pole. In addition to Laurence, there had been Liv Arneson, who made the journey solo and unsupported in 1995 and a team of four American women in 1993. Fiona and I, and Caroline Hamilton's team were the next women making the attempt. That year, Laurence would be starting out from the South Pole on 23 November for the French Station Dumont d'Urville on the Adélie Land coast, some 1550 miles away. Laurence was a full-time expeditioner and very reassuring about my doubts. She told me that the first two weeks would be tough, but that after that my body should have acclimatized to the cold and weather conditions.

That afternoon Peter and Tim were told that the season's first Twin Otter had landed successfully at Patriot Hills and the runway was ready. The Hercules was now set to make its first journey of the year and they would be the first on board. We all went down to the airport to see them off. They were both in all their Antarctic clothing and were very keyed up. But just as they were to board the plane the flight was called off. The weather had changed. Their disappointment was obvious. Each day of delay made it more likely that they would not be able to finish their journey.

On the fifth morning I had a ten-minute interview with Radio 5 Live. At the end of it the interviewer asked me what I felt about all the controversy surrounding me. "What controversy?" I asked. "Well, there's been a lot of discussion on various radio programmes that, as a complete novice, it is foolhardy to be on an expedition of this kind. Some people feel that you're being irresponsible." My immediate response was just surprise that my plans could have generated this kind of public interest. It was a question that I had not thought about and did not know how to answer. It troubled me for the rest of the day. Wasn't all unknown risk irresponsible?

Had not my journeys in Borneo and Jordan, alone and unprepared, been risks? Had it not been lunatic to try to cross the Thai–Laotian border? At least I was not alone and unsupported this time. I would be with a professional guide, a world leader in his field. With Geoff, we were in the best possible hands, and the risk was being managed; we were prepared for any eventuality. On reflection, this was probably the least risky and irresponsible adventure I had taken on to date.

It also struck me that I was not concerned about dying. Many people had asked me if this scared me, but no. While I was sure that if the situation actually arose I would be frightened, at the time I was not. In a very melodramatic and I suppose romantic way, it was almost an outcome I would not have minded — a dramatic finale to my life. It made me concerned that I was thinking in this way and I wondered why. I think I was terribly scared about returning. If I went back a failure, it would be very difficult indeed, when I knew I needed so badly to succeed at something. If I did succeed, I wondered already what I could do next. I had huge debts and no job to return to. I knew already from my previous travels how difficult it would be to make the transition back into normal life.

But I also thought of my brother. He had been obsessed by daredevil motorcycle touring. Even a serious accident and lengthy court case had not deterred him. He had been addicted to the danger. Yet, the minute he met his future wife he gave up and sold his motorbike. He had explained to me that he had suddenly found something worth living for, and for the first time was not prepared to take the risk of dying. Perhaps it would be the answer for me, too.

That afternoon we finally waved goodbye to Tim and Peter. They would fly for six hours in the Hercules to Patriot Hills and from there to Berkner Island in a Twin Otter to begin their long, long walk. We were to be on the next flight but, meanwhile, we had time to make a group video. Each of us spoke for a few minutes about our hopes and fears for the journey. This gave us all a really good insight into one another. Justin reiterated that his goal was to be at the South Pole for the

Millennium, and did not seem concerned with the journey itself. Being in Antarctica was not what the expedition was actually about for him. And he betrayed his impatience. "True to myself, I will want to see a way of getting to the Pole in twenty-five minutes rather than sixty-one days."

Steve was the only person really enthusiastic about the journey itself. When asked what we were most looking forward to, the rest of us replied seeing the Pole on the horizon and then arriving. But Steve was looking forward to everything; he couldn't wait, he had no fears; he was completely confident. Asked how the journey might change him, he said: "I know it will quite simply fuel my imagination to do more." I came to learn that his positive energy was absolutely genuine.

My comments were far more cautious. I felt extremely privileged to have the opportunity to be here and attempt this journey. But I was starting to feel afraid that I would hold everyone up, become a burden and then fail. I was terrified I wouldn't make it and I felt that exclaiming "Failure is not an option" on record to the British media before I left had been rash and foolish.

After a lesson from Geoff on how to go to the loo in freezing conditions, we had a team dinner. But what team? It seemed more like separate small groups to me. Because Mike, Fiona and I were sponsored, we had PR people. They were concerned only for their sponsors' products and cared little about the other members of the team. Mike and Fiona were calling their expedition the British Millennium South Pole

Expedition, whereas mine was supposedly the South Pole Millennium Expedition. The *Daily Telegraph* were following Mike and Fiona's story and the *Daily Mirror* mine; nobody was following the rest of the team, because they had all funded themselves and had no need for publicity. I knew it was our record-breaking attempt that made us attractive to our sponsors, so, embarrassing though it was for me, we had to advertise these pegs our trip was hung on — Fiona and I as the first British women, Fiona and her husband Mike, the first married couple.

But within the group it became a joke. Veijo thought, in his understated way, that he might be the first Finn to walk to the Pole. Steve thought he might be the youngest Briton, and certainly the first plumber, and Justin decided he would be the first bastard. It was Justin who astutely suggested that we should form our own single group identity now that we were about to set off. We decided to call ourselves Plebs to the Pole. It seemed only appropriate — we were to be the first group of amateurs to go. Our radio call sign became Papa Tango Papa, PTP, Plebs to the Pole. I have to say that Mike and Fiona dissented from this humorous title and still do. Their preparations had been so thorough — a visit to Spitzbergen, and extensive consultations with polar figures — they felt the title was demeaning and did not want to be seen as endorsing it. This was entirely understandable.

That evening I went into town to force more food into my body. I had only managed to put on half a stone before departing, rather than the two I had hoped. I was secretly getting worried about my weight and how thin I was. Since arriving in Punta I had started binge eating. I was drinking some horrible "gain weight" concoction and had found a hamburger diner we nicknamed Vomits, where I furtively guzzled four or more huge burgers a day, washed down with pints of chocolate milk.

As I was coming out of Vomits after my fifth burger, I noticed Pen and the British women's team in a café next door. Although I had been in regular contact with Pen, I had not actually seen him since the depressing evening when he told us his own expedition would not be going ahead. He was now logistics manager to the British All-Women. It was lovely to see him and interesting, even intimidating, to meet the women, knowing that we were all going for the same goal. We did not chat, I was too nervous and did not know what to say. They were going to the Pole as an all-women group, and without a guide. Their achievement would be extremely impressive, regardless of when they actually arrived. But they were booked on the second Hercules after ours. Depending on the weather, they would be at least a week behind. I realized that if the Plebs to the Pole did manage to get to the South Pole before the British All-Women, it would just be because of logistics.

We would be ready to go the next day. The Hercules had returned from depositing the Patriot Hills team, Tim and Peter, and fuelling up for us. Justin booked us into the poshest restaurant he could find, a few miles outside Punta on the seashore, for dinner with Geoff and Victor. The last supper, if you like. During the afternoon we packed all our equipment, sleds, skis and provisions on to a truck for the airport. Everything was weighed and loaded on to the plane. I furtively stood on some scales I found in the weighing room and noticed I had put on another stone. I was euphoric. "Hey guys, fantastic news, my burger eating has paid off, I've put on a stone and a half." Steve just blinked at me incredulously. Speechless, he pointed to the loaded rucksack I still had on my back. Only an hour ago Geoff had announced who would be sharing with whom for the first part of the journey. He had just heard I was to be his tent partner.

We ordered as much food as we could at dinner, knowing our diet would be dehydrated meals and butter for the next seventy days or so. I watched everyone round the table, Mike, Grahame and Veijo quiet and pensive, Steve his usual buoyant self, talking excitedly about the journey ahead. Fiona and Justin were in extremely high spirits, cracking jokes and roaring with laughter. They were totally unperturbed by the journey ahead, Justin because he had no idea and Fiona, as I was beginning to realize, because she was a glorious optimist. She was not a worrier and took on any new challenge with hearty enthusiasm. She was genuinely looking forward to the actual physical challenge and seeing how far she could push herself.

As for the guides, Victor was extremely upbeat and seemingly unworried, but Geoff was totally silent. He stared fixedly at some of the diners who had got up to salsa, but was clearly not interested. His mind was elsewhere. I wondered what he must be thinking. He was about to guide seven amateurs 705 miles across a freezing Antarctic wasteland, one that had taken many lives. It must have seemed a heavy responsibility.

I was quietly terrified now. I had been so completely absorbed preparing for this trip that I had never really thought about the realities of actually making the journey. All I had concentrated on was the next goal: getting accepted on the expedition, finding a sponsor, training, getting press coverage and finally getting to the airport and out to Punta Arenas. Back in England, I had been the naive optimist, gallantly declaring to the British media that, of course, I would make it — "failure was not an option". All well and good in the comfort of my warm, cosy London flat, surrounded by my party-loving friends who considered doggy-paddling the length of Clapham pool commendable exercise. In Punta I felt surrounded by people of apparently superhuman fitness and strength.

Geoff continued to stare as he watched his team on the dance floor in a haphazard and drunken attempt to salsa. "I'm not sure how this bunch of jokers think they are going to make it to the Pole, but I am happy to be proved wrong," someone overheard him say. I went out and had a walk along the sea. I could not take the general hilarity and high spirits at that moment. I needed to be quiet. I sat next to Steve on the way back. I had begun to open up to him about my doubts and fears of the journey and he was positive and extremely kind. He had noticed how quiet I had been at the restaurant and said, "You know what? You're going to get to the Pole, and when you get there you're going to want to just keep going all the way to the other side. You're going to have a ball, woman."

Nonetheless, that night I had a quiet word with Geoff. "Do you think I am mad? Do you honestly think I can make it?" He paused rather too long for my liking and then said, with words carefully chosen: "It is absolutely possible, Catharine. You see, on an expedition of this kind, it is not just physical ability that counts. Mental strength is as much if not more important. I would go as far as saying it's 30 per cent physical and 70 per cent mental. I've seen the strongest men go out and crack under the emotional pressure of the hardships of a polar expedition, and also seen seemingly physically weak people excel mentally and get through with persistence and determination. At this stage, I cannot say how *any* of you will perform out there."

On departure day, I developed a dreadful cold. We were told to stand by, so I just stayed in the hotel room and waited. I could do no more than just take to my bed and watch MTV. The suspense and anticipation were too much for anything else. It struck me that, normally, I spent every minute of every day abroad exploring the sights, and experiencing the people and nightlife. Abroad was a privilege. This was my first time in South America and, instead, all I had seen were the warehouse two miles out of town where we had been packing, the inside of my hotel bedroom and some cruddy pop videos.

At 2p.m. we had the call to go to the airport. I had one last cigarette and then left my box of 200 duty-free on the hotel bed for the chambermaid. Within half an hour we were on the bus in full Antarctic gear. The atmosphere was extremely highly charged. As well as us there was a four-man Singaporean team, also going to the Pole, and Laurence, our French friend. We arrived at the airport and waited. I had a whisky to calm my nerves. My last drink for two and a half months, I imagined. But within half an hour Faye, from ANI, announced that the weather had turned. It would be unsafe to land. Part of me felt disappointed and deflated. We were all so geared up and ready to go. But another part was relieved that the moment of beginning a journey of unavoidable hardship had now been postponed.

In one way or another this charade happened four more times. On Sunday, we did not even leave the hotel. My cold had worsened, so I did something I had never done before, I lay in bed the entire day watching dreadful films. The delay had caused us to exceed our accommodation budget, so on Monday we moved into a smaller hotel and all shared a very large room. Again we were told to stand by; we loitered forlornly by the phone, sweltering in our Antarctic clothes and enormous thermal boots. In the morning we tried again, but before we even reached the airport the weather closed in and the bus made a swift turn around.

The next day we did make it as far as the airport. In the afternoon, we were told to be ready by five. The

Hercules was fuelled up and the engines running. After a wait in the airport café we actually went through security and into the proper departure lounge. Strangely, we did not need our passports. I had assumed otherwise. We then clambered back on to the bus, which made its way over to the plane. Then I noticed Faye tapping the driver's shoulder. The bus stopped. Sure enough, the weather had changed again and we were to return to Punta for yet another frustrating wait.

By Thursday we were all restless, and everyone else had fallen into the pattern of only being able to watch cheap action films. But at half past two we got the call that it was a go. Once bitten, twice shy. We ambled on to the bus. At the airport we settled down for yet another "final" whisky, no longer really believing we would get any further. But this time we made it to the plane. Tentatively, we began to take departure photographs, still expecting the weather to change. We boarded. Suddenly, there was a real electricity in the cabin. The interior of the plane was mainly cargo, with a few seats bolted in. Our sleds were piled one on top of another. Rather than the entertainment headsets found on normal aircraft, we were given earplugs to drown out the deafening noise of the Hercules taking off. I felt a surge of terrified excitement.

After six hours flying above the notoriously dangerous sea of the Drake Passage, where many had been lost in shipwrecks, we landed on a natural runway. It was a huge stretch of blue ice, cleared of snow by winds from the nearby mountains. These winds were described as katabatic. They roared down the mountains at great speed. Their action was explained to me as being like the movement of a jelly on the top of an upturned bowl slipping down on to the table. Pilots were unable to use traditional braking techniques to stop the plane on ice. They needed to have enormous skill to land, reversing the propellers and very gradually bringing the plane to a stop, like back-pedalling on a bicycle. My heart was in my mouth, as I knew there was always the risk of the plane spinning round.

As I stepped out of the plane I was struck by how beautiful this place was. The sun shone, the sky was blue and even though it was incredibly cold, it was bearable because layers of thermal clothing, neoprene and Gore-Tex (a fabric that keeps moisture out but lets sweat escape) covered up my body. As far as I could see, there was a vast expanse of white. There were no other colours at all except a few dots of orange — the tents marking the base camp. It was an extraordinary sight to adjust my eyes to. Initially, it gave me an enormous high. It was such a contrast to the drab greyness of a British winter in London, which I had just left. Later on, the monochromatic landscape would nearly drive us all mad, but for the moment the blue ice runway was an awesome sight. The ice had been formed into ripples by the wind. It glistened in the sun and was easily mistaken for the sea.

I was quietly confident, because I was surprised at the favourable conditions. This was not at all the desolate bleak and miserable Antarctica I had read about in Scott's accounts. The base camp consisted of a series of tents erected for staff and guests who had come to visit Antarctica as a holiday rather than go on an expedition. It included a tent with a bucket, mirror and a bar of soap where one could wash. The toilets consisted of two buckets, one for each operation. Once you had finished, you were required to pour the liquid — or solids — into a barrel outside and this would then be flown back to Punta for disposal. It is the rule in Antarctica that no waste, even human, can remain if at all possible.

The communal cook tent was large enough to house about thirty people around tables heaving with exploration books. It was beautifully warm. At the far end was a kitchen where Ros and her assistant Jane produced superb "home from home" cooking. I learned that Ros had been the camp chef for some years — the short season allowed staff to have an ordinary life back in Blighty as well. Beside the kitchen, there was a communications tent, where the radio operator was in continual contact with Punta Arenas and with all the expeditions in Antarctica. A computer allowed a limited e-mail service. All this was run off petrol and wind turbine generators and solar panels.

Not far from the kitchen tent four aeroplanes sat on the ground, two Twin Otters, which seated nine at most, a wartime DC6, rebuilt with turboprop engines and sometimes used on excursions to see penguins, and a tiny Cessna plane which could take two people. This would be used to fly Laurence to the South Pole and if anyone needed to be airlifted out. At the end of the season, everything would be packed into an enormous

105

underground ice cave, leaving only six-foot pole markers showing. It was the job of the following season's staff, when they flew in, to locate the markers, dig by hand, unearth the ice cave and so renew the camp.

As we had arrived at midnight, we had just enough time for hot soup and home-made bread before putting up the tent and spending our first night in Antarctica. It was −26°C and still bright sunshine. I was already wearing three layers of thermal underwear and a fleece and was inside a down sleeping bag specially made by the manufacturer Rab. But I still felt very cold and could not sleep. I eventually applied an extra fleece, gloves, hat and another pair of socks and managed to doze fitfully for three hours. As the days passed, I did become used to the cold, and I was exhausted from each day's travel, so I was soon able to sleep through the whole night.

We spent the next morning checking equipment and our stoves and packing our sleds with enough food and fuel to last us four days. As soon as was possible, we were to fly in the two Twin Otters to a place called Hercules Inlet, right at the edge of Antarctica. This was twenty-seven miles from Patriot Hills. We would then begin our journey to the Pole, passing Patriot Hills on the way. In theory, this would give us four days' walk to test our equipment. The stop at Patriot Hills would allow us to check any physical problems with the base doctor. In practice, however, I knew also that if any of us were not up to the journey Geoff would have the chance to leave us at Patriot Hills to catch the next Hercules back to Punta. He would be well within his rights to do so, and even at this stage I was afraid he would be doing it to me.

In the afternoon I put on my skis and attached the sled to my harness. It was the moment of truth. This was the first time in my life I had put on cross-country skis and I was about to ski 705 miles in them. I took a few tentative steps. I did not immediately slip over, as I had feared, and the sled, admittedly nearly empty, slid smoothly over the ice. Steve advised me to imagine I was a grand-dad in slippers, shuffling around the house, not picking my feet up. But it was too early to feel confident. Once we returned from Hercules Inlet we would be filling our sleds with food and fuel — enough to last us for 325 miles, since we would be resupplied during our journey.

I noticed that although I was about to embark on a terrifying journey I felt extremely calm. I was hungry for the first time in months and actually craved food rather than having to force it down. I had not woken up with a nocturnal panic attack since I had arrived in Punta, and the thought of a cigarette had not entered my mind. My inner demons were at bay, then. While waiting, we waved off the Singaporeans, a friendly group led by a man called Swee Chiow. Another group of Singaporeans was climbing Mount Vinson. Both groups were very upbeat and excellent company. We were looking forward to following one another's progress, perhaps with some friendly rivalry along the way.

It was Friday, 5 November 1999, when we flew out to Hercules Inlet to make the first leg of the journey. It had become much windier and I started to feel the cold on my face. With the majority of my layers on, I was warm as long as I kept moving, but my hands were causing me problems. I was wearing a thin pair of thermal gloves designed for cycling in Britain under mountaineers' mittens with a fleece lining. I already regretted having shopped so hurriedly on the way to the airport.

In the morning we skied for about forty-five minutes away from the camp to test the radio. This might have been our only form of communication for the entire journey. However, Mike and Fiona were sponsored by Project Telecom, a communications provider, and had been lent an iridium mobile satellite phone. This operated on a battery charged by a solar panel strapped to their sled. So far it had worked perfectly — the reception was as clear as a local call. The radio, by contrast, was very heavy, as were the spare batteries. It took approximately ten minutes to set it and its aerials up outside the tent. It seemed that for expeditions of this kind the radio was becoming a thing of the past and was being taken over by the more reliable but much more expensive satellite phone. We got back to a departing feast of stew and apple pie and then set about preparing for our flight to Hercules Inlet.

Soon after lunch the plane was ready. I was to set off on the first flight with four team members and then the plane would return with the remainder. The flight over the Antarctic continent was wonderful. However, even though we were in the air for just twelve minutes, at approximately US$3000 it was the most expensive flight I had taken. As we approached the landing point I could only see ice. Geoff then pointed out a line, a crack separating the sea from the continent. The sea was, in fact, frozen. Our pilot made a few test touchdowns, delicately feathering one ski on to the surface of the ice to see whether it was smooth enough to use as a runway. When we actually landed, the plane ploughed through a small snowdrift causing plumes of snow to shower into the air. It was extremely exciting.

We waited for thirty minutes for the second group to arrive, moving constantly to keep warm. Within minutes of getting out of the warm plane my hands were painful again. My fingers felt wooden. In cold conditions, the body concentrates on keeping the core and the internal organs warm. It ignores extremities such as toes and fingers. I swung my arms round and round, like a windmill, propelling the blood back into my hands.

It was late by the time the remainder of the team arrived, so we decided to travel for just ninety minutes that night before setting up camp. The sky was blue, the sun was shining and the wind had calmed down considerably. Our sleds were light; we only had four days' food and fuel, of course.

That night we cooked our first meal. We began by selecting some firm snow and melting it, then poured the boiling water into packets of dehydrated food. We had various flavours — tonight's was shepherd's pie. It actually tasted quite good. With this, we had potato flakes, to which we added obscene amounts of butter, followed by very fatty flapjacks and army ration biscuits. Geoff had calculated that we should eat around 6000 calories a day, 4000 more than our usual diet in city life. The food was kept in boxes. Each box contained three days' rations for two people. It looked like a vast amount. But Geoff assured us it would not feel enough in two weeks' time and we would crave more. I slept well, absolutely stuffed.

Life was good. I was still quietly confident. I was extremely relieved that the weather was not as bad as I had imagined and read it would be. The journey had not been arduous so far. Perhaps those polar explorers had exaggerated the weather conditions and their own hardships for effect, I thought, as I drifted happily off to sleep.

CHAPTER
SEVEN

First Steps in the Snow

The winds were gusting and howling and whipping the snow up into a frozen blizzard. I could see nothing out of the tent. We had woken up to a whiteout. On this, just the second day, Antarctica was about to show us her true nature.

Whiteout is just that. When we started, I could see no further than the orange sled in front of me, which often, terrifyingly, disappeared into the suffocating white fog. I had experienced mist coming down during walks in Scotland before, but nothing like this. It was as if I were walking on the inside of a ping-pong ball. I could simply not tell which way was up, which down. The sky was exactly the same shade of white as the ground, the horizon could not be seen. I found the process particularly difficult as I felt I was skiing in pitch darkness, except it was white instead of black. It made keeping my balance difficult and I already imagined that days on end of it would do terrible things to the mind. The going was harder than before because the snow was much deeper. Instead of gliding smoothly over the ice, we had to use all the strength we had in our hips and backs to force the sleds through the snow.

It was a total shock. I was absolutely freezing and, within the first hour, I realized I was paying for my lack of training. I was the weakest and the slowest member of the group by far. The day was structured so that we would walk for one hour, stop for a five minute break, eat some chocolate, then continue. Each hour was timed and at the second the hour was up the leader would cross their skis in the air to indicate we were stopping. Even after I became more comfortable, later in the trip, this hourly signal was my Holy Grail, still what I longed to see.

It was too cold to stop for longer than five minutes before our bodies started to become hypothermic, and our hands to scream in pain, and each time I caught up that day, the break was always already over. I was too cold and in too much of a panic to eat; the simple task of opening my bumbag and retrieving my chocolate was too difficult. Because I was working so hard and my body lacking fuel I became hypoglycaemic — my level of blood sugar fell — and tearful, which made me more and more helpless. I fell over several times. Twice I was unable to put my ski back on and had to be assisted.

The wind, which blew steadily into our faces, and was to do so almost the entire journey, was so loud that I had to shout just to be heard by someone standing right next to me. It was so strong it could blow us backwards if we stood still. We walked for only three hours, but that short period was absolutely horrible. I felt weak, frightened and I was completely unable to keep up.

I would focus on the orange sled in front of me, desperately trying to keep it no more than a foot away, occupying my mind making anagrams from its sponsors' labels, much as car passengers make up words out of the registration letters of passing vehicles. I would then watch the sled drifting further away. The further it receded the more I panicked and the harder I tried to work. Eventually my body would be worn out and I would be forced to slow down to a snail's pace watching the anagram disappear into the white expanse.

At the last break it was so cold and windy we took refuge under an emergency bivouac shelter for ten minutes. This was just a big sheet of plastic that we all clambered under, sitting firmly on the sides to hold it down to stop the wind sweeping it away. It provided protection from the wind but little comfort as the plastic flapped wildly and very loudly against our heads. It also offered no respite from the temperature. I started to shiver violently. I looked around at eight very strained faces, all desperately trying to gnaw on frozen flapjack and chocolate.

When we set up camp I declined into serious cold. It was so windy that we could barely put up the tents. The others split into two teams of four, putting them up one at a time, but I was unable to do anything at all, so when the first inner tent was up Steve just shoved me in and lit the stove while everyone else put up the remainder of the camp. Fiona joined me shortly afterwards and sat with me to check I was all right. I noticed that she seemed not even remotely troubled and was happily chatting as I fell into a deep hypothermic sleep. When I woke up, Steve was settled, and the stove was on for dinner. He had covered me up with my own sleeping bag. "Bit of a nippy day, today," he said, as if everything were quite normal. I nodded glumly. "I know you are panicking," he went on, "but you'll be fine. You did well today, don't you worry."

I did worry. As I warmed up, I thought that I did not know how on earth I was going to keep up with the rest. We had talked about taking it really slowly — a polar plod as we called it — but it had still seemed a sprint to me. "I have been preparing for this trip for two years, I have raised £30,000," I mused, "and I think I am going to have to give up." For how was I going to survive another *sixty* days of this? Nothing, not Pen's or Geoff's briefings, nor the ANI lecture evening, had prepared me for it.

"At least leave that decision till we're back at Patriot Hills." Steve reassured me, "If it's any consolation, Grahame had just as bad a day. And he has flu or something. So we'll be taking it a lot slower tomorrow and having a nice short day." He cooked me dinner and tried to cheer me up with funny stories about his life as a plumber.

I kept waking up during the night in terror. I really did not believe I could go on. And what was I going to tell Trevor, who had put so much faith in me? I was very, very quiet the next morning. I tentatively put my nose out of the tent flap and noticed that, although it was no warmer, the wind had dropped. This made life almost bearable. Wind-chill, as it is called, makes outside temperatures feel much colder. But then the horrible moment came when the stove was switched off and we had to leave the tent, packing everything up into our sleds and finally taking down the tents themselves. I very nervously took my first steps with Fiona and concentrated hard on matching her strides. All day I forced myself to keep up with her pace.

Grahame was extremely unwell and Steve had unfortunately caught my Chilean cold. So the pace did slow down. We went five hours and, although exhausted, I managed to help make camp. I felt so much happier that evening. We all knew that these first four days were going to be a trial, acclimatizing to weather we had never experienced before. It was also uphill all the way — that day we had climbed to 1000 feet. I cooked for Steve, washed up and even managed to leave the warmth of the tent to give Grahame a Lemsip. He was looking very drawn and tired, confiding that when we had been under the bivvy shelter he had had hallucinations in which all of us had appeared as devils. This had naturally made him very frightened.

My back was giving me a lot of pain, however. I was filled with regret again. Pulling car tyres had sounded such a mad idea back in England, but I was now realizing how essential it was. No machine in the gym, no amount of training could have simulated the hard work of pulling a sled of provisions, and the weight would be going up sevenfold in four days' time. I could

115

put on a brave face now because our sleds were virtually empty and I knew in a couple of days we would be back in the fleshpots of Patriot Hills with Ros's home cooking. I also knew Victor and Geoff were monitoring me closely; they would rightly have no hesitation in leaving me at Patriot Hills if they felt I was not up to the journey.

After dinner I realized I must confront the question of going to the loo in front of Steve. Once in the tents at night, it was too cold to go out without putting on all the layers, face mask, boots and hat. So we had all brought plastic bottles, used for drinking in normal life, and were supposed to use them inside the tent. I had practised at home and found it very traumatic, as it was really difficult to get the aim right. I talked to Steve; he admitted that he was self-conscious, too. We then agreed that he should put his hat back to front over his eyes when it was my "turn". When I was finished, I would give him the all-clear and he would remove the hat. I would do the same for him, but, as in normal life, the operation is much easier for a man. It was relatively straightforward for him just to go sheltered by his sleeping bag.

We tried out the drill that night, but I had beginner's nerves. As I was putting the lid back on the bottle I dropped it, spilling the contents all over the tent floor. After my previous day's weakness, I decided I could not confess. So, in a complete panic, I hastily scooped up some of the snow which was to be used for cooking and spread it over the floor. It acted like a sponge and soaked up all the offending liquid quite quickly. I then gathered everything up in my hands and threw the whole mess out of the tent flap, all while Steve was still sitting there with his hat over his eyes, too polite to ask why I was taking so long. I gave the all clear signal. He suspected nothing. The drill was a success and we decided to adopt this very formal toilet procedure for the rest of the journey.

Defecating was a more tricky process. Up to now the need had not arisen, but with our change of diet, it became an urgent issue. Geoff had suggested that in the morning we wait until after breakfast and packing. One person for each tent should then dig a hole in the vestibule of the tent and deposit, while the other was sweeping the floor of snow. In reality I was always this second person and would begin faffing around with my wetwipes. Steve would then cover up his droppings with a layer of snow and I would go on top of that while he was taking the tent down around me. This was a tricky procedure that required military discipline, but it worked.

We now all had an attempt at navigating. Geoff turned on his GPS — the satellite controlled global positioning system that allows any skilled navigator to determine where he is anywhere in the world — to find our position and the compass bearing to Patriot Hills. He transferred this to a normal magnetic compass, by which we would then navigate. In the old days, exactly as with sailors at sea, position was calculated with the use of a marine sextant. The sextant measured the angle of the sun above the horizon, and using mathematical tables, positions on the globe could be calculated. This was an effective system, but extremely slow, and painful in the cold. In 1990, Geoff had navigated in this way over 4000 miles on his transantarctic expedition. Only ten years ago, he had not had the luxury of just turning on a machine that would simply tell him exactly where he was in the world down to the last 300 feet.

On a bright day navigation was relatively straightforward, as we would use our shadows. At six in the morning the sun was directly in the east, and therefore our shadows exactly to our right as we walked south. We would imagine our shadows were like the hands of clocks and, for each hour, the "shadow hand" would move round fifteen degrees. The shadow hand moved at half the speed of an hour hand. In twenty-four hours, the sun makes *one* complete circle of the sky; a clock hand, of course, goes all the way round in twelve. At midday, for example, the sun was behind us in the north and our shadows were straight in front of us. By six in the evening the sun was in the west and our shadows pointing exactly left. At midnight, the sun was in the south, our shadows directly behind us. We would position ourselves correctly to the bearing on the compass and then just look at where our shadows were in relation to our bodies. However, we did back up this form of sun navigation with the compass, and we made periodic checks.

Before embarking on this expedition, I had assumed that if we just set our compass arrow to south we should finally get to the Pole. But the Earth has a natural magnetism, and this causes a compass to point a few degrees out of true. This magnetic variation, as it is called, is slowly changing, and at present, the Magnetic North Pole — the place the compass thinks the North Pole is at — is about 700 miles from the true, Geographic North Pole. In the Antarctic, the Magnetic Pole is currently in the ocean, 1500 miles from the South Geographic Pole. Scientists calculate magnetic variation, but with the GPS, the instrument could just tell us exactly what the variation was, and so what the precise compass bearing should be.

When there was no sun to give shadows and absolutely no features on the ground to focus on, it was much harder. We would ski along, checking the compass bearing every five minutes or so, stopping and starting. Initially we led in pairs, one navigating and the other making constant checks behind to ensure the group was together. It would be easy to lose a straggler in a whiteout.

Already, Steve and I had the procedure of making camp down to an hour. We put up the tent together, asking for help if the wind proved too difficult. But it was not enough just to put pegs into the ice, however firmly. Steve would have to dig solidly, building a wall around our tent and shovelling hard snow on to the specially designed valance to stop the whole tent being blown away by the high winds. He would then adjust the guy ropes and place our sleds beside the tent where they could provide an extra protective barrier against the wind. It was not until all this was done that he could finally scramble into the tent for warmth. I

119

was immensely grateful that he always took on the undesirable role of outside man.

In the meantime, I would start setting up inside, inflating our mattresses, bringing out sleeping bags, food and the stove. As soon as Steve was in the tent we would light the stove — the first feeling of warmth all day. I loved this moment and would huddle over the fierce flame until dragged off in order to boil water to make a drink. This moment came to feel more pleasurable than anything I had ever experienced in my life.

The next day, the winds were ferocious and Geoff called a rest day. It was pointless to push ourselves at this stage, even before the journey proper. But in the afternoon he came round to inspect our tents. I was sure ours was beginning to smell by now and he instantly said, "This is a disgrace, if you don't get organized you'll die. Simple as that."

We looked around us. Food wrappers littered the floor and down sleeping bags and jackets lay dangerously near to the flame of the stove. I had already burned a hole in my sleeping bag. The feathers could have quickly turned into a ball of flame and burned the tent down in seconds. The floor of the tent was covered in snow that I had brought in with me after going outside for a box of food, because I had not bothered to clean my boots properly. There were wet socks, gloves and hats hanging precariously from string we had attached to the tent ceiling. The vestibule was covered in a yellow carpet of urine where we had

120

carelessly poured out our bottles. Geoff was right. It was quite revolting, a disaster waiting to happen.

We spent an hour clearing up and packing our rubbish into one bag, to be stored in Steve's sled and left at Patriot Hills to be flown out. After that, we would be carrying all our rubbish with us, as nothing was to be left or buried on the Antarctic continent. We packed away our sleeping bags, in which we had been lolling, and resolved not to bring them out until bedtime. This made the day seem less like one of my teenage sleepover parties. We then bored a small, neat hole in the ice of the vestibule. This would be our drainage system for every kind of liquid waste and could be tidily covered over on departure. After another long nap, Steve and I contracted cabin fever and decided to go out and brave the elements. It took us almost an hour to put on four layers of clothing, socks, hats, face masks, goggles and gloves, just to make the ten second journey to Mike and Fiona's tent for tea and chat.

In comparison to ours, their tent was immaculate. There was not a speck of snow on their floor. They had erected a very neat washing line from the four corners of the tent ceiling and hung up two pairs of socks carefully attached with safety pins. There was no rubbish and everything else was stored in two long sausage bags, which efficiently doubled as chairs or backrests. Their Antarctic home was like a new pin. On the inside of the tent, a diagram showed sixty-five marks in a vertical line, representing the sixty-five days we hoped we needed; three were now crossed off.

The wind had dropped and we ventured into the freezing evening for a walk. About half a mile away a DC6 aircraft had crashed in 1993. The plane had been carrying dogs and personnel for an expedition by the legendary Norman Vaughan. Vaughan had been dog sled driver for Admiral Byrd, when Byrd made the first flight to the Pole in 1929. In whiteout conditions, the DC6 pilot thought he was much higher than he was and flew into the ground. Mercifully, the wheels were not down and only one man was badly hurt, though two of the dogs ran off and were never seen again. ANI arrived from Patriot Hills and rescued everyone, but the plane had, of course, remained.

We walked for about ten minutes to reach it. Most was buried under snow, revealing just the top of the fuselage, the fin and some of an engine. I looked back at our camp and was suddenly frightened. Our tents were just five tiny yellow specks. Mike had taken a bearing, but had the weather closed in we could have been completely lost.

Geoff was very alarmed on our return; he did not know we had walked off so far. The next day, he told me a story from his transantarctic expedition. During a storm his partner Keizo had left their tent to check on the dogs, and not returned. Alarmed, the rest of the team roped together and started sweep-searching the surrounding area but without success. The next day with the storm still raging, Geoff found him barely a hundred feet away. When Keizo realized he was lost, he scraped a small hole in the snow with a pair of pliers he had found in his pockets and shivered out the night

122

in this tiny shelter. Overconfidence had nearly cost him his life. I instantly took the point.

Four hours later, the staff at Patriot Hills gave us a heroes' welcome home and it felt as if the expedition had actually ended. In reality, it had not truly begun. We were now to spend the next twenty-four hours making adjustments to skis and clothing and packing our sleds with enough food and fuel to take us to the Thiel Mountains, halfway between Patriot Hills and the Pole. This was to be our resupply point; we estimated thirty-five days for the 350-odd miles.

I was very quiet, in fear that I would be left behind. I spent the entire time waiting for an ominous tap on the shoulder, waiting to be led to a tent cleared of people and being told I was not up to the expedition. It took me back to waiting for a humiliating discharge after I had crashed the BBC e-mail system.

Well, I had improved, I reasoned, even if the mileage was low, the sleds virtually empty, and the weather reasonable. I knew in my heart of hearts that I was badly prepared mentally and physically, but I had decided in my less gloomy moments that I was going to give it my best. If I became a burden to the group I would bow out, but I refused to let my own fear, physical pain and misery get the better of me. Besides, it was one thing to fail through weather or sickness, quite another just to give up. Whatever strategy of self-justification I might adopt, and however kind and understanding people would be, it would be ridiculous to stop just four days into the journey.

That night, one after another, we visited the tent surgery of the camp doctor, Dr Kate, with blisters, mild frostbite and aching backs or joints. Despite her excellent bedside manner, there was only so much she could do. On an expedition of this kind pain was just one of the many unavoidable trials. I half suspected she would find something drastically wrong with me, and enable Geoff to abandon me, but she passed me fit. I decided not to speak to Geoff, or indeed anyone, about my own doubts, as if by keeping silent I would end up quietly tagging on the end of the team by default.

On 11 November 1999, we all left Patriot Hills at 3p.m. I almost felt as if someone would spot me and ask, "What is she still doing here?" The base camp manager, another Steve, wished me lots of luck and said, "Just keep going, Catharine. Before you know it, Patriot Hills will be out of sight. Then the Thiel Mountains will be out of sight and the next minute you will be at the Pole." I was really moved by our departure. We lined up, had our photos taken and then everyone came to see us off, waving for minutes until we were well on our way. But I found out many months later that nobody at Patriot Hills thought I would make it. They had even taken bets on how quickly I would give up. Victor had already suggested to Geoff that I be taken off the expedition, but Geoff had overruled him. Generally it was Victor rather than Geoff who accompanied me at the back — it was clearly good practice to have one guide at each end of the group — and from his "shepherd dog" duties he had seen my struggles close up.

From the moment I made that first tug on the harness I realized the change in weight was massive. No longer did the sleds glide over the snow, it was a case of having to haul with all one's might. It felt like pulling the sled over wet sand rather than smooth ice. The weight had all been distributed equally to every team member. The only dispensation in helping out on weight would be if a team member became ill or injured. It was up to me to keep up with the rest of the group regardless of my strength. Despite my struggles I was glad about this. Beside us were three mountains called the Three Sails. They looked like gigantic snow dunes topped by beautiful peaks, like icing on a Christmas cake. At the end of the day I was absolutely dead beat and very quiet. Steve asked me if he could take any of my weight, but I declined. I did not want anyone to say afterwards that I had got to the Pole because there were seven strong men helping me out. I wanted to succeed on my own merits.

But Steve was fast turning into my guardian angel. It already looked as if he was the strongest team member, and he saw this as a means of helping, supporting and encouraging me. His kindness and selflessness made me feel humble. Knowing that I was easily distracted from my misery by love stories and gossip, he spent the evening telling me about his girlfriend Catherine, who had stoically supported him in his polar quest. She sounded delightful. We covered a little over five miles that first day — I knew we had aimed more than to double that.

The next day, I woke up with a streaming cold, mucus frozen around my nose and where it had dripped into my sleeping bag. To make matters worse, my period arrived. I had decided not to take the Pill to stop my periods, but this purity, all well and good in the comforts of one's warm bathroom, soap and sanitary bin, was a very different matter at −25°C, living in a tent with a man I had only just met.

Every step that day gave me pain, in my legs, my back, my Achilles tendons and my shoulders. My diary described it as "The worst day of my life". I tried to make my mind wander on to pleasures, food, beaches, music, but I failed. The pain did not let me distract myself. I went through wall after mental wall, always convinced I could not get through the next half hour, but somehow managing, concentrating hard on just putting one foot in front of the other. I was very slow and aware the team was having to wait for me to catch up. But I was beyond caring. Geoff tried to be sympathetic and I knew he must be concerned.

By the end of seven hours, I was capable of nothing. I hindered rather than helped Steve in putting up the tent, and then he shoved me inside with a stove. I was already disciplined in not putting on the stove until the inside of our home was set up, beds laid out, food boxes in position and pee bottles at the ready. The cold added to the urgency and made us faster. But that day I could not wait to feel the blissful warmth of the flame making me human again. Ten minutes later, Steve came into the tent to find nothing ready, the stove roaring away, and his tent partner asleep. He had to cook and wash up again. This time, he told me funny stories of his life as a chalet boy in a French ski resort. I resolved that night that if I backed out, which looked increasingly likely, I would emigrate to Australia and marry David, who had lived through so much of my formative buffoonery that this latest failure would not trouble him.

Over the next three days the pattern became painfully apparent. Eight fit and strong members of the expedition skied at a reasonable rate for eight hours a day, covering a distance of around eleven miles, battling against blasting, icy winds and temperatures of down to −48°C, taking account of wind-chill. We pulled everything behind us in sleds weighing around eleven stone. Imagine that you spend your entire day dragging a full-grown man behind you as you walk about. There were no injuries yet, and although tired at the end of the day, the team was comfortable, and made camp quite happily. The next morning, we would pack everything up into the sleds and set off for another eight hours. Surprisingly, Justin, who had known nothing about Antarctica, was completely comfortable. He was exceptionally strong and his cavalier attitude of "training as you go" seemed to be working. I sensed he found my pace irritating. I was especially conscious I was an obstacle to his obsession with reaching the Pole for the Millennium.

The ninth member — that was me — was in quite a different position. I continued to find the conditions absolutely awful. I developed a chest infection and was coughing up a sinister fluid. No doubt this was because

I only gave up smoking after Punta. I was completely unable to keep up with the apparently gentle pace, and this meant the team had to wait on average three times an hour for me to catch up. I had pain in every muscle and was completely annihilated by the end of each day. I knew the team was getting cold waiting for me. In addition, we only had limited food, so we had target mileages, and I could not ask for longer breaks, let alone days off. Least of all could I "finish early" if I was too tired. I felt doomed. I also noticed that the tip of each finger had turned white and felt strangely wooden, a middle finger in particular. I decided to ignore the fact that I was probably getting frostbite.

Four days from Patriot Hills we came across a crevasse field. Geoff was aware this existed from a Japanese adventurer's hand-drawn map. He did not, however, know the exact locality. That day was a whiteout, I was miserable, and my mind felt unconnected to my body. In the afternoon, the wind started to pick up and the terrain became very icy. It became impossible to ski without sliding over so we took our skis off and walked. At this point Geoff was leading, and seeing a change in the surface twenty feet in front, he went ahead. With a ski pole, he probed a line of softer snow. The pole went straight through, opening up a small crevasse of about two feet wide. Below there was a yawning hole at least fifty feet deep. Geoff collected us together and told us to step over the crevasse and not be fooled by the soft snow bridge on top.

We found and crossed a number of such crevasses until we came across one almost four feet across, again, thinly covered with snow. This time Geoff spanned the crevasse with his sled to act as a handrail and had each of us make the step. I was utterly oblivious to my surroundings, locked in my own mind, concentrating on putting one foot in front of the other and keeping up with the sled in front of me. I was coughing continually now and my lungs and chest felt as if they would explode.

In this state of mind and because of the loud wind, I did not register what Geoff had said. Instead of stepping right across the crevasse I put one foot right on the snow bridge at the weakest point. As my foot plunged through I felt Geoff's hands just yank me into the air and on to the safe ice the other side. Crevasses narrow into a V shape as they deepen. Once jammed inside, rescue is extremely difficult. But for us to rope together in the way glaciers are normally crossed could have been as dangerous. Standing around and sorting out equipment could have very quickly brought on frostbite and hypothermia in such cold conditions. On the crevasse field, the line between control and disaster was a very fine one.

The next day, Fiona took one of my food boxes. It was an extremely kind gesture even though she was one of the strongest. Now I comprehended the enormous swallowing of pride attached to giving up a part of my load. First, it acknowledged that I was actually as slow as I thought I was. The others must have been discussing how to speed me up. Second, it was hard to accept help. Most of us want to be strong and capable, few enjoy being needy and vulnerable. I was used to helping and supporting others in everyday life. Finding myself helpless was a torment. But I gratefully accepted Fiona's offer.

We were now travelling eight hours every day, with four breaks. The breaks themselves proved to be stressful for me. In ten minutes I might have to go to the loo in front of seven men. Invariably, my hands were so cold I would fumble helplessly with the zips of my four layers of trousers. With my huge mittens I would often fail to tuck in the four layers of thermal underwear properly, so for the next session would have a bitter wind grinding into my skin.

I would have little time left to stuff as much food and drink into my mouth as I could with increasingly frozen hands. It took all my effort to undo the zip of my bum bag, pull out a frozen Nutrigrain, Pepperami or chocolate bar and put it into my mouth. The temptation was to pull off my gloves to make the whole procedure quick and simple, but to expose my hands at this point would have meant possible frostbite. They were already in agony simply because I had stopped moving for a few minutes. The breaks were strictly timed by one of the team members and at ten minutes there would be a shout of "Time!" We would have to put our skis on, and then haul ourselves up for the next two-hour march. My breaks were often shorter — I had used, perhaps, four minutes catching up with everyone while they were eating. At this point I was generally on the verge of tears, because I was so tired. But there was a real disadvantage if I actually cried. I found tears would freeze round my eyes and make it difficult for me to see properly.

I would spend the first ten minutes after each break moving my hands wildly to get the blood back in them and warm them up. I remember my friend Liza, whom I had met on Pen's selection course, and who had already had polar experience, advising me to "play the piano with my fingers" to keep them from freezing. Because I was exerting myself so much, my goggles would fill up with condensation. The condensation would then quickly freeze and ten minutes into the march I would be almost blind, unable to distinguish much through the thick film of ice.

That evening I set up the tent with Steve. I got out my pee bottle and discovered I stupidly had not emptied it from the morning. It was frozen solid. I put it by the stove to thaw; Steve did not bat an eyelid. A little later, we were having our first warm drink of the evening when Geoff poked his head through the tent door. He looked very serious. "Go for a walk for five minutes," he told Steve. "I need to talk to Catharine."

Quite where Steve was going to walk I don't know, but I knew immediately I was in trouble. It was that tap on the shoulder I had been waiting for. Hurriedly and awkwardly Geoff expressed grave concerns about my ability to continue. It was clear he felt I was quite incapable of making the trip and wanted me off the expedition. He left my tent with the words, "The plane is only sixty miles and a radio call away. I suggest you think about taking it." Steve came nervously back in. "Are you all right, Cath?" he asked. No, I was absolutely shattered. As ever, Steve was kind. I should not go, he argued, things would get better. Not wanting to impose myself on him at that moment, when he was so constantly supportive, I reapplied my five layers of clothing, three pairs of gloves, face mask and goggles and finally reached for a Nicorette chewing gum. Then I visited Mike and Fiona for counselling.

Mike and Fiona could have been sympathetic, but in agreement with Geoff. Then I would be off their backs and the team could continue without my holding them up. Instead, they were extremely supportive. Mike said: "Change your mindset, Catharine. You must have determination just to have come this far, so rather than feeling sorry for yourself, wake up tomorrow with a positive attitude. Geoff hasn't chucked you off; he's simply suggested you go. Show him that you won't, show him that what you lack in physical ability you have tenfold in mental determination. Fight him!"

Their encouragement was enough to strengthen my resolve to continue. I was overwhelmed by their support, especially by Fiona's. Their sponsorship relied on her breaking that record of being the first British woman to the Pole and she had been the only woman on the trip until just a fortnight before we left. Suddenly to have to share the possibility must have been galling and I had always been uncertain how she must feel about me. A lesser person would have wanted me off at the earliest moment. How selfless she must be.

CHAPTER
EIGHT

Earning My Place

I could hear the entire "zoo" of Zoë Ball's breakfast show. Knowing I was a fan of it, Steve was recreating it for me in the confines of a tent in the middle of the Antarctic wastelands to give me the best possible start to my day. It worked. I got up terrified but with a fighting attitude. I knew it was very likely my last chance. So my plan was to keep up with the sled in front of me, come what might. I would show Geoff.

I lined up between Steve and Fiona. Steve whispered "Good luck". Fiona told me to stick to the back of her sled like glue and not let it get more than three feet away from me. Mike gave me a squeeze on the arm and reminded me, "Just fight him." It felt like a self-assertiveness class I had attended some years before. I did as they instructed and out of nowhere I found physical strength. I thought about nothing except not allowing Fiona's sled to get away from my skis. My legs were burning and I was absolutely exhausted but I kept up. At the end of the day, Geoff gave me an approving nod before going into his tent. I went to bed so much happier. So I hid my middle finger, which had now turned black, from Steve. I did not wish to confront this and spoil my mood.

I took my box back from Fiona the next day. It is strange how small gestures like this one can mean so much. The day was not as easy as the previous one and still an immense struggle, but I had learned that determination and tenacity worked and I absolutely refused to go back into that destructive pit of self-pity. Geoff took me aside during one of the breaks and I immediately assumed this was to ask if I had made a decision about bailing out. But instead, he suggested that after twenty-five days, still another fortnight or so, I should give Steve a rest and move into his tent. I thought this was extremely noble of him. It was an oblique way of telling me he had relented about my staying on the trip, and I believe he also wanted to keep an eye on me.

I was pushing myself to the absolute limit and I was mindful I could not keep going at that level indefinitely. The breaks still continued to be as exhausting as the travelling itself. Nonetheless, when I managed to keep up for three days running, I started feeling positive for the first time; the simple fact that I was not trailing behind was an enormous encouragement. I remembered Geoff's suggestion that success on an expedition of this kind was 30 per cent physical and 70 per cent mental. I was sceptical at the time; now I was beginning to understand. Just as determination had eventually gained me the sponsor, now it would get me through the never-ending moments when most would have thrown in the towel. I noticed Geoff and Steve having a conversation about tent life with me. Geoff seemed nervous — for completely different reasons from before, at least.

Steve and I had now developed a good routine. I had speeded up when setting out the inside of the tent, so that by the time he clambered in I had the stove on and a pot of water boiling for our first drink. I hoped in time I could hand him the drink as he came through the door. It was extremely tough being the outside man, because at the end of a hard eight-hour day all we wanted was to shelter from the wind and snuggle down into warm sleeping bags. Instead, poor Steve always had another half-hour for the outside tasks.

We would then boil water and have a long, hot drink of juice. Juice crystals were all the rage when I was at school, loaded with sugar and additives, and something I would not have dreamed of drinking back home. Out here it became our delicacy, a treat that became a craving even more than cigarettes. I would start thinking about this drink during the last hour of the day, fantasizing over and over again about that moment of putting the hot orange to my lips. Steve had the same craving, too, and the moment we finally sat down, warm and content in our sleeping bags with Zuco, as it was called, in hand, was quite exquisite. I have tried to mimic that heavenly sensation since, but have never succeeded.

That evening I had let my glove slip off and Steve noticed my blackened finger. He insisted I went to see Geoff. I was very reluctant. I had been going well for the last few days and I did not want to blot my copybook again. I did not want to be the one who always had a problem and was always a worry to Geoff. So I decided to speak to Victor first, hoping he would brush it off as an irrelevance — something that was to be expected for an expedition like this. Instead he looked grave. "When fingers are white I don't worry, but black, we have problem. You must go and see Geoff. He can radio the doctor." Geoff looked serious, too. He was just about to give his nightly call to Patriot Hills; he told me to have my dinner.

When I went back he looked uncharacteristically anxious. "I have explained your injury to Dr Kate and she says that you have acute frostbite. She's afraid you'll lose your finger. She's going to talk to Dr Ann (the other doctor), but I think she will advise you must be evacuated." I tried to keep calm. It seemed the threat of that plane was always hanging over me. We radioed again; Dr Kate was already waiting.

"Patriot Hills, Patriot Hills this is Papa Tango Papa do you read, over?"

"Papa Tango Papa this is Patriot Hills, reading loud and clear, can you put Catharine on please, over."

It was the first time I had ever taken the handset.

"Catharine this is Dr Kate. I have consulted Anne Kershaw and my colleague Dr Ann and they both feel that your frostbite is too bad for you to continue. We think you should be evacuated. How do you feel about this?"

I was silent. Geoff took over and said we would think overnight and contact them in the morning.

I was in shock. Only two days ago I had put my all into proving I was strong enough to stay on the expedition. I had risen to the challenge. In his own quiet way, Geoff had given me a nod to stay on. Now I was being told I had to go again, this time for a reason that seemed out of my control.

"I'm not going, Geoff."

"I understand, Catharine, but it may not be up to you. The decision lies with Anne Kershaw. I assume it's a legal thing. If your finger drops off, technically you may be able to sue them for negligence. How and when did this happen, anyway?"

I explained that I had had hard white fingers within the first two days. I had taken off my outer gloves to put some food in my mouth and my inner gloves had become wet with snow. The wind had whipped through the wet fabric as if I had had no gloves at all and my hands had gone completely numb.

"You must look after yourself, Catharine!" Geoff despaired. "You are far too careless and sloppy. Exposing wet gloves for just two seconds in this kind of weather is enough to give you frostbite."

I knew this, but it was so hard to be meticulously attentive when one was freezing, exhausted and miserable. That was the real challenge. Maintaining impeccable standards, keeping the mind working, even when one felt so destroyed. Geoff asked me to think overnight. It was an interesting scenario. Never in my entire life had I been in so much discomfort. Every day I dreamed of home, and escaping the purgatory I had found myself in; now I was offered a dignified exit. I didn't have to "give up"; there would never be the shame of failure; I could blame everything on the doctor and on frostbite. In effect I was being told to go, and how could I argue with that? Glorious images of warm baths, steaming stews, being tucked up in a duvet in front of a log fire and watching vintage movies surged into my mind.

But when the novelty of being warm and comfortable wore off, I knew I would feel failure and massive disappointment. Club Direct's money would have been wasted, Sense would not be able to benefit, I would have to return all the sponsorship money and be unable to auction the teddy bear. I would sit at home watching the team's progress on the Internet. This was my one and only opportunity. I would never have it again. Another Nicorette gum, and time for another counselling session.

Steve and the Thornewills were again adamant I should fight but were keen I understand the implications of losing a finger. It was a strange conversation, one I had once had with two climbing friends, Tony and Mark, over a curry. We had been discussing how much we would be prepared to lose to reach the top of a mountain, or in my case a Pole. Mark said he would definitely be prepared to lose a finger and possibly his life. Tony, to Mark's scorn, was not prepared to risk anything. I, too, had been reticent about risking any part of my anatomy. To lose a finger would mean I would never play the piano again. I would not be able to type, which would be bad for my career. My hobbies such as rock climbing and sailing would become problematic. I had concluded that I would not take the risk.

Now that I was faced with the dilemma for real, piano playing and typing did not come into the equation. Losing a finger might just be part of the expedition I had undertaken. With the support of the team and now set in my own mind, I decided to challenge Dr Kate. To my surprise, Geoff confided to Mike he did not want me to go. He felt there was a good chance the frostbite would clear up and the finger would remain, but reiterated that the decision lay with Anne and that I might have no choice.

Then Mike had an idea. He came back into the tent after seeing Geoff. We wrote down intricate details of the injury, detailing the size, colour and nature of the frostbite. He then ripped up one of the food boxes and hastily drafted a document on the cardboard, in which I promised not to sue the expedition if my finger dropped off. He was, after all, a police officer, so he knew what to write. I signed without reading it. He then said: "Don't let them get you, Miss Hartley (as they now called me). Even if they come, just refuse to get on the plane. If they try to carry you on, tell them that you'll charge them with assault." His determination for me to fight was extremely touching, and the idea of my scrapping hysterically with two burly pilots in the middle of the Antarctic continent and threatening to sue them brought a huge and welcome smile to my face.

In the morning Mike and Fiona got up early and asked Geoff to call base camp on their iridium phone, rather than the radio. This would allow a free and relaxed conversation. Somehow, between the detailed analysis and the makeshift legal document, Dr Kate agreed to give me a week's grace. Should the finger get any worse then I would be evacuated with no argument.

The whole incident was particularly poignant for me. I was again bowled over by Mike and Fiona's generosity. I was certain any lesser couple would be quietly rejoicing at my pending departure. Steve was also protective, nagging me to keep my gloves on and making sure I was warm and taking care of myself. He had been instructed by Geoff to check my finger every night and report any changes. He took this responsibility on with diligent seriousness.

At the time my decision to continue was a minor triumph. The incident proved to Geoff that I was not going to give up lightly. He saw that what I lacked in physical ability I had gained tenfold in mental determination. He later said that it was at this point he knew I was capable of making the whole journey.

I noticed a change in Justin's attitude towards me, too. I had become increasingly nervous and wary of him. I was certain he wanted me off the expedition because of his Millennium ambition and my slow pace and felt extremely nervous telling him that I was not to be evacuated just yet. But, to my surprise, he was encouraging: "Good for you. I'm fully aware of how much you're struggling. I respect your determination to keep going, even with frostbite. Keep plodding." I felt I had been given a pardon for bad behaviour. I could have hugged him, but this would have been completely inappropriate, of course. A gentle nod of recognition was perfectly adequate.

A minor moment of triumph does not signify automatic success. My glory lasted approximately one day before the gruesome reality of man-hauling to the Pole took its grip again. My chest infection had now subsided into a constant niggling cough and was something I simply could not control, although Geoff thought I was playing up to gain attention. I had expected the sled to glide smoothly over the ice, but because it was so cold the snow particles that settled on the ice froze, so it felt as if I were hauling the sled over continuous speed bumps. I was utterly miserable. I would stick my head down and concentrate on putting one ski in front of the other.

That day, Victor asked me to stop while he filmed me travelling over some sastrugi — snow whipped up by the wind and formed into snow dunes, or moguls. For me these were a particular nightmare. I would use all my strength to haul the sled up the sastruga, and once I had reached the top the sled would tip over and come hurtling down the other side, smashing me in the back of the legs. During this particular two-hour stretch I had stuck to the back of Grahame's sled. I was exhausted, and kept myself going by singing the opera *La Traviata* from beginning to end. Occasionally I forgot to sing in my head and let out a ludicrous operatic warble. I was aware the team must be concerned about my state of mind.

When the filming was finished I was way behind and had no hope of catching up. The team just disappeared into familiar dots on the horizon. Eventually I saw them stop and wait for me dutifully. I was almost in tears. This was so unfair, I had been working so hard. I felt as if I was receiving the same rather pitying looks; I felt an undercurrent of disapproval. Later I understood that, in this environment, it was easy to feel symptoms of paranoia. I had read, too, that explorers often had particularly vivid dreams or nightmares. I suffered from these, too, once attending a whole Jamaican festival in my sleep.

Almost every day part of me still wanted to give up. I could never think further ahead than the next hour, never mind the next day. Quite often by the third hour, I had made the tentative decision to stop. One day I went as far as working out what I was going to say to my mother, my sponsors and my friends, but then a group of schoolchildren came into my mind. I had given a talk to them before I went away. What could I tell them? They were following my journey and had such faith in my success.

Each session varied according to the leader. Steve generally began the day with a very reasonable pace that I could just about keep up with. He was the perfect team member; he had nothing to prove and adjusted his pace to take in everyone's abilities. He was fantastically consistent, not so slow we would all get cold, not so fast that I would be left trailing behind. Halfway through the day Justin would take a two-hour shift, which I used to dread. Impatient with "polar plod" he would tear off. Most of the team members managed to keep up; I did not. Sometimes I would try, but burn out after fifteen minutes or so. By the time the end of the day came and I had got into the tent with a brew I invariably felt better and decided to put my decision of evacuation off for another day.

What was also worrying was that I heard that Mike, Fiona and Justin were considering making a faster breakaway group. After all, with the satellite phone they had independent means of communication. The wildest suggestion was that they should slip away one night while the rest of us were still asleep. Justin also suggested that we increase our hours from eight to nine. Geoff disagreed, we would burn out. Justin later admitted that Geoff was right and had he made a breakaway he would have undoubtedly been seriously injured and failed. I overheard the conversation as our tent was close to his and I was thankful beyond words. An extra hour a day would have certainly finished me off. But I felt responsible that they were going to this extent to look at ways of speeding up. I could cope with battling on with frostbite, nicotine deprivation and pain, but I could not under any circumstances continue in the knowledge that I was spoiling people's dreams and becoming a burden to them.

It was now nineteen days into the expedition and thirteen since we had left Patriot Hills for the second time. I had fantasized every day about a day off. My lower back was in considerable pain and my Achilles tendons were beginning to worry me. When we woke up that morning to a raging storm, I felt extremely hopeful that Geoff would call a rest. Steve left the tent, which we would share together only for another week, to find out.

Steve took delight in pausing far too long on his return, but a rest day it was. I secretly thanked the storm god. After a few seconds' delirious happiness, I sank into sleep and did not stir for another four hours. I cannot begin to describe the luxury of not having to wake up exhausted, haul myself out of the warm sleeping bag and put on freezing clothes. The outer shell clothing always froze solid overnight into a peculiar shape, arms outstretched stiffly like a sinister waxwork. Today I did not have to leave the cocoon of the tent and venture out for my eight hours' purgatory.

The choices now were all wonderful. Should I read, eat, wash my socks, have a tent bath or just go back to sleep? Steve inquired if I fancied a game of rugby. "If you think that on my day off I am venturing out into that cold, crap, indescribably miserable weather, then you're barking, utterly barking." But after just an hour's lie-in, Steve already had cabin fever. He loved Antarctica, the weather, the entire experience. I concluded that, in the nicest possible way, he was a psychotic maniac.

As for me, I decided I would eat. I was worried I was not eating enough as I had no fat to spare. I had lost weight, but in particular had lost all sign of having any breasts. They were completely gone; it was as if I had regressed to puberty. I ate four chocolate bars, one after the other, relishing the experience in luxurious detail. Normally the chocolate would be frozen and I would

144

have to hold it in my mouth for a few minutes to melt, so as not to crack my teeth. Now, as the tent was heated, I could squash them in my mouth. Melted chocolate oozed out of my mouth like foam from a rabid dog. I then cut some thick hunks of butter and laid them on top of the army ration biscuits before scoffing them as well. They were delicious, too.

Geoff had been absolutely right that our appetite would increase dramatically after two weeks. I was now eating absolutely all my daily rations and often still felt hungry. I have to say it was an obscene amount. It was extraordinary what the body now craved. Crisp salads and lightly steamed vegetables were a thing of the past, all I wanted was fat, sugar and meat. Our fruit cravings were kept at bay by the sugary juice crystals and dried apricots and raisins, which we nicknamed "laxatives" from their secondary purpose. Surprisingly, eating chocolate eventually became a struggle because it formed such an enormous part of our diet. We ate about five bars a day each, well over three hundred each over the journey.

After eating the majority of my day's rations, Steve and I decided to boil up some water for a bath. We had not washed now for about twenty-six days and I was surprised we did not smell to each other. The cold did not encourage smell but we had become immune. However, I felt like a piece of solid dirt. My daily ration of one wetwipe was completely insufficient. After we had boiled the water Steve gallantly left the tent and went round to Mike and Fiona's for a chat. Because the heat of the stove kept the tent warm, I was able to undress completely and sponge my filthy body in beautiful hot water with a tiny piece of towelling. It was absolutely wonderful. Layers and layers of black skin rolled off. With the remainder of the dirty water I washed my socks and knickers, and hung them up to dry. I then searched to the bottom of my personal stuff sack and produced the *pièce de résistance*, my only clean pair of knickers and socks. Putting them on was like slipping on a pair of silk stockings and knickers from Agent Provocateur.

I was basking in my new-found interpretation of heaven when Steve came back and said Justin had called a meeting. This sounded unwelcome and ominous. Half an hour later we were all in Geoff's two-man tent, contorted into ridiculous positions. In recognition of this formal occasion, Steve chopped up small pieces of flapjack, chocolate and brownies, which he set neatly out on a plate, decorated with nuts and raisins. The plate was handed round and we duly accepted a small piece each. I only just managed to restrain myself from shovelling the entire plate of "*petits fours*" into my mouth at once.

The meeting began. Justin explained that it was his and Grahame's goal to get to the Pole for the Millennium. That was why they were on this journey at all. He felt this conflicted with the rest of us, whose purpose was far more the actual journey itself. He said that without commitment from us at least to try for the Millennium, he and Grahame would definitely pull out. To help us, he had devised a strategy: to arrive at each degree of latitude by a certain date. If we fell behind, we would consider how to raise our daily distances. I feel Justin's thinking also gave a greater sense of purpose to the suffering he was enduring. He wanted to feel the misery was not for nothing, and that we supported him in his Millennium ambitions.

Everyone was surprised and taken off guard at this corporate approach, but we quickly agreed to adhere to his strategy as long as it did not cause us physical injuries. I was very quiet. Geoff asked how I felt. What could I say? It was taking every ounce of my mental and physical determination just to get through each hour. Of course, I wanted to try and meet Justin's targets. I would do my best, but I knew it was impossible. Geoff watched my reactions intently.

That evening I made the mistake of spilling a pan of water on to the tent floor. Luckily it did not spill into any of our clothes or sleeping bags, as they would have taken hours to dry, but there was still a mess. For the first time, Steve was furious, and, rather than shout at me, went into a stony silence, furiously mopping up the water with our valuable supply of toilet paper. I was mortified. Sharing with me had obviously taken its toll, and I did not blame him. The man had been an absolute saint, a constant source of positive encouragement; he had been patient and kind. Although I was nervous about sharing with Geoff, I was glad that I would be giving poor Steve a well-deserved rest.

I decided the best way to deal with this tense situation was to keep absolutely quiet. We went about our evening duties and then wrote our diaries. The silence lasted for about an hour, after which he went out and took some air — even at −25°C with a ferocious wind. When he came back he seemed to have calmed down and I had found an appropriate paragraph in the book about Shackleton that I had brought with me. On an expedition with Scott, Shackleton manages to do the same — to spill some water. Scott becomes so angry that he threatens to pull out of the entire expedition. I thought this hilarious and when I read it out, Steve was soon laughing, too.

Once the novelty of this blissful day wore off, I was again despondent. There would not be another day off for a long time and in view of my physical state, the possible getaway group, and Justin's corporate meeting, I wondered if I should really be there. There was still such a long way to go and I wasn't sure how long I could go, burning myself out day after day desperately trying to keep up with the rest of the group. It was physically destroying me and mentally eating away at my confidence. I was a burden, there was no getting away from it and that was a horrible position to be in. I lay awake for hours and finally decided I should offer to give up for the sake of the group. I would talk to Geoff the next day. It may sound weak to have considered giving up after pushing myself so hard, but the feeling of being a burden was a terrible one, and one that I could not escape, however hard I tried.

Fate was on my side, however, and two developments changed my fortunes completely. That night, Fiona and Mike had a terrible sickness and hardly slept. Fiona had vomited into a hole for nearly five hours. The majority of their load was shared out to the rest of the group the next day, but even then they could barely move. I suddenly found that they had taken their position at the back with me. Their weakness, ironically, gave me the boost I needed at a time when I felt so inadequate. Just for one day it caused an enormous emotional change. I was not the weakest, and rather than having just Victor behind me with the seven others up in front, I now had another two behind. It was to Mike and Fiona's credit that they managed to keep going at all. That night Steve and I helped them put up their tent. It felt really good to be able to do that, even if it was just a fraction of how they had helped me. So I decided to delay my possible evacuation talk with Geoff.

The second thing happened during the next day. Justin skied up to me and reported that Grahame was imagining I was about to bail out. If I did, Grahame had said he would be giving up as well. With that, Justin skied off to the front without another word, leaving me absolutely staggered. Grahame had been very perceptive, even if my struggles were obvious, but why should he go with me? That evening, I went to see him, while Justin was sent to my tent. Now Grahame told me that, without my presence, he would have been the slowest, something he would have been psychologically unable to accept. At the start of the expedition, he had imagined himself the weakest, and, all through it, he had the hardest of psychological struggles to keep going. It was only my own weakness that was giving him the courage to carry on.

In twenty-four hours, I had gone from feeling absolutely useless, inadequate and a burden, to earning my right to be there. I remembered how much I had enjoyed being in the netball team at school, with those girls who were hopeless at sport. We would all generally end up together because no one else would have us on their teams. I had no interest in winning the game itself, just in feeling comfortable about being no good at sport. Fortunately, there were three girls even worse than I was. While I was playing with them I had a certain confidence just from not being the worst. In any other company, I was the weakest and would take the brunt of everyone's abuse. If my weakness now served a purpose and enabled another team member to stay on the expedition, that was justification enough in itself for me. Nobody liked being at the back, but this was a position I now accepted.

With this new role I was determined to change my attitude. I started to take much more care of myself in the day, paying much greater attention to my clothing, doing zips up properly, and keeping my gloves on my hands. I learned to drink, eat and set up the tent with full mittens. I concentrated on keeping warm and also calm. When excessively cold, it is easy to become frightened and out of control. It is then one can often become unable to look after oneself. I was developing a strength of mind that when I did get too cold and felt my hands and feet go wooden, I was still calm enough to deal with the problem on my own.

By now my frostbite was actually improving. I had taken a course of antibiotics, the black swelling had then burst and, mercifully, the finger underneath was alive. Dr Kate said I might continue. Up until then, I had not wanted to know how many miles we had to go, it was such a huge figure. But now I started to take an interest.

The journey was measured in knots (nautical miles, slightly longer than miles on land) and degrees of latitude. There were nine and a half degrees between Patriot Hills and the Pole — from 80.5 to 90, and sixty knots in each degree. We were averaging twelve nautical miles though the team often spoke in kilometres. Kilometres were shorter, so there were more of them, and the higher numbers sounded more impressive. But to think of our journey as over a thousand kilometres horrified me. I broke the journey down into getting to just the next degree.

I used the same principle for my everyday journey. Everything revolved around just getting to the next break — this was what I lived for. The break meant being able to stop the pain for ten minutes. It meant food, which was now becoming an obsession, and drink to quench my continual thirst. Time played tricks on my mind while I was trudging along. I did wear a watch but the process of pulling back my huge mittens to read the time was actually more than I could manage — it took up valuable seconds, which was time I did not have when struggling so hard to keep up my pace. In any case my wrists had been exposed to the wind one day and had now become raw and covered in pus.

Without having a concept of time, the sessions had turned into obsessive speculation about when the two hours were up. Invariably, I would imagine after only an hour that we had been travelling for two, and would therefore be waiting desperately for a further hour for that signal of crossed skis in the air. I realized that if I had a better idea of time, the wait would be less tortured and I would therefore be able to let my mind wander more, something that was of fundamental assistance in distracting myself and enabling me to keep going. So I asked Steve if he would give me a signal when we had thirty minutes to go and then another when we had five minutes left. It worked really well. Often the thirty-minute signal came sooner than I had anticipated, which would give a real boost to my morale.

In the early days it was rare that anyone spoke during the day's march. The wind was too loud; I was always far too exhausted to speak. We were left to amuse ourselves with our own thoughts each day and each hour. I was too tired to think about anything profound or emotional. Instead, I fantasized about what I was missing. Every day without exception for the first two hours, I would have an imaginary cooked breakfast, lingering on each item in loving detail. I would sometimes eat at my mother's farmhouse, at other times it would be French toast and maple syrup in New York, or a huge pile of eggs, bacon and sausages at my local "greasy spoon" café. By the end of the two hours I swear I could actually smell the bacon. Then I spent many fantasy hours in Australia on the beach snorkelling and being served cocktails and would sing music in my mind, often a whole opera, which would take me through an entire session.

One day my reverie was interrupted by Geoff, intrigued to know what I was thinking about. He said I had a bounce in my step and my head was nodding as if in time with music. I explained I had been in the middle of a concert at the Royal Albert Hall where I was accompanying my hero Miles Davis on the piano. We were playing to a packed house and I was up for a Grammy award. He smiled in envy of my active imagination. "Yesterday I sang the first two lines of 'Three Blind Mice' over and over again all day. I couldn't even remember the rest of the nursery rhyme. It nearly drove me over the edge." I could imagine it probably would have.

The further inland we went the less wind there was, and with the passing days the team became more garrulous and animated. Fiona was a great talker and often chatted to me in the happy hour, as we had quickly named the last hour of the day. I always rationed my small bar of Kendal Mint Cake for the final break. It had an extraordinary effect and gave me a huge burst of energy to keep going until we made camp. During this hour Fiona would often ski up next to me and just talk. I explained that I could only respond with nods and grunts and was not capable of discussion but, nonetheless, I really looked forward to her company.

It was wonderfully soothing; it was like Radio 4. She would discuss topics like recipes, health farms and planning dinner parties. It was marvellous escapism. It

153

reminded me of when I was trying to raise money and was so stressed. Whenever I could, I would just stop at one forty-five each lunchtime to watch *Neighbours*. It was my form of simple therapy and, for that short period, I just escaped into the wonderful world of sun, barbecues, swimming parties and corny romances. It was invaluable.

I was learning more and more about controlling my mind. It was absolutely imperative to stay positive. The worst point, without a doubt, was getting out of the sleeping bag in the morning, donning all the Antarctic gear and stepping out of the tent to begin the day's march. It was imperative not to allow myself any negative thoughts at this point.

Each morning Victor would tap on our tent doors to make sure we were all up and then give us an analysis of the weather that day. "Good morning! *Dobri Utra!*" (for those of us that spoke Russian). "Weather today is −28°C and there is gusting wind of around thirty knots. It is a beautiful day and life is good." He was another Steve, perpetually positive and always happy. The trip was a breeze for him. The speech was always delivered at 7a.m. Steve and I had usually been up and getting ready for breakfast by six. We had until nine to melt enough snow for breakfast, fill our flasks with liquid for the day, sort out our day's rations, then pack everything up and venture outside. We now took it in turns to go outside first. The outside person would not only pack up — remember that this would be the moment for the inside person's loo break — but would also have to dig out the two sleds that had been covered by the night's snow. After this, the outside person would start to take the tent down around the toilet-going inside tent partner.

Surprisingly, Steve and I were often first with Geoff. We would, therefore, run around keeping warm for a few minutes while the remainder of the team made ready. During this time Geoff would report on the previous night's radio conversation with Patriot Hills. We all looked forward to this immensely. It was a welcome contact with the outside world, though a very selective one. The only news we received was of the Antarctic, and how other teams were faring. Sometimes, we would receive the odd message from a loved one at home via Punta and Patriot Hills. Steve often got loving messages from his girlfriend Catherine, which kept him smiling all day.

I also began to take much more care of my body. Most mornings and evenings I would spend five minutes or so stretching. I was terrified I would lose the advantage of my new-found confidence from physical injury. There would be no time to stop for a couple of days to let it heal, I would just have to keep going through it. Again, however, my improvement was being matched by a physical deterioration in the others. Most of them now were taking Ibuprofen, nicknamed by us Vitamin I, daily. Justin had shin splints and Veijo was frostbitten on his face and hands. Fiona had developed the most horrendous frostbite on her thighs, and the wounds were starting to open up. She never really regained her former strength, and Mike began to have severe problems with his knees and feet. I still usually remained at the back, but the gap was always small and certainly not enough to make or break our Millennium deadline.

When Fiona asked me round to her tent for cocktails, or rather hot chocolate and Zuco, I saw her injuries at close quarters. It was a very polite invitation and I felt it would be rude to turn it down, but the misery of leaving my nice warm tent, donning layers of frozen clothes and venturing out into a blizzard, seemed hardly worth the effort. Her left boot had been rubbing for the past two days, so badly it had worn a hole in the sock, soaked the heel in blood and left her ankle raw. It must have been absolute agony, but Fiona never ever moaned about anything. She was so strong and fit, she still continued to enjoy the trip. When we had met up on the journey to Chile, she was fully made up, with black high-heeled boots and even a vanity case. Her nails were painted. It was an intriguing transformation now, to the tough polar traveller whose hair was pasted to her head with a heavy layer of grease. I was very amused to find that she had smuggled in a mirror and some spot concealer, which she was now applying to her rugged, windswept face.

When the ice underneath our feet became hard and firm, Geoff suggested I try to take my skis off and walk instead. It was an absolute revelation. I had so much more leverage in my legs to pull the sled. It was far easier to keep up with the group. This was also the one advantage of whiteout days. Strangely, I had come to long for them because the conditions slowed the pace down. When visibility was so poor, we had to stick together. So I used secretly to dread the days when the weather improved, days that were absolutely stunning — blue sky, bright glaring sun and white ice, 360° around us, which sparkled as if it had been scattered with diamonds. But it would then be much easier to travel and the team would take off much more quickly, leaving me trailing behind praying for a blizzard.

It was time for me to move in with Geoff and I was very nervous. Steve was very concerned that I would think he had put Geoff up to it. "Honestly, Catharine, you don't have to go, I'm not pushing you out." After I moved, he still made a special effort to chat to me during the day, when he had the habit of skiing up and down the line to encourage the others. In fact, the idea was that everyone should swap companions to relieve any relationship problems, or simply to have a change. However, nobody wanted to. Grahame and Justin were very happy together in the "corporate tent", although I did wonder how Grahame was coping with Justin's urgency. Veijo and Victor seemed happy enough together and were even beginning to bicker like a married couple. They were the only two people whose first language was not English, which must have been hard for Veijo, and I wondered if it drew him to Victor.

That left Geoff to give up his solitude for a crazy girl whom he knew was going to be trouble, while Steve would now have the joy of camping alone. I did wonder if he would enjoy being by himself. Despite the immense difficulties I had during the day's travel I had come to really enjoy the tent life in the evening. Steve and I would sing and tell each other stories. I

157

remember laughing a lot, too. We had been nicknamed the Nursery Tent. This was partly because Steve's indomitable spirit kept my mood so positive and an atmosphere of fun in the tent, and partly because just before bedtime we would read a bedtime story, an entry from Robert Swan's diary, when he went to the Pole unsupported via Scott's route. It was, of course, an expedition of much greater magnitude, but it was interesting to compare his day with the one we had just experienced. I have incredibly fond memories of tent life with Steve.

At the end of the day, when we finally made camp, I went over to Steve to say goodbye. "Good luck," he said. "Thanks, and enjoy your freedom," I replied. Then I tottered over to my new home and new tent companion. Geoff's reputation for being extremely orderly and pernickety about tent routine went before him. So did mine for being clumsy. Geoff had done his homework. A couple of days earlier, he had quizzed Steve as to how I slept, whether I had any irritating habits and if there were any "women's things" that needed to be taken into consideration. Steve briefed him as diplomatically as he could and explained that the only privacy I required was in the morning, when Steve left the tent first and gave me five minutes "woman time". "I don't know what she does, but it seems to work," he said. He also explained about covering the eyes with a hat when I went to the loo.

Once in the tent I sat very quietly and nervously. You must remember I thought of Geoff as being on a pedestal and I was still raw from the moment he had wanted me off the expedition. I thus felt both apprehensive and very privileged to be sharing with him. Here was a man who had crossed the entire Antarctic continent — an expedition of gargantuan proportions. It would be a wonderful chance to learn.

Geoff had torn off a piece of card from a food box, written on it "Welcome to your new home, Catharine", and hung it from the tent washing line. Unlike the "relaxed" and erratic routines in the Nursery Tent, everything was extremely ordered. Every item had its place and the evening routine was carried out with military precision. Geoff had learned that this was the only way to survive in Antarctica.

By eight o'clock we had finished eating. There was no washing up as we used our dehydrated food packets as bowls, adding in cheese, butter, potato and water all at once. Clearly the days of cordon bleu recipes of cheesy potato and stew, using pans, spoons and bowls were gone. At 8.30p.m. sharp, Geoff turned on the radio for the nightly check with Patriot Hills. I hoped for updates on all the other expeditions and what the gossip was back at Patriot Hills. But Geoff clearly hated chatting. He spoke as little as he could beyond giving our position, status and the weather. Was I in for a very grown-up month?

CHAPTER
NINE

An Antarctic
Christmas

I was to share Geoff's home for the next twenty-five days, and I was sure I would drive him mad. It was an extraordinary situation, two people who did not know each other being forced to share a tiny space for such a long time, sleeping so close that each could feel the other's breath. It was much worse that I regarded Geoff as a hero, yet I knew I would have to lose every shred of dignity just conducting everyday life in his presence. I was desperate to impress and show him I was not the silly girl he must imagine me to be. But I felt there was little I could tell him. All I could offer was tales of a London girl who worked in TV, something very distant from the world of exploration, which was what interested him. I worried about being good company.

I once had a younger, charming boyfriend. I looked forward to our dates, but dreaded the conversation, so before each evening I would write a list of topics in my Filofax. This could be anything from gossip to international politics, which I would have swotted up in the unfamiliar *Guardian* (I was used to the *Mirror* and its showbiz column). During the meal, if I came upon an embarrassing silence I would excuse myself, go to the toilet, consult my list and come back and launch into another, perhaps rather unconnected, topic.

But this time my solution came from further back in my life. I remembered sitting at the kitchen table at home in my late teens, nearly in tears, simply because I had to go to a party. Parties frightened me — they meant socializing and the terror of being left alone with another guest. "Don't try to become a talker," my mum wisely advised at that moment. "You aren't, and if you try to be loud and extrovert you'll just make a fool of yourself. But you're a fantastic listener, and that makes you very easy to talk to. Everyone loves talking about themselves and the world is sadly lacking in good listeners. So tonight, when you find yourself alone with somebody, ask them questions about their job, their life, their hobbies, whatever, and when you listen, don't just nod in a distracted way, really listen and be interested. I guarantee you'll have a conversation for over an hour." I put her advice into practice. It worked; I use it still. So, of course, I decided to encourage Geoff to talk. He was happy to do so, though one night I saw him write in his diary: "Why does she keep asking me all these questions?"

Over the next two evenings we began to establish our tent routine and be more at ease with each other. Although I was easy-going, I understood the importance of methodical routine in these conditions. Surviving meant discipline — discipline in looking after equipment, hands and body, discipline while navigating. Tent discipline was an integral part of this; it was an absolute for Geoff. I worked hard as well and by the second night had managed to have the inside of the tent set up with the stove ready to light by the time he came in. And he usually kept his sleeping bag in its stuff sack (the bag which compressed it to a small size) till bedtime. He did not need to loll about in it all evening.

By the third night, I had memorized exactly where he liked all his belongings, even down to the placing of his mug and spoon. In turn, by the fourth evening we had established that what I craved at the end of the day was a mug of hot Zuco, and what he looked forward to was two army biscuits with his butter ration on top. So once he had finally removed all his frozen clothing and settled in I carefully cut up the butter and handed him his treat. He then poured me the Zuco. Not until this point did he visibly relax and settle down for the evening. It was a touching routine that continued religiously. I realized I was over-grateful to Geoff for taking me in, and hoped this was not showing in my behaviour.

For three evenings, Geoff entertained me with stories about Antarctica, his crossing of the Australian desert with camels and his life in Borneo. I felt I could offer little in return — the sort of amusing anecdotes my life story was built from seemed entirely trivial. We had now crossed 83°, but it was still 120 miles before we even reached the halfway mark at the Thiel Mountains, another 350 miles after that to the Pole.

I had started myself to become obsessed each night with how many miles we had covered that day, and become more sympathetic to Justin's talk of "strategy". In the evening, when the GPS had warmed up, Geoff allowed me the luxury of reading off our position and distance covered. We would then mark them off on a longitudinal map so I also had to face seeing exactly how far away the Pole still was. At least, as I wrote, I had managed 230 miles, and had neither given up nor been told to leave.

Of course I was now sharing my tent with the very person who had that power over me — Geoff. I did my best not to burden him with my paranoia that I would be thrown off. I knew it would be all too easy constantly to draw on him for reassurance and encouragement. But I knew I must not. Not only would it weaken my own resolve, which was now strong enough, but I could see it would greatly annoy him. Geoff was clearly not one readily to give sympathy or praise. He was tough and did not give the slightest hint of weakness. He expected others to behave likewise and I am sure this attitude strengthened me. Had he indulged me, I would have weakened, and as I lacked physical strength, the determination in my mind was certainly my only hope of success.

You will remember that usually Victor shepherded me at the rear. As I never had energy to speak, I felt bad that I made his time boring. Sometimes Geoff would relieve him and at such times I would watch as Victor bounced up to the front with the others and happily engaged in conversation to the extent the howling wind

163

allowed. Now I was keeping up more easily, I attempted to entertain Victor. As with Fiona, I explained I would not be able to converse myself other than in nods and grunts but I would be fascinated to hear about him, his family and his life in Russia. Victor turned out to be married to a beautiful woman called Lena. They had one son, of whom he was immensely proud, and lived in St Petersburg. He had studied geophysics and for many years worked for the Arctic and Antarctic Institute of the Soviet Union, overwintering on a Drifting Ice Station near the North Pole, working at various Soviet Antarctic stations, and exploring Siberia. He had been a guide and expedition organizer for ten years and felt immensely privileged to be a part of this expedition. The journey was easy for him; nothing suggested he was having any problems whatsoever. So he was always extremely cheerful.

Since the day of my tent move I had noticed Mike slow down. His knee clearly gave him pain and he had been getting cramp. Once or twice a day the pain would become too much; he would have to stop and take his boot off to massage his searing foot. Just before the last hour of my day with Victor, Mike's knee finally gave way and he collapsed on the ground. After a short break he continued very carefully at the back with me, terribly dispirited and even speaking about getting a plane out at the resupply point. I was shocked. He seemed a shadow of his former confident self, the Mike who had been so supportive and encouraging to me. To try to cheer him up, I mustered some energy to tell him an amusing anecdote about one of my disastrous love affairs. I usually succeeded in cheering people up like this, but in the excruciating cold, with infinite painful miles of desolate Antarctic wasteland still to come, it fell flat.

At the end of the day, Justin announced he had shin problems and would not be objecting to a day off. His attitude seemed to have changed, too. The following day, I gave Mike my whole ration of painkillers. He was running low and so far I had had no need for them. I had underestimated how good I felt giving help, especially when all I had done was take. The pills were a tiny gesture towards a huge debt, but it was a start.

After four days, Geoff had had enough of telling me stories. I was unnerved, but he, too, was an excellent listener and seemed surprisingly interested about my life in London. He made me describe a typical day as a location manager in precise detail. At the end he shuddered, saying he could never put himself through that kind of pressure. I found his response very funny when he was guiding a group of amateurs through the most isolated and harshest place in the world.

Then Geoff encouraged me to talk about my own travels and we discovered we had been to similar places. I gradually relaxed as I realized he was not going to be automatically bored. Finally, we got on to sailing. He enthralled me with a story of sailing round Greenland. I told him how I had sunk my dinghy when I was with Julian. He found it hilarious. And so I realized that while I would not even try to impress Geoff, I could, just by being myself, easily entertain him.

On 1 December I woke and barked "White rabbits!" "What are you saying, woman?" he asked in alarm. "On the first of each month you must say 'white rabbits' before anything else. If you remember, it brings you good luck, and let's face it, Geoff, I need all the luck I can get right now." "Well, I guess I've blown it then, but 'white rabbits' anyway," he replied. He smiled wryly through his balaclava. I wondered what it was like for him to share with a dotty woman, after being used to tough, professional male explorers. So far, we had had no cross words, though he was disgusted that I used my food bowl also to wash in and clean my teeth, and thought it cheap I had chipped nail varnish on my toes.

The white rabbits brought me one of my best days, or possibly it was just that nearly everyone else had ailments. The pace felt comfortable for the first time on the entire expedition. I managed to stay towards the front of the group for the whole day. It is odd to think how one's position in a team can have such a huge impact on confidence, but I felt fantastic. It was a real treat to feel important by being in the front. For one day — would it just be that one? — I had moved up in the Plebs to the Pole hierarchy with some dignity.

This evening Fiona climbed into the tent for the radio call. The purple spots on her thighs were absolutely revolting and had opened up into wounds weeping pus. It actually looked extremely serious to me, but I hid my feelings. She was always brave, however, and not for one minute did she ask for sympathy. She just wanted medical advice. We managed to speak to Dr Ann, who was sure it was a form of frostbite, perhaps reacting with her sickness. There was little to be done other than keep it well dressed and take aspirin to thin the blood. Seemingly this helped with cold injuries. But how could Fiona have such appalling frostbite on, of all places, her thighs? Geoff concluded it must be from sitting on the ice during breaks. Without a gap of air, the cold had penetrated the four insulating layers.

In the real world, especially in London, one's moods are constantly modified by the fast pace of work and life. It is easy to burn the candle at both ends, hard to find a single moment to stop and reflect. In the Antarctic, I was trapped in my own mind, in this vast empty wilderness with no distractions whatsoever. If, on a bad day, I had no escape from my demons, on a good day I felt all the advantages of serenity and space. As December continued, I found there was a pattern. The effort I was making meant that good and bad days alternated. I now felt the wish to give up only every other day. And more and more, my body's suffering was not so severe as to prevent me from either happy fantasies or simply mental peace.

However weak I might be physically, as yet I had no structural injuries. Grotesque blisters, yes, but my body was holding together well. In a way, my weakness was my strength. Since I was never fast, I was actually unable to put my body under excessive strain. I needed to stay like this. One serious problem would be enough to make me unable to keep up with the others. I concentrated very hard on my stretching exercises, morning and evening. Despite having nothing to distract my mind, mentally I had never felt healthier. It was better than any religion, meditation or spiritualism. Perhaps from Geoff's influence, I was starting to control my mind better, learning to plunge it into an almost trance-like state and just fantasize.

Antarctica had done this for me. All I did each day, I pondered, was put one ski in front of the other and move forward. All I did in the evening was put food in my mouth, repair my clothes and equipment and sleep. The only decision I had to make was whether to keep going, and I had already decided some days ago that I would as long as I was allowed. Since the frostbite incident, I had not even touched the Nicorette gum. I had not felt so at peace since childhood. Physical exertion has a wonderfully calming effect on the mind, too, and on the occasions when we could walk, not ski, I had a great feeling of power. Now that the wind was dropping a little and the weather slightly warmer as the sun rose higher into the sky, I was coming, if not to enjoy, at least to accept being there. It was a way of life that I was getting used to, one I felt I might almost miss when it came to an end.

In the tent that night Geoff informed me that some team members had suggested having a second resupply in order to help meet the Millennium schedule. We knew that the first few days after the existing resupply would be tough. By then, we would have got used to light sleds, our stores almost gone. The South Pole is actually 10,000 feet above sea level, so we were travelling uphill all the way. Most of the time the gradient is so gradual it goes unnoticed, but after Thiels it steepens considerably for a few days. So we would have to fight extra weight and gradient at the same moment.

Suppose we took on just eighteen days of supplies? At 88° we would then get a second resupply. It sounded wonderful to me. Geoff explained that there was no means of chartering a plane to make this airdrop just for us. We would somehow have to persuade Patriot Hills to organize a drop when they were landing the group skiing the last degree to the Pole. From what we could glean, this was a group of six men and one woman. The woman was Madelaine, whom I had met at my original selection course.

Geoff's task, therefore, was to have the plane make an extra stop to drop food — an extra landing and takeoff. This would be a big favour, so we had to put forward a good case. Aside from the team's desire to get there on 31 December, we claimed I was struggling and needed all the help I could get. At the time, this stung me. I had been working so hard, yet I was being used as leverage in this way. But a few minutes later I thought, to hell with it, I need that second resupply more than anyone. It would give me an edge, an extra bit of help that might just enable me to get to the Pole.

We had only our second rest day on 3 December, in a storm. I spent the morning sewing patches on to my disintegrating boots. Sewing and patching had become one of my greatest pleasures. I was absorbed, and allowed Geoff to enjoy much-deserved silence. Surprisingly, after an hour or so he tired of this and badgered me for more stories of my city disasters. Steve

169

very kindly loaned out his tent as a bathroom and I was able to have my second wash in six weeks by the warmth of two stoves. Once again the feeling of warm water and soap, even mixed with the muesli left in my bowl, was utterly, utterly delightful.

I hoped very much that in taking this day off we would not jeopardize our planned rest day at Thiels during the resupply. Seconds after I had this unwelcome thought, Victor knocked on the tent door saying that Justin would like another strategy meeting at 4p.m. I had visions of Justin vetoing any more rest days, but to my relief, he was relatively calm and had merely adjusted his mileage strategy. I knew this would mean travelling more hours a day. For some reason, perhaps the rest, there was a confident atmosphere. People spoke of what they would do when we arrived, and Veijo even asked if there was a souvenir shop. The whole conversation made me feel extremely uncomfortable. I could not allow myself such complacency, when there was so far to go.

There was also talk about Christmas Day. Victor had an idea that we should take the day off and build a snow cave, carving a Christmas tree inside. "Yes," said Fiona. "We could decorate the tree with sweet wrappers and then have dinner together, sing carols and play games." I was happily amused. If ever there was an opportunity for a party, Fiona was clearly dying to be hostess. I remained silent throughout, these were all self-indulgent events I might not myself have the opportunity to experience. It was foolish to tempt Fate.

Justin was muttering. He had not anticipated having Christmas Day off in his tight schedule. Victor calculated that, at our present pace, we would arrive at the Pole on 4 January. Justin finally began to accept the Pole as the goal, not the Millennium, and realised it was better for the team — now acceptable in its own right. The priorities had shifted just to arriving in one piece. I was quietly relieved at this unexpected development.

I looked around at everyone. Clearly, Justin was strong, and fast, too. He wanted to get on with this journey and be out of the continent as quickly as possible; he was getting absolutely no enjoyment out of the expedition whatsoever and was looking forward to a few days at a luxury resort on his return. Victor was just relentlessly solid. For him and for Steve, who was the strongest apart from the guides, the journey was an enormous joy and they were enjoying every minute.

I now knew Grahame was struggling daily. If he was having a particularly bad day he would call it a plane day, that is, a day when he wanted to be flown out. He had confided there were more plane days than not. But Veijo seemed as consistent as ever. He had black frostbite on his face and fingers but seemed not to acknowledge it. Like Justin's, Veijo's sessions of leading were always fast; I dreaded them. Veijo's problem was his spectacles. He was virtually blind without them, so rather than wear goggles, he put shades over his existing glasses. This was sufficient to prevent snow blindness, but it did mean there were areas around his cheeks and eyes that were exposed to the cold and gave him

171

frostbite. Moreover, his breath escaped on to the inside of his glasses and instantly froze. Within minutes he was trying to peer through a block of ice and would lose his sense of direction. At the beginning of the trip we often found him walking east instead of south and had to turn him round.

Mike and Fiona's initial strength and speed had declined. Both in his job and his leisure time, Mike was used to being a strong leader. Now that his body seemed to be failing him, he was becoming easily demoralized and continued to consider evacuating at Thiels. Despite her own considerable weight loss from sickness and her frostbite, Fiona was a rock. I still had not heard a squeak of complaint from her. Nor did she entertain the idea that she would not get to the Pole.

I found the emotional dynamic between them interesting. Mike had always been a great traveller, mountaineer and rock climber. He had spent a year with Operation Raleigh and his life revolved around outdoor pursuits. Fiona, by her own admission, lived for parties, for fun and socializing. Mike introduced Fiona to climbing and mountaineering, which she took to half-heartedly but completely competently. When he first introduced Fiona to his friends, her initiation was to hack up a mountain in Scotland. Seeing her in lipstick, nail varnish, and with immaculately coiffured hair, the outdoor lads were amused and sceptical, and set off expecting to have to drag Fiona up in tears. Instead, she overtook them all and made it to the top of the mountain first, without a bead of sweat, and with hair and lipstick still intact.

The polar journey had been Mike's idea in the first place, but I wondered how he felt now watching his wife cope with such strength and fortitude. She was mentally and physically stronger than he was. I think it helped Mike's self-esteem to look after me instead, as he was a natural giver and helper. I had been happy to grant him this role. It helped us both.

Geoff gave nothing away. Some nights, when he got into the tent he was clearly as exhausted as I was and would not speak until he had relaxed into his chair with his biscuits and a hot drink. But on the rest day, he let the mask fall slightly. "Sometimes I don't know why I am here, Cath. There are days when I think you would all be perfectly OK without me and I just want to get on a plane and get out." I was staggered. "There's not one of us that could have got this far without you and you've managed the team dynamics fabulously as well." Indeed he had. Apart from a few tensions about pace and date there had been absolutely no bad feelings whatsoever. "Maybe," he muttered, unconvinced.

Although I had nothing but admiration for Geoff's humanity, he was not always the greatest master of social graces. A few days later, Mike came to the tent to speak to Dr Kate on the radio. He was extremely worried because Fiona's wounds were worsening and she was clearly in great pain. "Well at least all her boyfriends won't want her now she's got horrible legs!" Geoff offered helpfully. "Sometimes your black humour is way off the mark," I thought as I glanced at Mike's horror-stricken face.

In one way I was lucky with my next bad day, as we were walking in a complete whiteout, where we had to slow the pace. Steve told me he always knew when I was having a bad day because my head hung ridiculously low as I stared fixedly at the tips of my skis. At the end of the first break that day he had picked up on my mood and he skied over and stuffed his Walkman in my pocket, put the earpieces in my ears and pressed "Play". Suddenly, the Monty Python classic "Always Look on the Bright Side of Life" bellowed into my ear. I cannot express how wonderful it was just to hear music again, nor how cheering the incongruous humour of the surreal comedians was in such surroundings. The relentless monotony was shattered and my disordered head was obliterated by the glorious sound of fifty men singing their hearts out, perched on wooden crucifixes — I knew the scene well.

I had been eyeing up Steve's Walkman for weeks but never dared ask if I could borrow it. I knew I now had two hours of magnificent entertainment. It was more than I could ever have dreamed of. "Tragedy" by the Bee Gees came next. I skied along in ecstasies, practically rocking. Barry Gibb was really doing his thing, purring harmonious falsetto into my frozen ears. Suddenly there was a clunk. I must have hit the stop button by mistake. Frantically I tried to put my enormous mitten into my pocket and switch it on again, knowing I had not time to stop and remove my gloves. It was so unfair. Just ten minutes into the session, the music had teased me into a state of euphoria and now it had been cruelly snatched away leaving me to sink back into the terrible boredom of another hour and fifty minutes. I began to sob quietly, but of course my tears instantly froze on my goggles. Great! I was now blind to boot.

That night I knew I was in for a scolding, when Geoff took his biscuits without his usual jovial thanks.

"Catharine, I am worried about your skiing. It is all very well walking when the ice is hard, but when we get to the Polar Plateau, the snow will be too thick. You'll have to ski; it'll be the only way and you have to learn to ski at the same pace that you walk. Simple as that."

"Fine, then I will learn to ski."

The next day I asked Steve and Victor to ski behind me for the first hour. "You ski with bent arms, as if you have arthritis or something," said Victor immediately. "Straighten your arms, you'll have much more strength and leverage." He also taught me to hold the tops of my sticks in a different way. The transformation was dramatic. "Oh my God, it's working," I screamed as I caught the others up. Steve and Victor looked absolutely delighted.

I have often been asked whether I found God or indulged in some sort of spirituality while I was there. My experience with religion had been relatively superficial. I had been a mischievous member of the church choir as a child, always eating sweets and giggling. Thereafter services were just for Christmas and weddings, but churches themselves were places where I always found peace. So throughout my travels I had always taken time to visit the local place of worship.

I had never relied on a faith. I believed that if I wanted something it was up to me, that my destiny was in my own hands. This was a frightening and rather lonely philosophy since I had no spiritual being to turn to when life — or choices — was tough. But I had already found this fear motivating. During the expedition to the South Pole, however, I was finding it impossible to ignore the presence of some kind of spirituality. Grahame, Mike and Fiona were all devout Christians and although they never imposed any of their beliefs on any of us it was impossible to ignore their convictions. I became strangely intoxicated by their faith.

This was highlighted one day when Mike was in so much pain with his knee that he was about to ask Geoff if we could make camp two hours early. During a break I saw Fiona place her hands on Mike's knee, bend her head and pray. I was intrigued. I watched him on the final two-hour stretch as his limp miraculously disappeared. The next day was one of my bad days and I struggled all morning. At the midday break Mike and Fiona said a quiet prayer for me without my knowledge and watched as I regained strength in the afternoon, finishing the day near the front. Whatever the true explanation, while I was out there, frightened and often miserable, gestures like these were comforting. It became hard not to contemplate religion quite seriously.

Sometimes I felt that I was being taken care of. Perhaps it was "imaginary friend syndrome", because I so desperately needed some sort of spiritual guidance when I was struggling by myself. I thought a lot about my father and whether he had a hand in all this somewhere. I hoped he could see me. He had only ever known the shy, frightened, underconfident Catharine. He had died just a few months before I set off travelling. I was sad that he had missed out on my transformation.

Unfortunately, that evening I opened my sled to find that one of my fuel canisters was empty. The lid had come off during the day and the fuel had leaked into the food boxes. I was horrified. In another age, this kind of inattention proved fatal. Scott himself had had exactly the same problem. In his case the party actually ran out of food and perished just eleven miles away from their final supply cache. Without fuel, you would not only freeze, but would not be able to melt snow to drink. I made sure I had Geoff's biscuits and drink ready before he even stepped into the tent. I waited until he had settled and then told him my unwelcome news. Silently, he went through the two contaminated boxes, testing flapjacks, chocolate, cheese and butter. Except for the dehydrated meals everything tasted of fuel and was inedible.

Geoff was extremely stressed. The stove chose just this moment to keep burning out and was clearly going to give us future problems. He wrote sums furiously on cardboard and concluded that if we kept on schedule we should have just enough food until the resupply. But any delay would mean trouble. I usually knew how to humour Geoff and get him chatting but I felt silence to be the most appropriate response. I went to sleep feeling absolutely terrible.

The next morning was similarly tense. There was silence apart from the occasional clinking of pans. Finally, Geoff broke the ice and said, "Look, Catharine, I don't blame you for this at all you know. The fuel cans were completely inadequate for an expedition of this kind. I'm afraid it was an accident waiting to happen." I breathed out a huge emotional gulp. "Thanks," I mumbled. Then I had a good day and at the end of it Geoff congratulated me. I felt as though I had been awarded a medal. The fuel incident was all forgotten, and that night we had a good chat about flatsharing. Geoff could not comprehend why on earth I would want to share my home with anybody else. I had to explain that with the right people, as Jo and Nikki were, it could be a wonderful experience.

But just the next day, the GPS broke. Since I was sharing his tent, each evening Geoff allowed me the pleasurable task of checking our position and calculating how many miles we had travelled that day. Often Geoff would then check again in the morning. Unfortunately, something seemed to be wrong this time, and as I was the last one to touch it, it had to be my fault.

We were, however, running a little late so there was no time to check till the evening. All day, I was anxious that I might have destroyed our only form of navigational equipment. This was the day when the Thiel Mountains first appeared, a welcome sight after twenty-five days of relentless flat, white wasteland. Not only was the change wonderfully absorbing, it also signified we had reached halfway. They first came into our field of vision at the midday break, when Steve pointed them out to me, but at that moment it was so windy and I was so exhausted I did not have the will to look round. Later in the afternoon, they did come directly into sight for me, their beauty much enhanced just because they were something different to look at.

We had learned that our supplies would be deposited at the same time as the Singaporeans' resupply. We would not meet the plane, so nobody would have the temptation of giving up. In all our cases insurance only covered a rescue if we were extremely ill and unable to continue. Being exhausted and miserable did not count, and as being airlifted out for the sake of it would cost thousands, hitching free of charge on the resupply plane was the only real option. Now this would no longer be available. I was relieved. Although I firmly believed now I was going to do my utmost to see this trip through, I did wonder what I would do if faced with a warm aircraft.

The evening was terrible. The GPS had indeed gone wrong. Luckily, both Victor and Grahame had their own GPSs, but I felt absolutely dreadful nonetheless. Geoff was extremely tense and silently continued to press buttons, trying to get it to work. But we both knew it was hopeless. I began to feel more and more ashamed. The only thing for me to do was to keep absolutely silent and just sweat the evening, or maybe the whole expedition, out. Mistakes that can be laughed off in the Lake District or simply in the retrospective safety of the pub, would be life-threatening here. In a landscape that offered only 360° ice and the sun above if we were lucky, it was a bad error to break the only useful navigational tool.

It turned out I was blameless, but we did not yet know this. My self-flagellation was a throwback to my many former errors and gaffes and was completely groundless. But my diary entry that night was peppered with expressions of inadequacy. In the morning, Geoff was still annoyed as he got up earlier than usual and started to brush the ice off the inside of the tent loudly and with unnecessary vigour, a job he normally left until I was awake. As we were about to set off I skulked over to Steve for some sympathy. "I've bust the GPS," I wailed. "Oh, dear," was all he could manage with a straight face. He busied himself retying his bootlaces, but I could see from his shaking shoulders he was helpless with laughter.

It was a stunningly beautiful day with blue skies, crisp ice and the mountains coming ever nearer when we reached our exact halfway point. Victor drew a line in the snow and filmed us all crossing it. It was incredibly exciting. I had not imagined I would ever have made it this far. We had another 350 miles to go, which was still difficult to comprehend, but I felt I had achieved something significant. If I could carry on just thirty more days, I would be there.

Shortly afterwards the DC6 flew over. On board it had the resupply for us and the Singaporeans. It dipped its wings in greeting and we waved our ski poles enthusiastically and screamed hallos. It was our first sighting of civilization for twenty-eight days. Justin was leading at this point and was on a roll, skiing at a great pace. He either did not see or chose to ignore the plane, pressing on in order to reach the resupply as quickly as possible.

Geoff worked out it would take us another six hours to reach the resupply. There, we would reorganize the food. We would leave in bags all the rubbish we had been carrying for nearly a month and anything else we no longer needed. Thiels was also used as a remote fuelling station, where barrels of aviation fuel were deposited early each season, so later on, a plane would remove what we left.

At the start of the day we could see nothing and I was sceptical that we could actually find it. It seemed incredible to me that the GPS could locate an area of just twelve square yards. But sure enough, in the middle of the mountain range, black shapes appeared. They were the barrels of aviation fuel and boxes upon boxes of food. In fifteen minutes we were there, put up our tents and spent a busy afternoon. Geoff sat in the tent with me and made me go through all my personal belongings, forcing me to leave anything unnecessary. He discovered my medical kit was still ridiculously large and was not amused that I had smuggled in my Anusol. He even suggested I saw off the handle of my toothbrush.

Geoff explained that much of what I was leaving was of negligible weight but helped me gain an attitude I needed to have. Even a single matchstick too many was an unnecessary luxury. The majority of my medical kit was left behind, although I later managed to hide some antiseptic ointment and Vaseline. The evening was relaxed, since we knew we had the following day for rest. Geoff was in high spirits, the broken GPS forgotten.

In our resupply there was a large envelope full of letters, faxes and e-mails from friends and family. It is hard to describe what excitement we felt receiving news from the outside world, when we were used to being so isolated. It was my job to divide the post into piles and distribute it and enormous pleasure to see everyone's face light up as I made the deliveries. It must be like this to be a florist on Valentine's Day, I thought. I had three letters, from Trevor of Club Direct, Liza and my mum. Mum's letter was full of news and I devoured every titbit. What would have seemed mundane in the real world became fascinating out here. Even her two new kittens became an extensive topic of conversation for Geoff and me later.

We left with enough food and fuel to last us until 88°. For the last week or so I had become used to a very light sled, so I was nervous again. I need not have worried. From somewhere I discovered enough strength, and kept up all day. Or perhaps the group was getting weaker. Because I am naturally skinny and slight — completely the wrong build for an expedition of this kind — I had worried that I simply had no weight to lose and would, therefore, quickly disintegrate into skin and bone. But I had discovered that our daily diet of 6000 calories was sufficient to maintain me, so my weight loss was minimal, whereas it was serious for large, stocky people like Steve and Justin. My frostbite was healed, too; it now looked like a bruise and nothing more. My chest and cold had cleared up as well.

As I continued to feel stronger, I saw the resupply had raised all our spirits. There was a dramatic change in Grahame, in particular. Getting beyond halfway was psychologically important and it seemed now that the press at home was also starting to take us seriously. *Blue Peter* had done an update and some of the papers were keen to hear from us. We were no longer foolish amateurs with no hope of success, already written off. More and more, I felt lucky to be away from London and the pressures of normal life. Sometimes, I was able to plod along with a completely empty mind. It must be a spiritual state that many devote years to cultivate, I thought.

That evening, Victor explained that the GPS was only supposed to accept thirty entries. We were now on day thirty-nine, no wonder the instrument had failed. Geoff also announced a rest day, because some of the team "were tired". I felt guilty, but I knew that Grahame and Mike had also been suffering that day. Geoff now confided that we would not in any case arrive for the Millennium. He was increasingly concerned about Justin's obsession and unsure how to manage it. He told me, as Mike had, that Justin hoped to sprint to the Pole after the second resupply. "But it's hopeless. Only Steve, Victor and Justin are capable of putting in that extra effort. Unless he intends to break away from the rest of the group. Oh God, I hope he doesn't suggest that again."

During the first rest day after the resuply, 14 December, I found dead skin flaking off me like a snake sloughing. It looked disgusting. We had another meeting summoned by Justin, but to audible relief, he announced he would not be discussing the schedule until we reached 88°. Instead, we discussed Christmas. But again, Justin disagreed with the rest of us. By having a day off for Christmas we were effectively saying he would not be able to be at the Pole for the Millennium. I found myself biting my nails for the first time in three weeks. In the end, we decided to delay thinking about Christmas until we had got to 88°. We all said we would then have a better idea how many miles we had to go and whether we could afford a day off, but in fact we were just delaying the unpleasant moment of disappointing Justin. I knew we all had our hearts set on a snow cave, games and festivities. We also decided to add thirty minutes on to each day's travelling. Then, every sixth day we would have a shorter day of six hours. It would be something to look forward to, a treat.

That night, a storm blew up and one rest day became two. Even though Geoff and I had developed a very comfortable routine, I sensed he needed space. I ventured into the storm in search of Steve and found him entertaining the Thornewills with hot chocolate and flapjacks. To my relief they all seemed comfortably resigned to the fact that we would not be arriving for the Millennium, nor would we be pushing ourselves to the Pole.

We then rewrote the "Twelve Days of Christmas" with Antarctic lines, most of which related in some way to frozen excrement. It is probably revealing that what we flush away from our minds and our houses in the city becomes an obsession when survival is such a struggle. After two hours of dedicated practice we went around each tent to sing. Victor filmed us and thanked us politely. And what seems improbable and surreal in retrospect — singing bastardized carols in a storm at −25°C — made perfect sense at the time.

For the second night in a row we could not make radio contact, but Geoff seemed unworried. This, I guessed, was the value of experience, he was used to intermittent communication. I hoped that it was not tonight that my appendix decided to burst. It was an irrational fear, but I knew many expeditioners chose to have the appendix removed before a long trip. This had seemed extreme when I first heard it, but now, I nervously eyed Geoff's penknife as he cut some cheese, and hoped he would not be doing cottage surgery with it next. It was only another twenty days, I reflected. One foot in front of the other for just three more weeks.

Fiona had been up all night with diarrhoea and Mike had not slept. Indeed, Fiona was on antibiotics, as her wounds had become gaping sores. I donated to her miracle tape and antiseptic ointment, causing raised eyebrows from Geoff, as I was supposed to have left the ointment behind at Thiels. Mike suffered more and more from a chafed groin. I soon donated to him my whole pot of Vaseline. Although he often looked like a pervert, hands stuffed inside his trousers as he rubbed the Vaseline into his crotch, nobody cared. Dignity was not an issue out here.

When we set off again on the 16th, we were all slow. After two days of lying horizontal, I was stiff. My elbows and shoulders were painful. That day we experienced our first snowquakes. These happen when layers of snow form on the ice. When trodden on, large areas collapse with loud bangs like cannon fire.

In the evening, Patriot Hills was glad to hear from us. They had considered flying in a plane to search for us, for the storm had been so severe, an eighty-knot wind had blown away nine tents. It was decided that in future, if we could not make radio contact, then we should use the satellite phone. We also learned that Tim and Peter, the Australians crossing the entire continent, were already past the Pole. They must have been going at a phenomenal pace; we were truly impressed. As for the Singaporeans, they were going solidly a few days ahead of us.

For the latter part of the journey, there was a new pattern. Justin, Veijo and Steve were the strongest and always at the front. Mike, Fiona, Grahame and I were at the back. Geoff and Victor would take it in turns to be around the front and rear. I was still the slowest, but not by much, and more often than not I was not the straggler, the one the team was waiting for. Except for Steve, Justin and Victor, we were all getting weaker. I did not think anybody would be capable of sprinting to the Pole, although Justin had not yet accepted that the two rest days off were enough to make his carefully planned schedule impossible. Although he could not have ever hoped to control the weather or our muscles in the way he had evidently managed his businesses, he was clearly frustrated and at times skied on far ahead.

A week before Christmas, it was Mike's birthday. We all signed a home-made card and yelled "Happy Birthday" over the wind before starting the day. That evening I made him a cake. I had no eggs, flour or oven, so snow was the main ingredient. With frozen gloves I moulded a cake shape on the stove tray and decorated the top with walnuts and dried fruit. I then put six matches on the top to act as candles. Steve was clearly unimpressed, "Yeah, a bit of snow on a foil tray with a couple of laxatives as cherries, I bet he'll be really chuffed." We managed to light two of the matches and then shoved it into their vestibule. Mike did look chuffed.

Geoff also brought up the subject of my moving out. Not that he wanted me to go, he added hastily, but he felt a change would be good. None of the others wanted to change tent partners, but I could move back in with Steve. In turn, I knew that Steve was more than keen to have the experience of sharing with Geoff, so, of course, I offered to camp alone. There was a look of horrified panic. "No! I feel that would be extremely unwise." I would stay with Geoff until Christmas Eve and then move back with Steve until the Pole. Until the Pole, I pondered. It is getting closer, it is really getting closer.

Our first "short", six-hour day, came on the 19th. It seemed a just reward for my continual improvement, but I was told off early the next day by Geoff for

187

attaching my skis too loosely to the sled. He made it quite clear that if a ski came off and was lost, I would have to be evacuated even at this late stage for when we reached the plateau that ended our journey, the snow would be too deep simply to be walked through. That day, we encountered monster sastrugi and a definite change in the weather. It was colder, so that much harder to warm up after each break. My foot had started to give me pain and I limped over to Geoff in order to set up camp. I turned round to open my sled and to my horror saw only one ski attached to it. One of my skis had indeed fallen off. I panicked. Geoff would be absolutely livid. He had reprimanded me only that morning. I considered saying nothing, but in the end, I confessed. "OK Catharine, when did you last have them?" he said, half-incredulous, half as if speaking to a very naughty child.

Geoff was trying hard to be calm. "I will reiterate what I said this morning. You cannot get to the Pole without your skis, so you and I are just going to have to go back out there and follow our tracks until we find it." I felt my eyes well up and the tears freeze to my face. I was absolutely exhausted, freezing and miserable, there was no way I could spend the next two hours looking for the ski and put Geoff through the pain as well. He looked at me and, not softening, said, "Come on, it's very windy. Let's go and help Steve put his tent up first before we set off." Emotionally, I explained to Steve what had happened, while Geoff started to erect his tent. Steve was silent for a moment and then shouted, "Sorry, Geoff, I can't carry on with this, it's just too cruel." With this, he turned round to his own sled and handed me my ski.

During the last hour, while I was walking like an automaton, the two of them had managed to pull my ski off my sled without my knowledge. They both thought it was hilarious. I had a complete sense of humour failure. After I had calmed down, Geoff tried to worm his way back into my favour with one of his chocolate brownies and by telling me that Steve's first idea had been to plant an empty fuel can in my sled. When I opened it that night, I would have assumed I had spilled its contents, as on the previous occasion.

By now, the altitude was starting to affect me. I felt short of breath. Despite the entertainment of an unexpected visitor, a seagull-like skua very far from its coastal habitat, tiredness put me in an appallingly bad mood. At one point I saw Justin desperately trying to warm his numb hands. He looked over to see Steve eating and pouring out a hot drink without gloves on at all. Steve did not seem to notice the cold. "Get some normal blood, you bastard," Justin joked. I started to giggle hysterically, rather too hysterically I thought. As ever, the line between sanity and instability seemed a very fine one.

Sure enough, I threw a tantrum the next day. It began when my face mask fell off. As soon as it hit the ground, it froze. A long icicle hung from the mouthpiece and a sheet of ice formed over it. Wearing it again would feel like torture, so, instead of replacing it, I pulled off my gloves and threw my ski sticks on to the ground in a rage, followed shortly by my gloves. I then stormed off again at a run, or rather attempted run, shouting, "This is all a load of absolute bollocks." I tripped over straightaway. Behind me, a gentle voice said, "I agree it's total bollocks, but please put your gloves back on, Catharine, you'll get frostbite." "No!" I snapped but, of course, I did force the gloves back on and set off again, in a huff. My mood lasted for the rest of the day, but by the time I was sitting comfortably in the tent with a cup of tea I felt extremely ashamed. It was the first and last time I lost my temper. More and more, I took to writing my feelings in my diary. It was the safest way to express them. I knew Geoff was doing the same; I dreaded to think what he must be writing.

Fortunately, Geoff made a joke of the whole thing, possibly because it was our last night together. He was kind and told me not to worry, just to keep on plodding. Then he told me about a diary entry from a week before. He had been so exhausted and in so much pain he had thought he would have a heart attack. "I'm glad Catharine is slow," he had written, "as she keeps a pace I can manage." It was generous of him to give me this insight into his own weakness, he knew how much it would help me.

I felt sad to be leaving Geoff's tent. It had indeed been a wonderful privilege. Despite his experience and the great respect with which he was held in the polar world, he remained utterly humble and self-effacing. That last morning, I reminded him that he had trained every single British woman that had set foot in the Arctic or Antarctic, the twenty-five members of the

190

Women's Polar Relay back in 1997, Caroline and her team for the South Pole and now Fiona and myself. He had never really thought about it like that. That day, he was in a wild mood, I imagine because he was thinking of being free again. He was, in fact, so exuberant that before the morning began, he took off his gloves and with a finger pretended to pee on the Australian flag attached to Grahame's sled to celebrate Christmas. Again, a very fine line between sanity and madness . . .

On my first night back with Steve, I forced him to stay up to make Christmas decorations. Cards for Geoff and Victor out of cardboard food boxes, trees and stars from the green army ration wrappers, stuck together with ski-binding glue, and star earrings to wear on Christmas Day. They all looked great. At 2a.m., we collapsed into our sleeping bags, Steve vowing to find a new tent partner in the morning. Justin had been overruled. The next day would be a holiday.

I slept really well after my creative endeavours and woke at nine on Christmas morning. Steve gave me a South American Picnic bar as a present. We had an invitation to go to the Thornewills for a Christmas service, which we both very much wanted to do, so we put on our star earrings. Geoff and Justin had decided not to attend, but the tent was already full of the others. Veijo gave us each a fridge magnet, which seemed entirely appropriate.

The service was wonderful. After initial awkwardness, giggling and general misbehaviour from Steve and me, regressing to our school choir days, we became really involved. We sang carols and Grahame and Mike

191

gave readings. It was informal and very relaxed and I didn't feel as self-conscious as I thought I might have. At midday, Steve, Veijo and Victor went off to build a snow cave. It was a beautiful day, the wind had dropped for us, and the skies were a clear blue, but to me they were absolutely crazy to put themselves through so much extra inessential effort. A lovely idea, but still barking, I thought. Instead, I took to my bed for several more hours.

In the afternoon, Mike asked whether I would like to use the satellite phone to call home. It was wonderful. All the family were there spending Christmas together, so I was able to have a very quick chat with each of them. I also had messages from Trevor, who had anticipated I would ring. He wanted to plan some telephone interviews and to organize a press conference on our arrival. The messages left me feeling uncomfortable. He was already assuming I would get there, and my reticence about and fear of being in the public eye came flooding back.

This was very much a personal journey for me, to fulfil a dream and move myself on. It was about the sort of character development I banged on about until four in the morning after slamming tequilas with my friends. I was not doing it for public recognition. But as Geoff reminded me, I was doing a job. My sponsors had helped pay for me in order to see me appear as much as possible in the media. He was quite right. I felt ashamed. I was extremely privileged to be in this position and I should not be allowed to complain. I was also concerned whether the PR would ignore the other people, and gloss over the fact that we were a guided expedition. Perhaps Fiona and my representatives would each want to play down the presence of the other woman. I had a chat with Mike and Fiona and they agreed to call their PR company and ask them to work with Trevor. I was determined that if I did get to the Pole, Fiona and I would be seen as a team and not separated.

At four we all went into the snow cave. It was simply incredible. The boys had been working solidly on it all day. From the outside it was hardly to be seen, but as we clambered down it opened up into a large cavern. They had even carved a large table and benches. When everyone was inside, we partially blocked up the entrance to protect us from the wind and a piercing blue light shone through. It was mesmerizing. Then we lit stoves for warmth and sat around our new table.

Aside from our extremely uncomfortable and squashed strategy meetings this was the first time we were all together. Justin had been up since the early hours making delicious Zuco fudge. Then, out of nowhere, Geoff produced a steaming Christmas pudding he had carried all the way out from England. He had decorated it with a piece of holly made from the increasingly versatile army ration biscuit foil. He then brought out a box of presents, so when we played games there were prizes for everybody. Mine were a clockwork frog and a set of miniature Winnie-the-Pooh books. Geoff also presented me with a small wrapped gift for putting up with him for twenty-six days. It was in fact a dried apricot, because I was always foraging for them in the bag of mixed fruit and nuts. I was extremely touched. We then gave Geoff and Victor their cards.

By now we were all freezing, even with stoves on, and our feet were starting to scream pain, so we cleared up and hurried back to our tents, leaving nothing but the piece of army ration holly stuck into the table. The cave would be here for years to come. We wondered if anyone would ever find it, maybe use it themselves. When it was Steve's turn to use the phone, he called his girlfriend. He was beaming when he came back into the tent. I already suspected he was going to propose when we returned. So it turned out to be one of the most special Christmases I had ever had. We were, we calculated, just ten days from the Pole and for the first time on the whole trip I allowed myself the luxury of fantasizing about the moment of arriving.

CHAPTER
TEN

Arrival at the Pole

On Boxing Day I would normally be recovering from a raging hangover, having spent the entire night talking with my mother. Today in Antarctica it was back to the routine of getting up at 6.30a.m. and beginning another day's march. I remembered saying to Steve weeks before, "Gosh, if I make it to Christmas Day I will be beside myself with excitement, as we'll be so nearly there." Now with ten days to go, the Pole still seemed far away, and I still had doubts whether my body would hold out, especially as my foot was becoming more and more painful. We crossed the 88° during the day, the only slight cause for concern that we were expecting our second resupply in the next day or so, but the weather was not allowing the plane to take off.

I did not often navigate, as I was inexperienced at it. I did not want either to risk the daily mileage targets or to make the others cold from travelling too slowly, so I rarely asked. But the next day, when we were in any case slowed by whiteout, I asked if I might lead the last hour.

It was the most extraordinary feeling walking into an abyss of white. There were no shadows to navigate by,

195

so we would take a bearing from the compass, and then focus on a piece of sastruga in the distance, skiing towards it with our heads up. This was very disorientating, balance was difficult, and I fell over twice. Also, because the white fog was so thick it was difficult actually to see anything to focus on. It, therefore, became more like guesswork. Mike had given me a tip — to focus on the fur ruff around my hood, take note of which way the wind was blowing the fur, and use that as the guide.

After a while, I stopped to take a bearing and Steve, who was skiing next to me, said, "Look round, Catharine, you won't believe this." We had left everyone way behind. Fiona was first to catch up, her goggles steamed up from the effort, while Grahame was panting and telling me to slow down. Justin merely said, "I think that's what's called proving a point." How had I managed this? Perhaps it was the sheer fear of holding people up that gave me the extra adrenalin and speed. Whenever I was given the chance to go first after that, my speed seemed to improve dramatically.

The next day, we were woken by Victor asking us to detail how much food we had left. We then had a meeting. Geoff was brief. Weather was bad everywhere, the Pole itself had been closed down to planes. We had eight days left, and looking at the list he was optimistic we would have enough food to get there anyway.

The reality was that most of us only had enough substantial food to last us another three days. We would then be on to nuts and Nutrigrain bars. Mike suggested trying to get a message to the Singaporeans, who were almost at the Pole, to ask if they had any spare food. He also suggested dumping three sleds to make our load lighter, and then picking them up on the way home. Both ideas were rejected, Geoff still certain we could get there on our remaining rations. Later, we discovered that Mike and Fiona had broken into some of their reserves; they actually had less food than the rest of us.

So that night we used up the last of our evening meals. When Geoff confessed he had no main meal, Steve and I put half of our shepherd's pie and potato into a bag and forced him to take it. Mike came round and asked if we would trade some food for some fuel. We tentatively accepted and gave him the other half of our potato. Unfortunately, the fuel we had received in the resupply was Chilean and smoked terribly, stinging the eyes and making them water. "Not sure if that was the best deal we've ever struck, Cath," remarked Steve, as the stove started to splutter out black smoke. "Our last potatoes in exchange for extra weight and a litre of tear gas."

We were now on chocolate, Pepperami and Nutrigrain bars. Rather than keep warm and suffocate we decided to turn our stove off and eavesdrop on Geoff's call to Patriot Hills. We shivered in our sleeping bags, hanging on his every word. But we could not glean much. It sounded as if the plane would try the following day, and at least throw some food out of the window. If, however, it could land, it would disembark the team walking the last degree to the Pole. I wondered if I would see Madelaine. "Or it's nut soup tomorrow, Stevie boy."

But the next day, the 29th, was very cold. We kept travelling as fast as we could on half rations. Mike was low in energy. Like me, he found it very difficult to function on little food. I guessed that his blood sugar was very low as he began to behave in an irrational way. I spent the majority of the day speculating how I could turn nuts and powdered soup into a delicious and appetizing meal and drawing a blank. But when we made camp we had just seventy miles to go.

Suddenly we heard the familiar hum of a Twin Otter. It dived down to let us know it would be back and soared off again to drop the other team. Madelaine later said that she was looking out of the window and saw me. It was an emotional moment for her, as she remembered so vividly starting out together at Pen's selection course in England. From the air, she could see how close I was to my goal. We set up camp and ate, as we could not tell how long it would take for the plane to return. When it did, ninety minutes later, Steve was beside himself with excitement, and was quickly out of the tent shouting for me to follow.

The plane landed only feet from the tents. It was a mad scramble, boxes came hurtling out, but the engines were not shut down, the pilots were to be here only a few minutes. As we came to the plane door we noticed Peter and Tim on board. They were very subdued. Apparently, shortly after passing the South Pole their fuel had leaked into their food boxes, making everything completely inedible and they had been evacuated. A resupply would have invalidated their attempt at an unsupported crossing. At least they had

198

made a record fastest journey to the Pole itself. We stayed up very late to sort out all the food, finding endless packs of spicy Thai noodles and very little else.

And so, on the 31st, to Justin's final disappointment, we were still not at the Pole itself. Of course, to see in New Year we had a ceremony. No one really knew what to do, but we had received a cake in the resupply, so we cut it ritually in the cold night, linked arms and in a reserved and awkwardly British way sang "Auld Lang Syne". Very soon after we scurried back to our tents, too cold to carry on. Steve and I did visit the Thornewills. So this was the Millennium. It was a New Year I had thought about since I was at school. I vividly remember discussing it with a friend at lunch break. "Blimey, we'll be so old," she said. "You'll be thirty-four, for God's sake, what do you think you'll be doing?" "I suppose I will be married, hopefully to Stewart (my then boyfriend), with four children. Definitely not working. I'll live in a cottage by the sea and make my own bread."

"What about New Year's resolutions?" Steve asked. Fiona's was to learn the piano. Mine? I was used to big, ambitious New Year's resolutions. But the list of character faults I had to remove from eight years previously was almost all ticked off now. I did not know what my New Year's resolutions were, I really had no idea. One thing was certain, it was the first sober New Year I had had since childhood, and the first time I had woken up without a hangover, an empty packet of cigarettes and a bucket beside my bed.

Insanely, Steve had decided to sleep outside to see in the New Year, wearing all his clothes inside his sleeping bag and knowing there was little wind to chill him in the open. I stumbled over him as I got up at 6a.m. to go into Fiona's tent for an interview with *Live and Kicking*. I had worked as a stage manager on the programme for the previous two New Years with the presenters Zoë Ball and Jamie Theakston. What we were planning now was the first ever live satellite link from Antarctica. Mike and Fiona, loyal as always to their sponsors, were working out how to plug them live on air. I pictured the producer's horrified face if we used our live thirty-second slot to thank Project Telecom and Potton Homes without talking about Antarctica. "Don't do that. I beg you. I may never work in Children's TV again," I pleaded, remembering how seriously the BBC takes its public, non-commercial obligations.

We turned on the phone and then just had to wait for it to ring. I was imagining Scott from the sound department in the gallery trying to get through to us while live on air. Eventually we spoke to Steve Wilson, the presenter. After a brief explanation of where we were, he said he had someone there who wanted to talk to me. It was my mum. They had brought her and my brother into the studio on New Year's Day to speak to me live on television. We had enough time to say that I was fine and was going to get there. And then it was finished and the line was dead. I was overwhelmed. It remained one of the most memorable highlights of my trip.

We stopped to take our "New Year" photos, but Justin did not join in. He sat quietly on his sled away from the rest of us, obviously disappointed that we were not already at the Pole as he had hoped. That evening I overheard Geoff speaking about Fiona and myself. He had heard our conversation on Christmas Eve when we had talked about our PR people co-operating. He vehemently hated any kind of media attention, and had taken the conversation completely the wrong way. In fact, he thought we were planning some kind of celebrity lifestyle on our return. "The truth is," he was saying, "if it wasn't for the men on this trip those girls would not get to the Pole. It's those women back there (Caroline Hamilton's team) that deserve all the credit, not Catharine and Fiona." I was horrified. I had just shared a tent with Geoff for almost a month and in that time had become very close to and fond of him. It was so important to me that I had his respect and approval and I had worked extremely hard for it. I felt completely rejected.

I spent the entire evening thinking about this and discussing it with Steve. There was absolutely no doubt that Caroline's team was admirable, and what they would achieve more substantial. I was on a "commercial" expedition, if you like; I was paying to be guided to the Pole and, yes, I was in a mixed group. Caroline and her team were all female and they were guiding themselves. It was true that Fiona and I would, indeed, be the first British women to walk to the South Pole. But this was really chance. We left two weeks before the others. It had always been impossible for them to catch up; it had never been a race at all.

On the other hand, Fiona and I were doing exactly what everyone, man or woman, guide or amateur, must do when walking to the South Pole. We man-hauled all our supplies to the Pole ourselves, without the aid of machines, dogs or Sherpas, and I myself had spent fifteen months trying to raise sponsorship, alone, without the help of a team. Apart from a moment in the first week, I had pulled the same weight as all the men, and Fiona certainly had. In some cases she had even taken some of Mike's load.

I would certainly not have reached the Pole without our team spirit and the enormous mental support I had been given, especially by Steve. But I was aggrieved that anyone had felt the need to compare. This was in every sense my personal journey, and my personal achievement. Although my fondness for Geoff gradually returned the next day, I still felt let down. I knew I would have to speak to him about it, although perhaps not until we had arrived. But I felt I must try to get it in proportion. I could not let it ruin the triumph of getting to the Pole. Only two days later, I was going to experience the most incredible moment of my life. In the event, Geoff's obvious pleasure at my success when we arrived made me keep silent.

I spent the rest of the night making wedding invitations. Yes, really. Mike and Fiona had decided to renew their marriage vows at the Pole. As there was no clergyman there, Grahame had received dispensation to officiate. A suitable order of service had come in with our second resupply. It took me hours. I cut out sweet wrappers and pasted them in a mosaic pattern on the back of a piece of card. I cut flowers out of the ever-useful army ration biscuit foil and pasted them on to the front. Then I lined the edges with the "Fixomole" tape used for Fiona's wounds. *Blue Peter* would have been proud of me. Steve then braved the cold to deliver the invitations to each tent.

During the final two-hour session of the next day, 3 January, there was a sighting of the Pole — three black shapes on the horizon, about ten miles away. I was right at the back, and could not see anything because I did not have my glasses, but it was really exciting watching the team at the front waving ski sticks and scanning the horizon. I dutifully followed suit, and waved my sticks also. All the boys immediately tore off into the distance, skiing at top speed, and leaving Fiona, Geoff and me lagging behind, as if we were minding trolleys in Sainsburys. "There's far too much testosterone on this expedition," I said to Geoff, as I watched them getting further and further away.

Steve and I spent the evening with the Thornewills. Finally, Mike and I allowed ourselves to believe we would make it. I was now only too happy to talk about our arrival. We all agreed that it would be wonderful to have at least a day at the Pole, perhaps two, and then about four at Patriot Hills. We started to fantasize about Ros's cooking, having a wash, reading books and sitting in the communal tent chatting to everyone else about their expeditions. Justin had other ideas. He wanted to get off the continent as quickly as possible. He hoped the Twin Otter could be waiting at the Pole and a connecting Hercules at Patriot Hills. At Punta Arenas, the first international flight would take him for his beach holiday. But Mike said, "I've waited thirty years to get to the South Pole, there's no way I won't spend time there."

This last night Geoff came by with news. The Singaporeans had arrived safely at the Pole and were already gone. The last degree party would be leaving tomorrow, but because of their late arrival they had had to be deposited much nearer to the Pole than 89°, to make the Millennium. Geoff anticipated that it would take us seven hours to get to the Pole. We would stay there for about twenty-four hours, but he anticipated we might have no time at Patriot Hills. ANI's Hercules was booked to leave immediately for Chile. The thought of going back to civilization so soon upset me. A sudden return to the familiar from great changes is disturbing; a gentle transition is always preferable.

It did take us exactly seven hours. We were all awake by 6a.m., and all excited. I was completely dazed. It was an absolutely beautiful day, −33°C but bright sun and sky, with not a breath of wind. We took it at a deliberately slow pace, so that we could really enjoy the day. And we each had a chance to lead. I have to say that there was a phenomenal pleasure to be had from leading the group at the same time as watching the Pole get nearer and nearer, and hearing the noise of the scientific base get louder and louder.

Mike came up beside me as I was leading and said, "Really enjoy this moment, feel it, remember it. You'll never have a feeling like this again." Soon the Pole became even clearer. It spurred me on. What we could see was a two-storey dome, the living quarters of the 200 base workers who stayed there during the summer. For us, this was the real Millennium Dome. Around this, there was something that looked like a construction site, where the scientific research took place. During the last hour, Mike was on the phone giving a live commentary to his website. Unknown to me, my whole family was at home having a party while my brother read out my progress. They had a magnum of champagne waiting on ice.

It was decided that Steve would lead us in. He had led most during the journey and had provided support to all of us when he sensed we needed it. As we were arriving, a representative from the base came bounding up to meet us. He was greatly excited; he had always wanted to greet an expedition. He escorted us to the ceremonial pole, a red and white striped podium surrounded with flags, with a mirrored ball on top. Here we took a very quick photograph.

It was 4 January 2000 and 9.20p.m. GMT. With Fiona, I had become the first British woman to walk to the South Pole. We had walked 1126 kilometres (over 700 miles) in average temperatures of −30°C. The sun was shining, and it was −37°C. I had wondered in my head every day for sixty-one days what this moment would feel like. I wondered whether I would cry, or go completely berserk. Most of the time I hadn't dared believe that I would experience this moment in anything other than a dream. I do not think anyone thought I could really pull it off, least of all me. Veijo turned to me and, in the deadpan way of Finns, said: "So . . . you made it, that's good."

There are two South Poles: the ceremonial pole and the real one. During our photo call, we unwittingly removed the "real" South Pole from the ground. Its geographical position changes slightly and is recalculated each year. This position was marked by a wooden sign commemorating Scott and Amundsen, but also by an old iron post, unsightly in our photos, which we pulled out, unaware of what it really represented. But then a scientist ran out shouting, "Guys, please put that back, it's the South Pole."

In fact, the "moment" was all very civilized and, in retrospect, extremely British. We all shook hands and then, completely exhausted, were taken into the base for coffee. I tried to give Geoff a hug. It resembled what I felt hugging a tree would be like. He shook my hand in return. Steve was, as expected, absolutely exuberant, bounding around the base. As a plumber, he marvelled at the pipes and plumbing in the canteen loo. Grahame was quiet, but moved. Veijo was intent on finding souvenirs for his children and managed to get the base to open the shop. Fiona was terribly cold from posing for photos, so Mike was helping her to warm up. Victor looked ready for a vodka celebration, and Geoff was quiet, dignified and emotionless, betraying no feelings at all. Despite his urgency to leave Antarctica and get on with a hot beach holiday, Justin — I know — was chuffed. As we walked to the Pole itself, he had written

"Plebs to the Pole" on his thermarest and was holding it as Victor filmed us.

And me? I was so utterly incredulous that I was there, alive, successful, that I could not speak or communicate in any way — I had never felt such relief, such satisfaction, such pride and such happiness all in one moment before. So I just sat in a chair drinking coffee, staring into space, feeling utterly high on caffeine and also completely disbelieving that I was at last experiencing this moment.

The natives were friendly. They offered us the hospitality of the base. Being inside was the most surreal experience of my life. For two months we had only seen ourselves and the infinite expanse of white ice 360° around us. Now, suddenly, we were in the warm with artificial light, being stared at by distantly amused base workers over their breakfasts. We felt as if we had conquered the world; it was just another working day to them. We were given a tour of the base before being politely asked to leave. Only the scientists could live there, and US government rules meant that we now had to go and set up camp again a minimum of a quarter of a mile away from the base.

We could not sleep, of course. We were too excited. And for the next two and a half hours the satellite phone did not stop ringing. Interviewers from every TV station seemed to call. Fortunately they all seemed to want to talk to Mike and Fiona; it seemed the "first married couple" angle appealed far more than "first British women". I did get my interview with *Blue Peter*, however, which felt extraordinary. Katy Hill, a

207

presenter whom I had looked after as a stage manager for two years, interviewed me live. I had watched many a satellite link-up with Chris Bonington at the top of a mountain or Tracy Edwards from her yacht. I had never imagined there would be one with me. At 11a.m. we had Mike and Fiona's marriage blessing at the Pole. Grahame led the service and Justin gave a reading; it was a touching moment. Unfortunately, it was so cold I spent much of it flailing my arms about like an albatross and running on the spot. Inappropriate behaviour indeed for a civilized marriage ceremony.

Twenty hours later, the Twin Otter arrived to take us back to Patriot Hills. Mike's police uniform was flown in. He was in fact very late back for work, but had resolved to send them a photograph of himself on duty, at the South Pole instead of Nottingham. The flight back from the Pole was a dream. I was on the plane after all, not alone in disgrace as I had feared so many times, but on my way home with everyone else. We flew over much of the wasteland that we had walked across. I stared fixedly out of the window in absolute wonderment nearly the whole way back, looking out at this massive continent I had successfully walked across. I watched the sastrugi, the Thiel Mountains, the Three Sails and then finally the Patriot Hills Mountains came into view. It took us just six hours to fly back, a journey that had taken us sixty-one days to walk. We had one interruption, from the *Daily Mirror*. Jane Ridley had tracked me down and was now speaking to the pilots about doing an interview.

Everyone at Patriot Hills came running out to meet us. Madelaine was in the lead to greet me, then came the Singaporeans. It was so good to see them all. The first thing we did was eat. I had a full English breakfast, the one that I had been fantasizing about for the entire duration of the journey. I then moved on to a main meal. We all ate far too much. Mike was sick and I had to leave the tent for air. Sadly for me, the Hercules was already on its way. It would land and then we would have to set off soon after. But although the plane arrived, the weather closed in and it could not land. It, therefore, had to turn round and fly all the way back to Chile again, costing ANI thousands of dollars' worth of fuel. What was a welcome respite for me was very bad news for Justin, and Anne Kershaw.

Steve, Fiona, the Singaporeans and I stayed up all night talking, dissecting our journeys in minute detail. I finally went to bed. Before doing so I rummaged through my bag for a bottle of perfume I had saved for this moment. I also came across my packet of cigarettes. I threw them straight in the bin.

In the end we spent four days at Patriot Hills, and it was the best holiday of my life. We ate, chatted with other expeditioners and I somehow even managed to climb a mountain. I had a bath of sorts, but waited to wash my hair. On our fourth day at Patriot Hills we were told that the plane had just left Chile to come and collect us. To my surprise, I was completely horrified at the thought of leaving Antarctica, of returning to normal life again. The expedition was more challenging than I could ever have comprehended and I had cleared

209

more hurdles than I could ever have imagined. I had never felt so mentally cleansed. All I had had to do was concentrate on putting one foot in front of the other and make mileage. In the evening our only duties had been to cook, write our diaries, and repair our deteriorating bodies and equipment. There was no stress, no rat race and no relationship nightmares. Those evenings spent getting smashed on tequila, smoking endless fags and then waking up in the morning feeling wretched and having disgraced myself were mercifully distant.

The continent had completely bewitched me. Perhaps naturally enough, I did not want to face mundane, everyday life again; besides, my future back in the city was very uncertain. I also felt strangely alone. When we reached the Pole, I was suddenly aware that the rest of the team were going back into the arms of wives and girlfriends, and their secure lives. My reality of going back to debt, no job and former pressures became glaringly evident and unattractive. The easiest thing to do in these situations is, of course, to panic, bury one's head in the sand and put off the moment of return as indefinitely as possible. I asked if I might see out the season working in the canteen at the base. Steve, the camp manager, agreed that I could. My mother and my sponsors were horrified. A little later Geoff came over to my tent and found me wrapped up in my duvet jacket, sobbing. It was all too much. He came over, patted me on the head and simply said, "I think it would be better if you came back with all of us." "Do you?" I asked. "Yes, you've got to face the music sometime, you know. Come on, let's go and get some more chocolate cake and go and put your mum's mind at rest." "OK, then," I conceded. Geoff clearly had insurmountable experience in how to deal with deranged and erratic women. I boarded the plane with the others.

CHAPTER
ELEVEN

Between the Poles

My fantasies for two months had been of cascading hot water, bubble baths and shaving my legs, and of being able to wash my hair. But the entire youth hostel had just one shower. I was too tired to think about anything except sleep. So, though I had imagined the first thing we would all do was wash off two months of filth, I actually went straight to bed, smelly and rank.

We had arrived back in Punta Arenas at 1a.m. And the problem was we were now broke. So we had to forgo our fantasy hotel suites with their private bathrooms and, instead, Fiona, Steve, Mike and I all crammed in one room. But the next morning we were up early, as Justin had offered us all breakfast at the best hotel in town. It was odd seeing everyone suddenly scrubbed up, beards shaved and smelling of cologne.

One by one, we went home over the next three days. I loathe goodbyes; I will do anything to avoid them. I always find them awkward and embarrassing, and prefer to exit quietly, unnoticed. But I wanted to give Geoff a proper farewell. Saying goodbye to him would be a wrench, but at least I could do it in the right way. So Steve and I got up at 5.30a.m. to see him off.

Even at this emotional moment he did not drop his guard. He shook my hand and then gave me just the sketchiest of hugs. I lost my dignity immediately. I began to witter about how much I wanted to see him on my return and how I could not envisage our being apart now the expedition was over. I finally plucked up courage to ask him if I could stay with him for a couple of weeks when we were back in England. There was a pause. "Well, not if I can help it," he said with a wry smile. The month we had spent together in his tent had clearly left its mark. And then he was gone.

Three hours later I had to see Steve off, too. We drove to the airport together. Without him I would not have reached the Pole, it was that simple. I wondered if the strong bonds we had all made over the last two months would ever be reproduced back in the real world or whether we would all just drift apart. Sadly, I rather suspected the latter.

I myself was flying back with Mike and Fiona. I was very nervous on the last leg of our journey from Madrid to Heathrow, but as Mike had managed to get us an upgrade to business class, I had the chance, after months of abstinence, to get completely drunk on champagne.

I knew my mother would be there at the airport to meet me, but had she asked if I would like a big gathering and a party, I would certainly have refused — the idea of being the centre of attention still left me absolutely cold. So what I expected was just to see my mum, my brother and his wife. Nevertheless, Fiona insisted we go into the first airport toilet and put on make-up. We then went through, I tottering and swaying from alcohol, nerves and tiredness. Suddenly, there was loud cheering and I saw my entire family and all my closest friends, champagne glasses in hands, waving billboards saying "Congratulations, Catharine!" Even my grandmother had turned up, with balloons flying from her wheelchair. There was a similar reception for Mike and Fiona from their friends and family. A glass of champagne was thrust into my hand; I gave interviews and chatted.

I could not believe everyone had turned up to see me. I can look back and say without hesitation it was the best moment in my entire life. As a friend I was loyal but reserved and aloof. I very rarely showed how much I cared. Now, I not only had the chance to relax and celebrate my achievement, I could also do so surrounded by all the people I loved, who were showing so obviously they cared for me, as if it were my birthday, or Christmas. I was completely overwhelmed. I suppose I had made my polar journey so much for myself, and inconvenienced so many of the people who loved me in preparing for it, that it did not occur to me they would be so happy for me in my success. When I saw the evidence in front of me, I was just really moved. My family had organized a party in the Radisson hotel nearby, where we stayed drinking exorbitantly expensive gin and tonics until two in the morning.

"Marinating in a bath of essential oils for several hours, then buying a cottage and growing basil!" I told the reporter from the *Telegraph*, in answer to the question, "What are you most looking forward to doing now?" On our return, there was enormous media attention, which also greatly surprised me. We spent the first week giving interviews, and the very first of them was my triumphant return to *Blue Peter*. To my delight, my old colleagues there were really proud of me, especially because I had managed to plant the *Blue Peter* flag at the Pole and wear my much-loved *Blue Peter* Badge on all the photographs. To my amazement I received the ultimate accolade — a Gold *Blue Peter* Badge. While I had been working on the show, I had nursemaided the Gold Badges for Damon Hill, the racing driver, and Michael Bond, the creator of Paddington Bear. "That makes it all worthwhile," I said on camera. Aside from my airport party, this was the proudest moment in my life.

Next, I had Christopher, my Beanie Bear, auctioned on the new Sotheby's website. When I set off, I had removed his tag from his ear, deciding it looked unsightly. Only now did I learn that this had greatly decreased his commercial value for collectors. In the end, he raised just £500.

There was more. Fiona and I, together with the British All-Women team, who had also successfully reached the Pole, were invited to the *Daily Mirror* Pride of Britain Awards. It was a huge privilege to be recognized in this way, since the other award winners were not celebrities but ordinary people who had displayed great bravery or public-spiritedness. I think all of us felt almost fraudulent and undeserving to be there. Nonetheless, it was a wonderful ceremony. Chris

Evans presented us with our award, and Mike gallantly gave a speech on behalf of Fiona and myself. It was recognition for Plebs to the Pole.

By now, I tended not to drink, aware that I found moderation in anything difficult. But whether it was nerves, awe or excitement, I succumbed that afternoon. The ceremony ended and everyone started to take their leave. The next thing I remember was waking up on the floor of a toilet cubicle in the Hilton Hotel, not knowing how on earth I had got there. I had no coat, no bag and no award. Mike and Fiona were nowhere to be seen. Ashamed of my behaviour, they had clearly just abandoned me to my fate.

I limped out into reception and then back into the ballroom to search for my belongings. The hall had been packed up already and only three or four cleaners remained, hoovering up the debris. There was certainly no sign of my possessions. After finally finding my handbag in the reception, I staggered to the tube and passed out on a seat, surrounded by commuters going home. Shortly before arriving at Clapham Common I was woken by an irate passenger whose shoulder I had fallen asleep on. I surveyed the scene. There I was, dribbling and just awake from my drunken stupor. I was still clutching a basket of red roses that I had clearly stolen from one of the Hilton tables, as well as my prized ceremony brochure. Was I the Pride of Britain? No, I was a pathetic and shameful sight. I hoped to God I had not been photographed by a tabloid journalist.

The next thing I had to learn — and fast — was public speaking. I was invited to give talks by my sponsors and the charity. It was a terrifying prospect. I knew I could not have stood up as Mike had done at the awards. Remember that I was somebody who flinched at telling a story to four friends in a pub, let alone a whole roomful giving me all their attention. I gave a first talk to my friends, family and climbing club, about seventy people in all. Somehow, I got through it, and at the end my mother said to me, "You know, I am almost more proud of you having the guts to get up in front of all those people and speak, than I am about you walking to the Pole. I know how much it terrified you."

Jane Fleury, my wonderful boss who had been unfailingly supportive throughout my South Pole exploits, gave me my job back as a location manager and, initially, I settled back into normal life well; indeed, I had a huge desire to be conventional, perhaps to conform at last. Four years on from when I had felt they were settling down, my friends now seemed all to be marrying and having children. I was thirty-four, but I was still flatsharing, behaving irresponsibly and dating unsuitable men. My disgraceful charade at the Pride of Britain Awards was another wake-up call. Time to behave.

It did not then strike me that I had led a wonderfully rich life since leaving school. I could only see my friends had solid, lasting gains from their adult lives, and I did not. Going on one's travels, being unconventional and adventurous are hardly faults, but part of me felt a strong desire to conform. So I bought a flat, the first one I looked at. I saw it on a Saturday, put an offer in on the Sunday and had it accepted on Monday. My BBC job was enough security for my mortgage lender, which conveniently ignored my debts; my family gave me the deposit. Nikki, who was also having an attack of conventionalism, in response to signing up for drama school at the age of thirty-five, bought a flat at the same time. When she opened the door to her new home, the previous owners had left it spotless, with a bottle of Châteauneuf du Pape and a vase of flowers on a gleaming kitchen table. My owners had not done likewise.

When I took possession, I was faced with a disgusting pit. Pictures of naked women covered the kitchen wall, there were condoms under the bed and dirty underwear strewn around the bathroom. It gave me a very concrete focus for the next three months. I painted and redecorated it into a beautiful penthouse. But it felt like somewhere I could only refurbish and rent out, not settle into. Being conventional at first was fun. For the first time in my life I revelled in conversations about paint samples and DIY. But soon the novelty of having the time to read books, socialize and argue the benefits of B&Q versus Homebase wore thin.

Soon after my return I was invited for two interviews to study Speech Therapy, and was accepted at City University to start that year. It seemed by far the best option — to quit while I was ahead, turn my back on the whole travelling world and direct my energies to something cerebral, yet substantial, instead. I had had the ten years' travelling and partying that I knew I had needed before settling down. The mischief was out of my system, and in my own mind, Speech Therapy was a new direction and a challenge for which I now felt ready.

Yet, however many scented baths I took, I could not drown my restlessness. Instead, I had time to reflect on my journey to the South Pole and I became aware, too aware, of the glaring fact that there was a North Pole and no British woman had walked all the way to it yet. Mike and Fiona had also noted this, and had financial backing. They tentatively made plans to go the following year. We all contacted ANI, who agreed to organize a trip to the North Pole, should we want to go. So did I? Could I?

The drawback of the North Pole was it was tougher — by a long, long way — and because I had struggled so hard in Antarctica, I really doubted my abilities. Rather than flat terrain, the Arctic is a frozen moving ocean. This movement, essentially caused by ocean currents beneath, frequently breaks up the ice into massive walls and rubble called pressure ridges. These ridges often shift and can extend for miles, to a height of up to forty feet. More often than not, they cannot be walked around and inconveniently for the northbound traveller, they generally run east–west, right across the line of travel. The only way forward is to push and haul one's eleven-and-a-half-stone sled up and over them.

In addition, the temperatures are much colder to begin with. The Antarctic is visited at high summer, when it is least cold and most light, but a frozen ocean is best traversed when it is most frozen, provided there is any light at all. So there is a very small window between the first week in March and the end of May, into which one must fit a two-month journey. It is a journey often lengthened by drifting ice. Very often, a traveller goes to sleep, only to find when he wakes that he has drifted back in the night the entire distance he journeyed the day before. There are the constant dangers of falling through the ice and of polar bears, which will gladly devour polar explorers.

Scott and Shackleton are part of English mythology. They were not just the most famous Antarctic explorers of their generation, but arguably the most famous British explorers to go to any continent. The Arctic holds no such place in the British imagination, but it has an equivalent draw for Americans. Perhaps we remember something hazy about the North-West Passage, but the most famous British Arctic explorer, Wally Herbert, though idolized by the polar community, is scarcely known to the lay public, partly because his greatest achievement unfortunately coincided with the Moon landings. But for Americans, Robert E. Peary, a US Navy engineer, and Frederick Cook, a New York doctor, are names to salute.

Since the North Pole is ice, not land, it is even in dispute as to who the first man to reach it might have been. There is, after all, nowhere one can leave a flag. So we cannot talk of a simple race, as between

Amundsen and Scott. Peary made several attempts, but on 1 March 1909, he set off with 24 men, 19 sledges and 133 huskies. He later stated he had reached the Pole on 6 April, but on his return, he was dismayed to find that his rival, Cook, was claiming to have got there with two Eskimo companions, a year earlier, on 21 April 1908. Peary said this must be false, and soon Cook, who also had a very tendentious claim to be the first to the summit of Mount McKinley, the highest peak in North America, was discredited. Peary had been sponsored by the *National Geographic* magazine, which unreservedly supported him.

Unfortunately, Peary's proof was not solid either. His only means of navigation was by observing the height of the sun, so his calculations could be easily falsified. As we were to find, the closer we came to the Pole, the more often corrections needed to be made. Peary did not take sufficiently frequent readings to have given himself such a chance. Next, the distances Peary claimed he travelled each day were enormous. No one before or since, and certainly not Peary himself, equalled on any single day the distances claimed as the average. So the claims of both Cook and Peary continue to be debated and the matter is unresolved.

In 1968–9, Herbert and three companions made the first surface crossing of the Arctic Ocean, from Alaska to Spitzbergen. He took forty dogs on a sixteen-month journey that extended for 3600 miles, though rather less as the crow flies. It involved camping on the ice during the polar summer when the ice was too broken to travel. It has been described as the last of the great explorers' journeys, since Herbert did not know what he would find. Some even claim that he became the first man to reach the North Pole, which shows how confusing the issue is, and how few people go there at all.

If there have been few men, there are even fewer women. Before we went there, only three women had been all the way to the North Pole. Ann Bancroft was an American who, in 1986, travelled 1000 miles from the Northwest Territories in Canada with a dog team. She was the only female member of that expedition. Then, in 1997, Matty McNair and her Canadian assistant Denise Martin were the guides for the British Women's Polar Relay. Whereas the British women all travelled for around ten days each before they were air-lifted out, Matty and Denise, both North Americans, skied the whole way.

There is a further source of confusion. You will remember that the Earth's magnetic variation causes the Magnetic and Geographic Poles to be in different places. The Geographic North Pole, the "true" one for explorers, is the hardest to reach. In the Antarctic, only the Geographic Pole is of any interest, but in the shifting conditions of the Arctic, the Magnetic North Pole is a valid, but much lesser challenge.

The Plebs all went back to their jobs and back to their normal lives. I remained in contact with Mike and Fiona, attending two of Fiona's many excellent parties. I spoke frequently to Steve on the phone, just needing to maintain some sort of contact. And I made intermittent visits to Geoff in the Lake District, always on the pretext of doing something else, visiting ageing aunts or any other lame excuse which would make him feel more relaxed about my visits. In turn, he sent me a congratulation present. Since he knew I had a phobia about spiders, this was a tin of chocolate ones. At first, I could not open it, terrified. But several weeks later, I came home one night with irresistible food cravings. I opened the tin very gingerly, just to be sure that the spiders were indeed made of chocolate, that it was not some terrible joke. Even then, the thought of putting one into my mouth proved too revolting so I left the cellophane intact. Thirty minutes later my hunger became overpowering and I nervously chewed on a leg. Five minutes after that the tin was empty, all ten spiders now in the bottom of my tummy.

In June, we had a reunion, which everyone was able to attend except Grahame, now living in Australia. No one spoke of any further trips, except Steve, who was hungry for more and was planning his own unsupported expedition to the North Pole with Swee Chiow, the Singaporeans' leader.

As for my own ambitions, Anne Kershaw, although encouraging, was noncommittal.

"OK, Catharine, I think the best thing to do would be for you to try and raise the money this summer and then talk again around Christmas time. We'll then know if we've got a team, who the guide is, and whether he is willing to take you on." Mike and Fiona were not committing themselves to ANI either; they were looking at the possibility of setting up their own, completely independent expedition. But I knew I myself had to be part of a guided trip, if I was going to have any chance of getting there.

The thought of starting again on raising money — £25,000 this time — was almost more than I could bear. It was also extremely hard to motivate myself to ask for money when I did not even know whether the expedition existed or not, let alone whether I would be a part of it. What I was sure about, however, was that this time I should train properly and that meant starting immediately.

When I was looking for locations in my job, I chose as many as possible within a twenty-minute radius of a Hertfordshire farm, itself used as a location, which had agreed to let me train there. Remember that my schedule as a location manager was punishingly long, starting work at around 5.30a.m. and finishing between 8 and 9p.m. But every other night, I would drive to the farm, put a harness on, attach four car tyres to it and then plod off dutifully into the fields for two hours. There was a particularly steep and muddy hill on the farm; this made hauling my tyres all the more strenuous and useful. The film crew would look on with great amusement.

On the nights that I was not pulling tyres, I would run six miles and then go to the gym for two hours' bodybuilding. I never told the gym what I was training for, merely instructing them to write me a programme to build my muscles to the size of Arnold Schwarzenegger's. Twice a week, I would train with the army. So, this time, I was in excellent condition physically, and financially up to my ears in debt.

Moreover, I was still completely undecided whether I should take on the huge challenge of the other Pole. Did I really have any chance of success?

I read some of the accounts explorers had written, always in the traditional diary form. Their journeys to the North Pole were portrayed as sheer misery. I took advice from those who had been there, hoping for some encouragement — in particular from Geoff and Victor, of course, but also Robert Swan, who, you remember, had impeccable credentials as the first man to walk to both Poles. They, and others, were all men and what they said was without fail extremely negative. I had fondly hoped one such beard would be my patron. "I will eat my hat five times if you make it to the Pole," he bellowed good-humouredly instead. His reluctance was completely understandable. I was of course talking to someone who had spent several years training and travelling in the polar regions. He himself had truly earned his place in the history books.

When I was interviewed by ANI, Steve, the base camp manager from Patriot Hills, who was working for them as a consultant outside the short Antarctic season, was very direct. "The reality is, Catharine, you'll get three days in and then have to be bailed out. The way I see it is that it is one big waste of money." Anne was more supportive, and advised me to wait for Geoff, who was arriving the same afternoon. "I think he will look at ways to make it happen," she encouraged me.

But even Geoff was equivocal. I was embarrassed enough by the idea he would be put in the position of being the one to turn me down. I spoke to him privately the next day. "I am certainly not ruling it out, Cath, but I think your chance of success is very slim. You must think hard how you would cope with failure. You may just want to quit while you're ahead or maybe you'd rather try and fail, than not try at all." So many British heroes had made their names through failure — Scott and Shackleton had, of course — but did I have the courage simply to try?

Then, in November 2000, I gave a talk about our Antarctic expedition at the Royal Geographical Society and met a man who was himself speaking about the Arctic. He was a tree surgeon by day and a sculptor and drummer by night. He spent any spare time he had mountaineering and travelling in the Arctic. He was a ball of positive energy and was himself training for an expedition in May 2001 to become the first British man to cross the Arctic region of Svalbard. He was adamant that I should make the North Pole attempt and convinced that I could succeed.

After our meeting my mind was consumed by his encouragement. And it was also awash with violins, red roses and hearts pierced with Cupid's arrows. I bounced back to Jo that night and announced that I would be walking to the North Pole, after all. She allowed me a few minutes of inane rambling, then calmly commented: "Cath, you can't walk to the North Pole *just* to pull a man. Ask him out for dinner like any other normal person. This isn't 'Bridget Jones Goes to the Arctic' you know." Of course, she was right, but it had given me the positive push I needed.

The very next day ANI called to say that a distinguished French Canadian called Paul Landry would guide the expedition. Anne had discussed my possible participation with him at length and Paul was happy to take me on board. Fiona and Mike had decided to join, too. There would be just four of us this time. However, with three months to go before departure and only milk bottle tops to offer for money, the chance of stumping up £25,000 seemed remote.

Arctic Tree Surgeon continued to encourage me over the following months and I continued to pursue him. Two days before I left for the North Pole we finally "got together". Afterwards, he hung an ivory polar bear around my neck for luck. Two weeks after my departure, he would leave for his own expedition. It was unspeakably romantic.

So I began the task I had sworn never to do again — finding a sponsor. And I was very late starting. It was something that had taken me a year and a half, not three months, to achieve for the South Pole. The first thing I did was hire Tina Price, who had already been my publicist for the South Pole expedition and its aftermath. She was an impressive, feisty woman, who had taken me in hand shortly before my departure to Antarctica and guided me through the whole terrifying experience of dealing with the media and of whom I was now deeply fond. Once she decided to be a part of my project she was infectiously enthusiastic and put everything into doing the right thing for me.

I also decided to work with Sense again. They had been delighted with the coverage they received and I was still raising money for them from giving talks. So Georgia, their press officer, Tina and I put out a press release saying that I was returning to the snowy wastes and taking another furry friend in the form of a tiny polar bear. I named him Oliver, after my brother.

It was the same routine as before. I would sneak off with my mobile during work, telephoning any marketing manager that would speak to me. Because of my South Pole success, I easily aroused interest, but everyone was incredulous I was supposed to be leaving so soon. No one could help.

Georgia set up a press call on a rainy afternoon. I had managed to escape from work, telling my production manager I was going off to look at locations. Nobody ever questioned where I was or what I was doing as long as I actually came up with the locations. I can really recommend it as a job, should one need to pull the wool over anybody's eyes.

Georgia had wangled the use of the bear department in Hamley's. So there I sat in the middle of fifty cuddly polar bears of all shapes and sizes. I smiled and smiled at the ten press photographers, trying to look like the cuddliest bear of all. But actually I was no starlet in a mink coat, I was suffocating in a sea of fake fur fabric. I could not imagine that any paper in its right mind would buy the picture. But I was lucky, London's *Evening Standard* did.

The idea of sending out proposals and letters was a luxury of the past — I had no time. Every second I had I was on the phone, begging for money, spinning a story, selling my soul to gain interest. But the answer was still no. Tina almost succeeded. One lead got as far as the interview, but just before I was about to walk into the office to meet the board, the idea was axed and I was sent home.

As before the South Pole, I needed to be around those who encouraged me and to avoid those who thought me a lunatic. My friends in the climbing club knew more than most about what I was up to, since they were witness to my training. Their sense of adventure made them very supportive of my ambitions. It was a period when I was vulnerable, even undecided, when a few words from my climbing friend Mark and from my old guru Pen were of critical importance. Mark sensed my apprehension one evening, and responded in the same positive spirit as in the conversation where he had spoken of achieving a mountain summit being worth losing a finger. Pen rang me, and when I asked him if I was mad, told me: "Do not back out! I am absolutely convinced you can succeed. Go! I know you will do it." Pen had always been completely supportive about my ambitions, and was the most important single source of encouragement I had. He had a generous spirit and a very genuine desire for women in general and myself in particular to succeed in the polar field.

With just two weeks to go before departure and my deadline for ANI, the *News of the World* came forward and offered to sponsor me. They were one of many who had been intrigued by my picture in the *Standard*. But seven days later they pulled out, when the editor returned from holiday and vetoed the deal. By now I was back to my insomniac habits, waking up at 3 o'clock every morning. I would smoke two cigarettes and drink a glass of brandy to go back to sleep. When the alarm woke me at five o'clock I would have another cigarette before I even got out of bed. I was stressed beyond belief. But by this point I was utterly focused on going.

I had handed in my resignation to the BBC, remortgaged my flat to raise money, let out my own room, and bought all my plane tickets — nothing was going to stop me. I tore around London in a friend's car, trying to barge my way into the marketing directors' offices of any company that seemed to have plush offices. Sometimes I lied to receptionists just to get into the building proper, barged unannounced into what seemed to be the right office, and started talking before I could be asked what I was doing. I obviously looked desperate, as everyone was very kind. I was offered tea and my cheek was sometimes admired, but at this short notice, no one could help.

Six days before my scheduled departure, Liza Helps, my friend from that first selection course, telephoned me. She had already walked to the Magnetic Pole, so had applied to come on our Geographic Pole expedition. The same day that I had talked to Steve from Patriot Hills and to Geoff, they had gently told her in her meeting that she had insufficient experience for the harder challenge. She had been very disappointed, especially as she had been training hard with the help of the army. Now, when I explained my situation, she said without hesitation: "I had a company

230

lined up to sponsor me if I was accepted and they're now hanging on in case I do something else. Call them, they can help you instead. I know your need is the greater." This was the most selfless act of kindness I had ever come across; I was absolutely dumbstruck. I made the call.

It was a day and a half before I was supposed to go. Manugistics was "a software provider for supply chain systems". I had no idea what that meant, but I had contacted its marketing director, Simon, arranged a meeting, attended it and was now sitting in my kitchen, smoking, waiting for the phone to ring with an answer. I had spent the weekend in the Lake District with my climbing friends, who were astonished I had no idea whether I was actually going. I was rather quiet, but I carried on training with a locally sourced truck tyre and by fell-running. I had chosen not to tell ANI, Paul or Mike and Fiona of my predicament; somehow I just had to get this cash. At 6.30p.m. the phone finally rang, Manugistics were going to give me just enough to enable me to go. I would be financially ruined on my return; I would worry about that later.

I now had exactly one day to pack, get all my equipment together and move out of my flat. I was teetering on the edge. By eight-thirty the following morning I was bundled into the car, barely having slept or eaten for three days. I looked a mess. I met up with Mike and Fiona at the airport, and checked in. Before going airside, I gave an interview to *Newsroom South East*. Of course I was asked how I was feeling. Far from being composed and positive, I just said, "I don't think I have ever been so frightened in my entire life."

Since there had been such doubt about whether I would be able to go, I had kept most of my friends in the dark. I had not told many people that I was even thinking about making the journey. The first that they knew was now, when I frantically telephoned as many as I could from the airport and announced that I was on my way to the North Pole. Everyone was shocked.

Anne had been able to reassure my mother, and Paul's reputation made her feel I was in safe hands, but my worst moment in this period was having to tell my grandmother. She was now ninety-two, and although she had enjoyed following my Antarctic trip, she knew the North Pole was much worse.

As I went through to the departure lounge I knew I was really going. A huge weight was immediately lifted from my shoulders; all my efforts had finally paid off. Air Canada kindly let us into the VIP lounge and even more kindly, but dangerously, let us loose on the drinks cabinet. Mike, from concern for my sanity, poured me a quadruple Jack Daniels.

In the plane, warm, comfortable and relieved, I decided to have a glass of wine, then another and another. No sooner had one glass been delivered than I would press the bell and ask for the next. Somewhere over the Atlantic, the cabin staff refused to serve me, but the galley was nearby so I staggered there to help myself. By the time we landed at Ottawa I was completely paralytic. I had to be helped off the plane by Mike and Fiona and a very concerned member of airport staff. It was no more than release from stress, but I could not have chosen a less appropriate time. I guess I was also unconsciously aware that the expedition represented an escape from real life for me.

On arrival at Immigration, I was sick into a bag. Then I was taken to a side room and refused entry into Canada as an undesirable alien. Mike sat with me for over an hour trying to persuade the authorities to let me in. He began by explaining that we were on our way to make a historic journey to the North Pole, and if we succeeded Fiona and I would be walking into the history books as the first British women to achieve such a feat. He explained he was a police sergeant. This caused even more annoyance; the whole story could only be a fantastical fabrication. Finally, after telephone calls, computer checks and endless questions, they believed him. He said that I had been under extreme pressure, had not eaten or slept for three days, had drunk only a single glass of wine on the plane and then, with the cabin pressure, had had a bad reaction. They decided to allow me to stay.

Then they spotted my ski poles. Fool that I was, I had not washed off the mud from the field in Hertfordshire where I had been training — and this was in the middle of Britain's outbreak of foot and mouth disease. Back to the side room and a further hour's wait while they decided what to do. By now, Mike was nearly in tears. Eventually, the authorities weakened and took away my poles to be disinfected.

I was put to bed, and awoke fourteen hours later ashamed, sheepish and grateful. There was nothing I could say. It was an absolutely appalling start to the expedition. At least I knew they would find it funny before long. They could and would dine out on the story for the rest of their lives. But now I was strangely excited for myself. If nothing else I knew the High Arctic would be a fascinating place to visit. I had hoped to come here for years, and had indeed planned that cycling expedition. I wanted to find out more about the Inuit culture and would have loved to have had more time travelling around, exploring the communities as well as just walking to the Pole. I could not lose, I thought; whatever the outcome I would have a wonderful time.

CHAPTER
TWELVE

Into the High Arctic

Our goal was to reach the Pole in sixty days. We would spend the first two weeks travelling six hours a day when the weather was at its coldest and the terrain at its toughest. We would then work up to eight and then even twelve hours a day when the going became easier. We were told that the first two weeks were completely grim and it was during this period that most expeditions bailed out. My old polar guru Pen had written me a note of encouragement as he had for the South Pole. Survive the first ten days, it said, and you will make it. I kept this, and a humorous card from Geoff, in a bag with my corn plasters, and referred to them daily.

Paul Landry, our guide, was married to Matty McNair, who had herself guided the British Women's Polar Relay in 1997. Paul had guided various polar treks since 1985. He was meticulously organized, efficient and completely self-controlled. But he also had a lighter side. He was an ex-hippie who had spent some time in London in the seventies. He loved music and films. He told us that in the past his blunt frankness had offended Brits, since we are so used to being polite and avoiding confrontations. Indeed, it did take me a long time to get used to this new, typically direct French Canadian manner without taking it personally.

And so we began with a week's acclimatization and training at Paul and Matty's home in Iqaluit. The temperatures, though around −25°C, would come to seem tropical compared to what we would encounter on the journey itself. The house was beautiful and full of both polar exploration books and Bob Dylan albums. Their children, Sarah and Eric, were charming. The bottom of their garden backed straight on to the frozen Frobisher Bay, named after the famous explorers who sought unsuccessfully to discover the North-West Passage, the mythical seaway "round the top" between the Atlantic and Pacific. Paul's garden shed was therefore his ski store and sled garage, and the hitching post for his huskies. The family lived there all year. Temperatures rose to around +5°C in summer. The children sledged or sailed according to the season.

Both Paul and Geoff had worked extensively with husky dogs and were very fond of them. "They became your friends," as Geoff used to say. Geoff had kept one dog from his transantarctic expedition. Thule was the only female on the team and made an excellent lead dog, because all the males ran fast to catch her. Unfortunately they succeeded, and she had to be evacuated to have her puppies. Thule lived with Geoff in the Lake District. He loved her and took her to talks and presentations, where she was in turn adored by the children in the audiences. When Geoff took her to meet his mother in the Channel Islands, Thule ran away while on the beach and disappeared. Geoff braced himself, knowing that so hardy a dog would be a loose cannon in so genteel a place. Sure enough, the phone rang. It was the owner of one of the luxury homes on the island, phoning from South America. "I have just been informed your dog has eaten one of my peacocks!!" she bellowed pompously. Geoff managed to replace the peacock, but Thule was sent back to England in disgrace.

Paul was an enthusiastic advocate of Peary's claims to be the first man to the North Pole. Indeed, he spent many evenings on the subject with us. In 2000, he had recreated Peary's journey to show that it had been possible, and had taken care to use the same number of dogs for each sled as Peary had done. Only oceanic drift had prevented him reaching the Pole in the same time as Peary. Paul took forty-seven days, Peary thirty-eight.

The question of animals or no animals remains a vexed one in polar exploration, ever since Amundsen's success over Scott was partly attributed to his use of dogs. Scott, of course, had used ponies at an earlier stage, but had only man-hauled to the Pole. Dogs are now banned from Antarctica as a non-native species intrusive to the environment. Tractors and Skidoos — scooters with skis — have replaced them, to the sadness of many, who think that the dogs had a positive emotional effect quite beyond their capacity to pull loads. In the Arctic, there are not the same delicate political considerations — the Antarctic is an essentially uninhabited continent administered by many countries — and in any case, there have always been dogs.

We practised pulling the sledges on this new terrain, thoroughly testing our equipment, and went through the routine of putting up and taking down our tents several times a day. It was absolutely essential that our drills became second nature because at −45°C it would be much too cold to have any delays. Following Geoff's advice in England I had upgraded all my own equipment to be appropriate for the colder conditions. It was dark for much of each day, but the sunrises and sunsets, just a few hours apart, were beautiful.

Each time the sun rose, it would sit only just above the horizon and give off an extraordinary array of reds, oranges and pinks. The colours would then reflect on to the white snow, turning it a deep shade of pink. Moreover, you could not hear a thing. It was so quiet that the noise of the blood rushing in my head was deafening. It was utterly hypnotic and soothing. On several occasions I had to be woken from a meditative state where I was not aware that time had passed.

To my relief I discovered that my hard training had paid off. The tyre-pulling had given me muscles I never thought I had. Several days in a row, we weighed down our sleds with huge blocks of husky food and set off round the extensive wilderness of Paul's back garden. We needed to adjust ourselves to this very new form of polar terrain — to the pressure ridges — and simply to the idea we were not travelling on land, but over the sea, the top of which had frozen in the cold winter.

When we came back in May, Paul assured us, much of what we were now standing on would be water.

The pressure ridges in Frobisher Bay were already a good introduction to what we would be experiencing on the Arctic Ocean. I had bought a new pair of skis for this trip and I knew their strength would be tested to the limit. While sometimes we would be hauling our sleds over these pressure ridges on foot, at others it seemed more straightforward just to keep our skis on, using artificial skins attached beneath them to give friction. At this stage they seemed very resilient, but we had to avoid the danger of putting too much pressure on them and snapping them in two.

So for one week we practised and practised. We were all going to share a single tent, and we would ski for an hour, set the tent up with everything inside, boil up snow for tea and get into our sleeping bags. Then we would pretend we had just had eight hours' sleep, pack everything up, put on our skis and set off again for another hour. We would repeat this exercise three or four times during the day until it all became second nature. It was all very straightforward carrying out these tasks at −25°C, but at −45°C we knew they would prove very difficult. We would have to work extremely quickly not to let our bodies cool down and until the weather became warmer we would not be able to take our gloves off at all.

Initially, the three of us were relieved at the ease with which we had transferred from the Antarctic to the Arctic, but were extremely worried how we would deal with the cold. The lowest ambient temperature we had experienced on our way to the South Pole was −30°C, and although wind-chill occasionally might make it feel as cold as −45°C, we were used to the minus thirties. Besides, there was no wind inside the tents; no wind-chill meant that it was always warmer there. On our journey to the North Pole there would be less wind but the temperature at the beginning would always be in the range −45°C to −50°C and it would be no warmer in the tent at night. We knew that sitting still in these temperatures would be intolerable.

We spent some time in the one and only coffee bar in Iqaluit. When Paul first spoke to us, he had been very open about being nervous about meeting the three of us. He knew that our common Antarctic experience had given us a very strong bond, he could not know where I fitted in as a single person linked with a couple or how he would fit in at all. But coffee seemed to be an addiction for all of us. The coffee bar was the place where we could find our ease with Paul and make him feel comfortable that we were not a nasty cliquey Antarctic gang. He knew that this form of team-building was at least as important as the physical training.

It was Paul's encouraging attitude to me that struck me most. I had spoken to him two weeks before departing. I spoke completely honestly of my terror and doubts about making the journey, and I had berated myself for taking on such a ridiculous challenge. But now he told me not to doubt myself. He had spoken at length with Geoff, who had continued to express some concerns about my physical ability, but none about my fortitude. Paul agreed with Geoff that 70 per cent of success in an expedition of this kind came from sheer mental determination. With this mindset, and because I had already survived sixty-one days on the ice in Antarctica, Paul believed my chances were as good as anyone's. I was delighted.

There are two traditional and quite obvious walking routes to the North Pole, one from the northern tip of Russia and the other from Ward Hunt Island, the equivalent in Canada. As soon as one sets foot on the Arctic Ocean, the journey begins. Our base camp would be in Resolute Bay, and Paul phoned Aziz, the man who would be our base camp manager there, to hear who else would be attempting the Pole that year. There would be Dave Mill, making his second solo and unsupported attempt, and Swee Chiow, our Singaporean friend from the South Pole, not with Steve, who had not succeeded in raising funds, but with Armin Wirth, a German who had done considerable professional guiding in Greenland. The two of them had only first met at Ottawa airport and were now in Resolute organizing the logistics. Swee had been very active. Since his return from the South Pole, he had climbed the last two on his list of the "seven summits" (the highest points of each continent), so the North Pole was in the way of a final challenge.

From the Russian side, a Belgian woman, Bettina Aller, was setting off solo and Pen himself was guiding a client, called Ben, unsupported. The Norwegian, Borge Ousland, had already skied to the Pole in a previous year and was now crossing the entire Arctic

Ocean via the Pole, all the way from Russia to Canada solo and unsupported. This last was a truly awesome challenge, quite beyond my comprehension. In addition there was a Japanese man, Hyoichi Kohno, who was walking from the North Pole back to Japan over a period of six years.

In the polar world it is imperative that the expeditions are billed correctly. There is an enormous difference in achievement between whether an expedition is supported — that is, whether supplies can be flown in during the journey — or unsupported, so the poor expeditioner has to pull everything he needs from start to finish. It is even more important whether the trip is guided; whether it is in effect led by someone with professional experience who is responsible for the navigation and for making the decisions. As for "solo", that is self-explanatory, but it is clear that "solo and unsupported" represents the very hardest category.

When we returned from our South Pole expedition we discovered that many of the newspaper reports failed to print that there were, in fact, other people on the trip and that the expedition was guided. Many implied that Mike, Fiona and myself had been alone. To the lay public, these might seem trivial issues, but within the polar travellers' community, of which we were now a part whether we liked it or not, these mistakes had been extremely embarrassing for us and understandably upset some people.

Two days before we were due to leave, we took publicity shots in the back garden. This felt quite fraudulent. We had to act as if we had already arrived at the Pole, holding the Union Jack high above our heads. The photos were then sent to our publicist, Tina, who would store them for the actual moment of arrival. It made me feel extremely uncomfortable, forcing a look of triumph on to my face when I was so scared and before I had even taken one step on to the Arctic Ocean. I always hate tempting Fate. In view of our previous publicity confusions, I was adamant that Paul should be in every single shot, so there would be no doubt that the trip was guided.

After eight days, by which time it felt as if we had tested our equipment a million times, we left for Resolute, where we would stay for just one night before taking a Twin Otter to Ward Hunt Island. We packed our sleds and drove everything down to freight at Iqaluit airport.

Before we boarded our flight the four of us had a final cappuccino in the coffee bar. I turned down the offer of whisky. I had been completely dry and nicotine-free since my cataclysmic arrival in Canada, and felt much better for it. Paul initiated a very sobering conversation about our wishes should a member of our family die, as to whether we would want to stay on the ice or be flown out. I had simply not considered this, and did not want to. I felt I would not be able to answer this until it actually arose.

Our own lives were not to be risked at any point, the same position as with the South Pole trip. A guide not only navigates and organizes his clients but also has a duty of care to them. He certainly cannot kill them off. So Geoff and Victor had been, and Paul now was responsible not just for making decisions, but for keeping us safe.

We set off for Resolute Bay on 10 March 2001. Resolute is a tiny community, but an important jumping-off point for expeditions to the High Arctic. All expeditions to the Geographic and Magnetic Poles from Canada are based here; it is the second northernmost settlement in Canada but has much better facilities than its more northerly neighbour, Grise Fjord. After the Second World War, a weather station and an airstrip were established here. In 1953 the first Inuit families were relocated here from northern Quebec by the Federal Department of Northern Affairs and National Resources, and more came in 1955.

For many years the government suggested that this had been done purely in the best interests of the Quebec Inuit, who had experienced immense hardship in their homeland. They were told that the High Arctic offered better hunting conditions. But this was not the case and many of the Inuit actually starved. So there continues to be resentment and controversy. The Inuit have claimed that the government instigated the move for reasons of sovereignty, as no civilians had previously lived in the Canadian High Arctic. As it became clear that the Inuit experienced more hardships in the High Arctic than they had ever done in Quebec, many of them returned home.

Since the 1950s, Resolute Bay has also been a centre for scientific research and then became the operations base for the Polar Continental Shelf Project, a multidisciplinary programme of Arctic research. In the 1960s, a school opened and a major housing programme began. So Resolute now has a population of around 200, of whom two-thirds are Inuit.

The Inuit lived by hunting seals and selling the proceeds. But, largely because of animal rights activity, the world market for all sealskin products collapsed, especially after the EEC ban on seal imports in 1983. Since then, Inuit hunters everywhere have been hard pressed to make seal-hunting pay and employment in many Inuit communities is, therefore, at an all-time low.

I sat on the plane reading my in-flight magazine. Instead of the usual features on conference facilities and glitzy shopping centres, or advertisements for hi-fi and jewels, there were articles about the ban on the seal trade, husky sledding and research projects in community health and caribou habitats. I thought back to my similar flight from Punta Arenas to Patriot Hills. I felt very different. I had worked hard this time and I felt much more as if I deserved my place. I was no longer embarrassed or apologetic. And finally, after surviving my appalling drunken arrival, I no longer felt I was a burden to the others.

Resolute was a remarkable place. At this time of year it was quite bleak, completely white, but made grey by the storm. Downtown consisted of a collection of small modern buildings, many with polar bear skins hanging outside on lines, instead of washing, which would, of course, have frozen instantly. There was a school, a church, a health centre and a co-op which sold everything from hardcore Arctic clothing and survival equipment down to pretty hair clips with glitter on them.

The town was simple. Inuit women wandered around with their babies sitting in their coat hoods, and boys tore about on motorized Skidoos. It had a part-time, transitory feel about it, almost as if the occupants would soon be leaving to return to normal Western lives. But for the majority, it was their permanent home and with the shameful curiosity only a cosseted Westerner could have I wondered how tough their day-to-day lives must be, especially in the harsh winter when they would not see natural light for two months. The whole winter would be spent looking forward to spring when they could embark on their traditional lifestyle, travelling over the ice hunting seal and polar bear, and to summer when they could travel by boat to hunt further afield.

Resolute fascinated me in the same way that the small villages in Borneo had done. I had spent a long time in them and I instantly wished I could spend a long time here. I realized that this aspect of the trip almost interested me more than making the journey to the North Pole, and vowed then to return to the High Arctic one day. Aziz took us to his hotel in "downtown" Resolute. Downstairs, the main room was, as one would imagine, full of radio and navigational equipment. Strewn around the floor were boxes of food and camera equipment. There were two large sleds. These belonged to Swee and Armin, who were making

246

final preparations before setting off the next day for Ward Hunt Island with us.

The main room also had a pool table, a computer with games and the Internet and a large cinema screen supplying cable television. Aziz had made a haven for the local Inuit children to come any time to escape the harsh Arctic existence. Upstairs, the hotel bedrooms were a surprise, all were ensuite and some even had Jacuzzis. The decor was very pretty, too, more that of an English country hotel than the expected rough-and-ready style one might have imagined of an Arctic town serving hunters and explorers.

We had not felt the cold so far, as we had been rushed from the airport in a heated jeep into an equally tropically heated hotel. But when the jeep arrived with our equipment, we had to go outside to unload. It was dark, as we were barely out of winter, and the wind was ferocious. I eased open the door cautiously, but the cold still affected me as if I had been physically struck. That all too familiar searing polar pain started to rush into my hands and quickly numbed them. We had to move fast, first to keep warm and second to get the job finished so we could get back inside. By this time the next day, we would have no such escape for two months. Oddly enough I felt more reassured than dismayed. It was at least no worse than I had feared.

We spent the next couple of hours checking and rechecking our food and equipment before putting it back on the jeep to be weighed for the Twin Otter flight. Swee and Armin were doing the same. Swee looked tense. We had not set eyes on him since we waved him goodbye in Chile as we all stepped off the return Hercules from the South Pole. "Wow! It is good to see your happy faces!" he said. We started to eye up one another's sleds, and then unashamedly felt the weight as if competing for fairground prizes. Their sleds were shaped like canoes, because they hoped to use them as boats to row across any stretches of open water. We noticed they were much heavier than ours. All this was cause for great banter and discussion.

Most of all, we also noticed the dramatic difference in the amount of fuel our two teams were taking. Paul decided we would travel to the Pole with a very different approach to the adventurers before us. He wanted us to travel "in style", and was keen to abandon the traditional, male ideal of travelling with maximum hardship and with just enough fuel to keep alive. Instead he wanted to take almost more fuel than we could ever use.

You will remember that weight is thought to be of paramount importance when embarking on a journey of this sort. If you recall, Geoff had me sawing off the handle of my toothbrush in the Antarctic. But Paul was insistent that the first twenty days of the trip would be extremely cold and very tough. First, he wanted us to be able to dry our clothes at the end of the day. We would not be able to avoid sweating and the sweat would immediately freeze into sheets of ice. It was critical that we put on dry clothes in the morning. Not to do so would not only be insufferably miserable but could cause frostbite and hypothermia. More importantly, we could look forward to sitting in a warm tent at night. An essential reward at the end of each day. To sit shivering at −45°C for four hours before then trying to sleep for a further eight would have been unbearable.

So, to last us the eighteen days till our first resupply, we would take fifty-six litres of fuel. Swee and Armin were taking just twelve. "What the hell are you going to do with it all?" asked Armin, astonished. "Burn it," replied Paul without a trace of irony. We calculated on using three litres a day, where most expeditions burnt just a half. "Right now they think I'm an idiot," he told us later. "Two days into the journey they'll be asking us for fuel, mark my words." We named our expedition "North Pole in Style". I thought we certainly deserved to be a grade up from "Plebs to the Pole".

We all went to bed early. I had a long, hot bath in my luxury suite and then sat at my desk to make last phone calls. It seemed utterly absurd that I was leaving this beautiful warm cocoon to go on a long, miserable journey — again. I must be out of my tiny mind, I thought. Absolutely barking. What the hell was wrong with me? Why in God's name was I putting myself through this misery again? I must be a masochist. I vowed to have therapy on my return. I called my mother, Tina and then finally Geoff. "Hi Geoff, just to say I am leaving for the North Pole tomorrow morning, and I wanted to say goodbye." I forced myself to make my tone light, as if I were just off to a Butlins holiday camp for a relaxing week. To my astonishment, he was almost emotional in his farewell. I speculated he must just be scared to death on my behalf.

On Sunday, 11 March, we all got up at 5a.m. and had breakfast in silence. I chose sultana bread and fried eggs, Mike ate an entire carton of cream. An hour later we were told the weather was good — we were going. There would not even be any delays. Oh my God, we are really doing this, I thought. Now we filled our water bottles with hot liquid and put chocolate and salami into pockets we had sewn on to our thermal underwear next to our chests. In the Antarctic, we kept food in bum bags, but here, it would be too cold, the food would freeze. The next time we eat, I thought, will be when we are walking to the North Pole. Before leaving the hotel I picked up a glossy magazine with an article about Tom Cruise and Nicole Kidman. It would provide much-needed mental escape during the flight. Nobody said a word on the journey to the airport.

It was dark and freezing when we boarded the Twin Otter for the six hour flight to Ward Hunt Island. I spent the first, dark part of the journey with my nose in the magazine, forcing myself to concentrate on Tom and Nicole's pending divorce. It was the only way I could keep calm. After two and a half hours we stopped off at a small scientific outpost called Eureka to refuel. A handful of scientists came out to meet us, desperate for a chat. When they found out what we were up to, one said, "Gee, you guys are just absolutely crazy, you know that?" I would have preferred not to have been reminded. The temperature was already noticeably colder than at Resolute. I could not imagine how it could become any colder.

When we finally touched down on Ward Hunt Island, the northernmost tip of land in Canada, we were at latitude 83°06′ South and 74°12′ West. We had 414 nautical miles to walk to the North Pole and were hoping to make the journey in around sixty days with two resupplies — airdrops of food. Mr "Five Hats" had done his journey in fifty-six days with five resupplies. I would have loved more resupplies myself, since this would obviously mean carrying less between each, but the price of chartering the Twin Otter was too steep. We had already cut costs by sharing the plane to Ward Hunt Island with Swee and Armin, and if we continued at a similar pace it might be possible to be resupplied together as well.

Here we saw Ranulph Fiennes's hut still standing. Ran is, of course, one of only a handful of household names in British polar exploration. I still prize the letter of encouragement he sent me at an early stage. The previous year, he had tried what was the very hardest challenge — solo and unsupported to the North Pole. It is a feat just two men, the very same Borge Ousland and Hyoichi Kohno, have achieved. But just a few days into his expedition, Ran's sled fell through the ice. In trying to retrieve it, he immediately contracted frostbite on all the fingers of one hand. He just succeeded in retracing his steps to the safety of his hut, and rescue.

My biggest concern was how I was going to cope in such extreme temperatures. We prepared to leave the plane, but I was very loath actually to make the move, and faffed around, shuffling my bags about in an aimless manner. Paul gently eased the magazine from

251

my terrified grip and said delicately, "You won't be needing Tom and Nicole out here, Catharine." We had barely packed any reading material for this first section of the journey. It would simply be too dark and too cold to read.

CHAPTER
THIRTEEN

In Which We Are Very Cold

The pilot was quite unable to let go of my hand as we shook hands on parting and he wished me luck. I will never forget the look of extreme concern he gave me. As we walked out of the plane the thermometer read −48°C. For two minutes it was actually bearable — just because we did not have the winds of Antarctica. "My God, this is OK, I'm coping!" I shouted to the emptiness around me. But then my body started to shut down and that too familiar pain began to seep into my hands and feet. It took no more than thirty seconds to become agonizing.

There was only one way to deal with this. It was not to panic, but to throw my body into violent action, flinging my arms round like a windmill, literally throwing blood back into my extremities while running around as if sprint training. I was compensating for my body's reluctance to send blood out of its core. We waited until the plane took off. Then, with as much speed as we could muster, without speaking and desperately trying to keep calm in the cold, we attached the sleds to our harnesses and set off, Paul in the lead, I instantly and automatically taking my place at the back. Swee and Armin skied beside us. I wondered how long we would stay together and at what point we would go our separate ways. I predicted that before long they would leave us far behind.

After ten minutes of fast skiing my body started to warm up and the pain in my hands subsided to a dull ache. I looked around me. My God, I thought, how absolutely beautiful. The sun was just peeping up in a semicircle over the horizon. It was deep orange and threw a glowing pink light on the white ice around us. I am walking to the North Pole, I thought, I am really doing it, I am really walking to the North Pole. I was incredulous.

After an hour and a half we had completed two and a half miles. We decided to make camp. It became apparent very quickly that we could not stand still for even five minutes. Slowing down to the pace needed to put up the tent made us too cold. So in between working, we ran at great pace on the spot or jogged for a few minutes in the deep snow, just to warm up again. We were then able to carry on for another five minutes before repeating the cycle. I was extremely thankful that we had rehearsed the camping drill so many times in Iqaluit. It was way, way too cold to have to think out how to do things, one just had to do them.

The tent went up, Paul clambered inside and fitted a pole in the middle. We then put in six pegs and I started digging furiously, putting snow on the valance around the tent as a means of securing it if there was a storm.

Mike secured the guy ropes and Fiona unloaded our sleds and set up inside the tent. I kept digging and then cut out big blocks of snow, which we would then use to melt into water. Now Paul put up his own one-man tent. He had decided the tent was too small for four and I think he also valued the privacy.

What happened now became our routine. Once we were all in the tent we would light the stove. Because it was so cold, the gas in the lighter would not ignite until the lighter itself had been warmed in the hand or next to our chests. We then leaked a little gas into the stove bowl, but this, too, would not light until it was itself warmed with the lighter. All this would take five minutes, during which we waited impatiently, desperate to see the flame, getting steadily colder. After one stove was on, we lit two more. Slowly we started to warm up. The tent had no floor, which had alarmed all of us back in Iqaluit, but Paul knew a floor would provide no insulation from the cold. Instead, we sat on our rolled up sleeping gear, while drying our clothes and eating dinner. In the first days, we would also light a halogen lamp, but we knew that the days were lengthening so fast it would soon be light at all times.

Paul loved to cook, and would rarely let any of us share the task. The food was dehydrated, but surprisingly tasty. The GPS and satellite phone — Mike and Fiona had the same sponsors — would be sealed in bags and hung up to prevent condensation. After an hour, we would telephone Mike's mother, who was keeping a record of our position for the expedition website, and, once a week, we would also speak to Aziz and to Matty, Paul's wife.

The subject of going to the loo quickly came up. It was quite clear that we could not possibly go outside. Paul looked faintly amused that we were even discussing the subject. "Just go there, where you are sitting," he said. "What, without using a bottle?" I asked indignantly. "I'm British, damn it, I have my dignity to think of." His withering look told me I would have no chance of instigating any system to give me privacy, let alone the hat ritual I had had with Steve and Geoff. His no-nonsense attitude to life did not allow for this sort of English reserve or modesty. Paul was always efficient to the point of military precision. On the two occasions on our journey he briefly took weight from my sled to speed me up, he made no concessions to my pride; what was best for the expedition was everything to him.

Mike had bought David Hempleman-Adams's account of his expedition to the North Pole. Like us, he and his Norwegian companion, Rune Gjeldnes, had made a supported journey with two resupplies. Each day, he had made a diary entry and, in the evening, one of us would read it aloud. They seemed to have had a miserable time. We were all quietly incredulous that we were enjoying ourselves. Surely we were not supposed to? But none of us dared speak our thoughts in case we tempted Fate. After a while, we discovered we were making better progress than they were, and despite my long-held scorn for competitive sport, I was ashamed to find myself delighted.

So, during each evening, we would bet on how many miles we had covered that day, write our diary entries — very short ones because it was so cold — talk and have our reading from the Hempleman-Adams book. It was all extremely civilized, a genteel dinner party whose only *faux pas* was that during the course of the evening we all urinated on the carpet and then slept on top of the results. At bedtime I would get out my toothpaste and wetwipes and thaw them by the stove out of their solid condition. We would then boil up a final pan of water and pour it into our water bottles, taking these to bed to help keep us warm. The extra fuel was instantly making all the difference.

Getting into bed was a time-consuming affair, rolling out bedding and trying to fit the three of us together. Once we were finally cocooned into our rolls of insulation, Paul would turn the stoves off, and dive outside to his own one-man tent. I never ceased to think it extraordinary he had the resolve and strength of mind to make that last trip outside each night and back in the morning.

The first night was grim indeed. This was to become my routine. To sleep I wore five layers of clothing, a hat, a face mask, gloves and socks. I then got into an inner bag lining, something that was a vapour barrier and prevented any body moisture getting into my goose down sleeping bag. When already in the sleeping bag, I would climb into a further, outer bag providing a final layer of warmth.

Now the stoves were off, the heat in the tent dissipated all too quickly, and not all my layers, goose

257

down and thermals could keep the cold at bay. The exertion of getting into bed kept me initially warm and allowed me to sleep for an hour but then I would wake up freezing and have to run in my sleeping bag for a minute or so to warm up. This allowed me another hour's sleep until I woke up again to repeat the process. Imagine, every hour, every night, for those first days.

That first night, I had to take a pee at three in the morning. I opened my eyes and found I could barely move my head. I had a collar of ice around my neck like an Elizabethan ruff, where my breath had frozen around me. Forcing myself out of my freezing cocoon into an even more freezing "room" was more than shocking. I still struggle to find words to describe the excruciating feeling of cold at that moment, the sense in which its grip made me almost physically and mentally paralysed within seconds. It took me ten minutes to wrench my way out of the bag and find a small patch of snow. Unfortunately, the only one available was immediately next to Mike's head and the noise woke him up. I was mortified. It then took me another ten minutes to work my way back into my bag and another ten of running in the bag to warm myself back up. By six, after eight hours' attempted sleep, we were all awake and so cold we could not wait to get up, get our harnesses on and start walking again.

At seven Paul came in and lit the stoves. How on earth had he managed to move between his tent and ours in such cold? The stoves went on and we began to relax for the first time in eight hours, as we felt our bodies start to thaw. Even before I had ever camped, I knew that to climb into a warm sleeping bag at the end of a day would always be a wonderful experience. That was true everywhere except here. Here, it was to be the most difficult part of the day. What struck me as odd was that my sleeping bag was wet, as were my clothes. I could not understand, first, how on earth I could have sweated when I had been so cold and, second, how the moisture had got through my vapour barrier liner. Mike had had problems with this on our training trip and in the end he went up to the local police station in Iqaluit and borrowed a body bag. It was really sinister to see him zip himself up over his head. I felt very disconcerted, but to my relief this did not work either.

We were all terrified of sweat getting through past the vapour barrier and into the sleeping bag itself. Our bags were filled with down, which ceases to have any warmth if wet and would be impossible to dry out. In our case, we had the additional problem that as soon as they left our tent, any moisture in the bags would freeze into blocks of ice, and add extra weight. This could cost the expedition.

Part of the morning was spent eating and part drying our clothes. Again, the extra fuel allowed us to be warm, so we could actually speak, and to thaw our clothes. My outer coat, however, was completely frozen. It had formed into a solid sculpture with the arms sticking out oddly. It would be impossible to dry and I had to force my way into it as if it were a suit of frozen armour. I could not imagine what it would have been like to put on frozen gloves as well. We then chopped up our chocolate into bite-size pieces, put them in a bag and then put the bag into our chest pockets. We had less dried fruit than for the South Pole — mostly raisins, in fact — but we also had pitta bread and salami. I had never seen such fatty salami in my life, but in this cold it looked delicious. Very quickly, my body craved two things, chocolate and fat.

Emerging from the tent that first time was alarming and a shock for our bodies. The minute the stove was off my hands and feet went into immediate pain. We all had to run for a couple of minutes to warm up. It was actually frightening, and the atmosphere was tense. No one spoke, we concentrated on dealing with the cold. I later realized that coping with this kind of temperature was a real psychological exercise. The most important thing was not to panic, but to keep calm and carry on thinking logically.

I looked around. We were all cold but were all fighting it quietly and by ourselves. We had come a long way from our days in Antarctica. To panic, cry for help, break down or do nothing would be unacceptable and dangerous. In the midst of packing up and keeping warm I had to find a minute to go to the loo. I dug a hole and pulled my trousers down. I was frightened about exposing my raw skin at that temperature. At home, my friend Charlie had warned me with a straight face that faeces freeze as they come out at −45°C, and many polar explorers had died this way. It was a ridiculous fabrication, but seemed all too plausible as I sat feeling extremely vulnerable and trying not to panic. I had put my packet of wetwipes into my chest pocket, which I managed to pull out with my teeth, for I could not remove my mitts. By the time I had removed a wipe, it had frozen solid and become useless. Paul had recommended we use snow instead of loo paper, but I found the idea too horrifying.

As soon as we set off, we were plunged into piles and piles of ice rubble. Paul nicknamed it "cauliflower". On that second day there were no flat pans at all, and several days passed before we could put our skis on. We worked alone, or in pairs or as a single team, helping one another pull the sleds over the rubble. Often the sleds would become wedged between blocks, but it was always important to guide them gently, so that they did not come crashing down the far side of each slope, and cause damage or even injury to the person in front. Once I let my sled go, and it came crashing down behind me into the back of my shins, knocking me off my feet. It was no easier to try to weave one's way through the blocks because soft, thick snow was piled in between, a very poor surface over which to pull the sleds.

By the end of six hours I was absolutely exhausted, yet we had only covered three and a half miles. We managed to stop just twice for a break. It was barely possible to stand still for long enough to eat our chocolate. Tired or not, it was preferable to keep going while eating, than to stop and become cold. The next day I tried to take a photograph. I had a small point-and-press given to me by Olympus, worn round my neck next to my skin. I was able to take it out just long enough to take one shot, before the battery went dead from the cold.

While surrounded by this giant ice rockery, we could not clearly see our way, so we would climb up on to tall pieces of ice and use them as lookout points. On a clear day we could see for miles, and the sight was often uniformly depressing. It was hard to tell how long the rubble would last, a few hours or more likely several days. So I quickly understood what Geoff and the others had been telling me about the hardships of this journey. It would be a combination of the soul-destroying cold and the immense physical demands required. And yet, I considered, after three days in Antarctica, I was in despair, whereas here, the beauty of the journey was outweighing the effort and I was almost enjoying myself.

I was also proud to say that I had taken on the role of the "outside man" when we made camp, digging out the snow for twenty minutes and placing it on the valance. It is not something I could possibly have done in Antarctica, where I skulked inside unpacking while others did the heavy work. I often wished Geoff could have been there to see me, though I suspected he would not have been able to believe his eyes.

My final task before going inside was to cut out blocks of snow to melt for water. In doing this it was important to choose unsalted rather than salty snow — snow that had fallen from the sky, or which had collected on very old pressure ridges, so the salt had leached out, not that which had frozen out of the sea. Hard, compacted snow was also much more efficient than fluffy snow full of air bubbles. Initially, all this had to be explained to me, but as time passed, I became extremely fastidious about the quality of "my" snow and determined not to ruin the quality of the food with too much salt.

We needed the same quality of ice for cooking and for camping itself. The old, good ice tended to have snow drifted on it, whereas new ice was darker and more colourful, the blocks had sharp edges rather than being smoothed over time. The older the ice, the thicker and stronger it was. During the summer, the ice cracks into huge pieces, sometimes several miles across, that do not have time to melt before winter comes. These become stronger and, therefore, more stable as the years pass. This, the so-called "multi-year" ice, was the ideal, stable platform for pitching a tent.

What struck me about the Arctic was its staggering beauty. Again, in all the polar accounts I had read about this journey, I had only heard about hardship and misery; there seemed little reference to how stunning this place was. Rather than the vast flat expanses of white in Antarctica, the Arctic was an explosion of blue ice. The pressure ridges themselves were impressive sculptures, on which the light played. I could continually see an infinity of deep shades of blue, turquoise, green and aquamarine. In the sun the ice sparkled.

It was often the ground that was the most striking — white hard snow that looked as if it had been sprinkled with diamonds and jewels, because of the reflection of the light. It was even colder than the Antarctic, so the snowflakes literally froze on the ground in beautiful lace shapes — the classic snowflakes we have all drawn at school. It was extraordinary to see them in real life, perfectly preserved all around me. And even better, the harsh driving winds of Antarctica were absent. This made an enormous difference to our comfort; even in a city it is wind-chill that is the prime source of cold.

I think, too, that I enjoyed the variety in our travel. The monotony of putting one ski in front of the other for eight hours of identical landscape had been tough for me not only mentally but also physically. It had been a relentless physical strain. A similar comparison, I suppose, would be the monotony of walking up a hill day in day out, compared to a technical climb on a rock face or mountain. The first would be easy, but require sheer endurance just to keep going hour after hour. The second would be much harder, but the technicalities would provide respite, both physically and mentally.

An ocean has life, mood and, above all, movement. And so there were not only ridges where the ice was forced together, but also open channels where the ice cracked and split apart. These were called leads. Leads could open and close with dramatic speed, could be of any width, and up to hundreds of miles in length, and like the ridges, they usually ran from east to west. When Geoff was training the Women's Polar Relay he had seen one on the satellite photograph stretching all the way to Greenland.

There are plenty of tales describing how parties have been separated crossing leads, or of travellers falling in. The ocean beneath is three miles deep, the water is freezing, the heavy polar clothing a terrible handicap. Many Inuit had died in this way, usually travelling alone, and either unable to pull themselves out, or trapped beneath the ice. It was a horror for all of us that we might fall through the thin layer of safety and be swallowed up into the dark ocean. None of us wanted to die out here. Mike talked about this openly. We knew that the behaviour of these leads was unpredictable, and there was always a danger one would form under our tent while we were sleeping.

For the first month or so, it was so cold that as soon as a lead opened, it froze again. Usually, salt water ice is tough, even if it has a little give in it as one walks across, but it can also break without warning. So all leads and thin ice must be tested with extreme care. The earlier an expedition to the North Pole on skis sets off, the safer. Once the ice begins to melt and break up in the warmer weather, more and more open water and leads appear, and travelling becomes impossible, or painfully slow, without a boat. Conversely, by starting early, as we had done, we had to face much worse cold and suffer many more hours of darkness.

We were very tentative at the first lead, just as Paul, with his experience, was confident, especially after he had prodded the ice. Then we had a pleasant surprise. A frozen lead was a natural ice rink, over which the sled could skate smoothly and with little effort from us. Whenever we could find a frozen lead running in the right direction, we gained many miles. Some leads were not entirely frozen; their surface might have the texture of rubber, which bounced back up under our feet, or of wet cardboard, always threatening to disintegrate. I gained a perverse excitement when we were forced to cross these kinds, a sort of Arctic Russian roulette.

The leads could be incredibly beautiful. Often a thick carpet of hoar frost covered the ice, resembling from a distance an infinite spread of white lace sprinkled with sequins and pearls. When inspected more closely, the lace compositions were revealed as the most stunningly intricate flower shapes with spiky, delicately fashioned petals. They stood about two inches off the ground; they were absolutely exquisite. It seemed sacrilege mowing them down and crushing them back into the ice with our skis. I felt as I would stamping on a field of snowdrops and trampling them with muddy boots.

Over and over again, I realized how right Paul was to bring all the fuel. Every evening, we had respite from the cold. And this was borne out by Swee and Armin's story. On the very first night, they used up a whole litre of fuel, and sadly realized they did not have enough. At their request, Paul gave them a litre and a half of ours the next morning, but, thereafter, he was keen to keep his distance from them when they appeared. When, one day, I wanted to invite them in for tea, he refused. I understood this. Paul was there to look after us, and it would have been wrong of him to take on the responsibility for others, especially as they now clearly had insufficient fuel.

By the fourth day, Swee was struggling with the cold, and I could see in his blank stares when I spoke to him the same despair that I remembered in myself in Antarctica. More and more, they camped next to us at night and we travelled together in the day. I was shocked to find that although Armin was usually second in line, Swee was generally behind even me. As we regularly worked in pairs to move the sleds over ridges, I was often in Swee's company, but I found the situation difficult. His sled was enormous, and, therefore, so heavy I was always afraid I would injure my back manhandling it, while I felt awkward asking him for help with mine when he was having so difficult a time himself. Lifting and pushing could cause back problems, and it was all too easy to trip up on one of the many ridges.

One evening, after a week, stoves on and tea in hand, Paul told us that Swee was having difficulties. We knew by now that they would run out of fuel by the theoretical day of the resupply, and we also imagined they must be having extremely unpleasant, because cold, evenings in their tent. They had barely enough fuel to cook, so were quite unable to dry their clothes. Their sweat was not escaping fast enough through their Gore-Tex jackets, and was instead freezing into a thick coat of icy armour round their bodies. All their clothes were frozen blocks of ice each morning.

Swee acknowledged, too, that they had bought far too much equipment and he was struggling with the weight. He tried to think of ways out, asking if some of Paul's dogs could be flown out on the first resupply, and making a joint expedition. Paul was forced to explain that dogs were useless without trained handlers, and that he could not possibly abdicate his original responsibility for us. We were fond of Swee and we

267

admired him; we had responded to his warmth and magnetism in Antarctica, where he had been a charismatic leader.

In the event, Swee and Armin lasted only eleven days. We were astonished. They were only a week away from the resupply, when they could have had virtually unlimited fuel brought in. Mike tried unsuccessfully to talk him round, making the effort to visit their tent after dinner, but Swee had had enough of suffering and resolved to return the following year, with dogs, and perhaps with Paul himself. He wanted to be able to enjoy the journey, to film and appreciate the beauty of the Arctic. When Mike returned to us, he confided he had to agree. Their tent was so cold there was no chance of drying clothes, which were hung up but just stayed frozen. Swee and Armin were despondently huddled in their bags in many layers and face masks. As Mike peeled off his layers and joined the warmth and high spirits in our tent, he felt the contrast could not have been greater.

Armin seemed extremely tough and seemed to be thriving on the hardships; we doubted that he wanted to leave too. We suspected he would ask to join us, and Paul asked us to prepare our response. Sure enough, Armin did ask. He hoped to return to Resolute, to reorganize the supplies, and return on the resupply plane. We had decided we would be happy to take him, but we also had to make clear that since ANI had organized the expedition, it was Anne Kershaw's decision, and Armin would have to contribute to the overall costs. All this left him disconsolate, and though we promised to speak when he was in Resolute, we knew lack of money would prevent him returning.

A few hours after we had left our friends behind, waiting in their tent to be evacuated, we heard the engines of the Twin Otter. To our surprise, the plane came looking for us, and 300 feet or so ahead, with the plane's belly almost stroking the ice, a package came hurtling out. What had they left us? It was a can of fuel wrapped in a piece of foam mattress. Even with all they suffered, they had taken the trouble to repay our fuel. Swee kept his word to himself, too. The next year, he returned, indeed with Paul, and they completed the journey in record time.

The next day, the twelfth, we were at 84°10′ and we felt terribly isolated. We missed our two companions, we felt deflated by their departure; we were now the four northernmost people in the entire world. Pen Hadow and Ben were still trying to begin their journey from the Russian side, but we knew were delayed by a massive open lead. We had no news of anyone else; it actually made us feel rather frightened and lonely.

It was, however, exactly the day when there was a fundamental change in the terrain. The enormous pressure ridges lessened and gave way to flatter pans. We had reached the end of the so-called "shear zone". Here, where the ice shelf deepened, there were especially ferocious currents and, therefore, especially chaotic ridges and rubble. The ice often cracks into an enormous lead at the shear zone and many are driven back at this point. Peary came across this and named it "The Big Lead". Luckily for us, it was frozen, so we could cross it with ease and safety. Once over this, the terrain was older, tamer and more stable. We were able to travel seven hours, and progress around nine miles each day.

But it was still cold, relentlessly so. Even breathing lowered the body temperature, and breathing through the nose could cause frostbite and pain in the nasal passages, so we breathed through our mouths as much as we could. Even in the three-second journey from my pocket to my mouth, a piece of chocolate, warm and soft when I picked it up from being next to my skin, would freeze. Before I could swallow it, I had to hold it in my mouth to thaw it, and at such moments I could not avoid the pain of breathing through my nose.

Often if my eyes watered my eyelids would actually stick together. My breath would freeze instantly as it came out of my mouth and nose and would form a long horn. Although we had all sewn large pieces of fleece on our mittens to serve as handkerchiefs for our permanently running noses, on the coldest days I did not even have the strength to lift my hand to my nose. The mucus would freeze into a second horn. It made me look like a grotesque ice rhinoceros.

The difficulty of going to the toilet in those early days never lessened, we always had to plan our visits carefully. As it was always too cold to remove my gloves, I had to prepare the toilet paper in advance. All my zips had long strings attached to enable me to pull them in mittens. Afterwards, I had to make sure all thermal tops were tucked tightly in as any skin left exposed would freeze, yet I had to do it in haste so as not to cool down too much from standing around. I often left a piece of skin uncovered out of haste, and it would immediately turn into a painful blister. During these first days, we were all obsessed by the simple task of defecating, and by the need to avoid constipation, because squatting for any length of time exposed our bottoms to frostbite. Fiona and I were already suffering in this way. One day, I also tripped and stepped into my own droppings. They froze instantly to my boot, and to my companions' disgust, could not be removed. My boot was refused entry into the tent.

Less than a week after setting off I had also had my period. Sanitary pads can only be changed with gloves off, but even inside the tent, my hands became stiff within seconds, while the cold made the glue on the pad completely useless. I was forced to broadcast my condition in order to ask the others to ignore me, and then hide in my vapour barrier liner. It gave me about as much cover as removing a bikini on a beach behind a face flannel. Fortunately, no one was even vaguely interested in my predicament.

You know already that frostbite arises because the body's priority for its blood supply is the core, not the extremities, but cold affected everything, not just the skin. The lack of blood also made our muscles weak and sluggish, so it tended to make us clumsy. It also made us less efficient, less motivated and could drive us mad. I found my greatest challenge with the cold was mental. If I was too cold I would find concentration impossible and get irritable and often I would feel very emotional and tearful, just unable to cope. One could not predict these psychological changes. I recently heard from a polar guide of an extremely successful career man, who had spent much of his life mountaineering, who went on a supposedly straightforward five-day expedition to walk the last degree to the Pole. At −35°C he lost his abilities and his guide had had to do everything for him, from putting on his skis to helping him eat.

I was surprised at how I had managed the cold so much better than anticipated, thanks to my experience in Antarctica. I remembered how frightened and helpless I had started off there, how unable to look after myself. Steve and Geoff had helped me with my coat, my zips and my food and I would often feel very emotional. Here I could take care of myself. In the morning, I still stayed in the sleeping bag until the last possible moment, and I was still the slowest, but my speed was close to that of Mike and Fiona. We all skied at our own pace and caught up at each break. It made a great difference not having the pressure of trying to reach the Pole by a given date, or battling to keep up with the others. It was a new and pleasant feeling to be able to look around me and appreciate where I was. I reflected that as I had not made such enormous sacrifices simply to suffer for two months, it was important that my everyday experience should be positive.

I threw only one tantrum, though this time it was much earlier in the trip. On day thirteen, for no apparent reason, and no doubt ground down by the cold, I threw down my sticks and gloves at the first break, followed by a Mars Bar whose frozen condition irritated me beyond measure in my hunger. Paul picked it up and handed it back to me. "Don't want it," I spat out. "Fine, I'll have it then," he replied, and calmly ate it, leaving me salivating and with a rumbling stomach. At the next break, he decided I was too slow, imagined I was intentionally so because of my mood, took the tent from my sled and put it into his. My temper worsened. Not until I was warm again in the tent that night did I feel sheepish and guilty and apologize to the others.

I cannot stress too strongly the importance of controlling one's emotions when in the kind of isolation we were. There was simply nowhere one could go to let off steam, to release anger or unhappiness. At home, whatever one fears to face, there are reliable distractions at any time of day or night: cinema, television, socializing, hobbies, working all hours. Any number of artificial substances can obliterate memories, senses and feelings, and delay the need to make decisions. Here there was absolutely nothing between me and my thoughts, between me and myself. I was completely raw; so I felt vulnerable. I had stupidly even forgotten my Nicorette gum. So I had no choice but to face my concerns, not bury them. It was unnerving, but something I started to realize was healthy.

It was not possible to lock oneself in a darkened room for an hour or to go for a walk to cool off. Either one had to inflict one's feelings on one's team-mates, which carried an obvious risk, or keep one's emotions to oneself, which could lead to insanity. I learned

273

towards the end of the South Pole expedition to write everything down in my diary, and this was an adequate solution. But on this expedition, strangely, I seemed much more emotional. Maybe I was unconsciously more frightened of what awaited me on my return or maybe, as I was struggling less physically, I had more mental space. I found the best ways of dealing with this were first to eat every hour to maintain my blood sugar levels, and to talk openly about what was on my mind.

One day in particular, I developed the old fear I was slowing the others down and became convinced Paul was concerned about my abilities. Overnight I had worked myself up into a real frenzy about it so, in the morning, I asked Paul to ski with me. He was surprised by my openness, and after ten minutes of reassuring chat I felt the world lifted from my shoulders. Later on, as my inescapable return home drew nearer, all three of them were a wonderful sounding board for my worries. I am normally extremely reserved about self-revelation, but in these unusual and privileged circumstances, I touched on subjects with them that I have never discussed before or since.

It was now only a few days to the first resupply. The Twin Otter from the company First Air was extremely expensive to charter. As it would be carrying only a few boxes of food and cans of fuel, we had the idea of inviting guests to hitch a lift on the plane for a twenty minute visit and so make better use of our investment. First I thought of Geoff, since I knew he was due in the Arctic, but he would be going from Russia, not Canada. Then it occurred to us that our mothers could come out, one per resupply. My mum screamed with excitement when she heard my suggestion. She had a little time to prepare. Mike's mother, who would come on the first plane, had to leave immediately.

We had not had to worry much about preparing runways in the Antarctic. Apart from sastrugi, the surface was generally flat. On the Arctic Ocean a suitable runway was much harder to find since it had to be at least 1000 feet long and 160 feet wide and any bumps had to be ironed out. At both ends, the runway had to be clear of pressure ridges. We spent several painful hours laboriously digging out any undulations, transferring the ice into our sleds and then towing them well away from the airstrip. We then flattened down the result using spades or our feet. Finally we marked our chosen airstrip out with ski poles, black bin liners and sleds to guide the pilots in. Pilots sometimes rejected the land travellers' landing place and chose their own. It would be, we hoped, very close by, since we could not make much more than an average of one mile an hour. Then we would have to pack up and hurry across to the plane. The pilots could only wait for so long in such conditions, even with engines running. We also knew how careful we should be to avoid unnecessary injury. It was easy to see what problems there might be trying to carry to the nearest possible airstrip a person who had become immobilized in a large area of ice rubble.

In preparation, we boiled our largest pan of water and had a wash. I went through the delightful process of putting on my spare, clean set of thermal underwear, knickers and socks, saved specially for our first resupply. I had a new clean set arriving in my resupply bag, which was also to contain more film and wetwipes. It was a special occasion. We had completed eighteen days of the expedition. Apart from Pen, all the "experts" had predicted I would have given up by then; few thought I would last beyond ten days.

"This is great," said Paul, as we were waiting. "I expected us all to be sitting here desperately trying to talk one another out of getting on to the plane and bailing out. The fact is we are two days off getting over the worst part, and nobody has even considered bailing. We are in fact all having a good time, crazy really." We had done the worst "in style", with plenty of food, fuel and dry clothing. Before the expedition, we had all trained exhaustively. During the expedition we had taken exceptional care of our equipment and ourselves. The journey had been as comfortable as it could possibly have been under such freezing conditions.

We heard the noise of the Twin Otter overhead. Mike was beside himself with excitement. Quickly, we put on our five layers of clothing, face masks, goggles, hats and gloves and ran out to see it land. After all our hard work, the pilot obviously did not like the runway we had prepared, and chose his own a short way away. We ran over as the plane taxied to a halt, leaving one engine idling. I stood back and watched as Mike's mum and sister came out of the door. We already knew this would be the most adventurous thing his mother had ever done. As Paul, I and the pilots unloaded the plane and sorted out our second batch of food and fuel, Mike and Fiona took his mother and sister to see our "home". After only twenty minutes on the ground they were shepherded back on to the plane. I hoped very much that in three weeks' time I would be seeing my mother, too.

I sensed a feeling of anticlimax for Mike and Fiona, understandably so. The visit was very significant and special for them, despite being so short. We hurried around taking our new supplies into the tent and seeing what other goodies had been packed. Aziz and Nick the Chef had packed an enormous feast of beef stew and dumplings, chocolate Easter eggs, smoked oysters, smoked fish, fresh fruit, cake and pie. We gorged for four hours solidly, trying to eat as much as we possibly could.

There was also a pile of faxes and e-mails from home. I had forgotten just how wonderful it was to receive word and stories from friends. My flatmate Jo had a possible new boyfriend, I was beside myself with excitement. My mother's cat Primrose was due to have kittens next month. They would all be given Arctic names. Nikki was preparing to go to drama school, also a life-long dream. The foot and mouth crisis was still raging.

There was also a fax from Arctic Tree Surgeon, obviously sent just before he left for Svalbard. It was friendly, chatty and completely indifferent. Only one kiss and not even a suggestion of romantic emotion, what does that mean Fi-Fi? "Well, judging from the letter I don't think he realizes he's marrying you, love," she said gently. Later, Mike noticed I had pensively read the letter for the sixth time and said, "Getting disappointing letters when you're out there doing something crazy with no means of communicating is hard, isn't it? It's too easy to read it over and over again, examining every nuance, but don't interpret too much into it, wait till you're both back on the ground before you start thinking about wedding dresses." We all went to bed feeling utterly stuffed and also rather sick.

The next morning the tent was a tip, reminiscent of the morning after one of my London parties. Instead of clearing up half-empty glasses and overflowing ashtrays, as I was so used to doing in my Clapham flat, we packed up all the remnants of food and Easter egg wrappers that we had devoured the day before. Breakfast was chocolate cake, cookies loaded with butter and bagels with high fat cream cheese.

We spent the morning repacking the sleds with enough provisions to last us the next twenty days. To have to pull full weight again came as a shock, and, when we started, Fiona and I struggled to put one foot in front of the other. Our journey was one third over.

CHAPTER
FOURTEEN

The North Pole In Style

Everything was changing. The temperature rose dramatically from −40°C to −30°C. Spring was here. Our journey became radically more comfortable, but for the first time, we faced the danger of pressure ridges collapsing on — or underneath — us as we were crossing or, worse, sleeping.

When we came across our first batch of moving ice, we could see high piles of stunning aquamarine ice actually in motion. The noise of the ice breaking up and grinding in this way was deafening, very like standing in my local launderette with washing machines and tumble dryers going at full power. It was important to move away as quickly as possible. The ice could open up under our feet separating the team or taking one of us down into the ocean, before crashing together to form a new pressure ridge.

As we knew we would, we also started to meet open water, leads that had not refrozen or huge cracks through which we could see the ocean foaming beneath. When everything had been frozen it was easy to have the illusion of being on land. Now we were being shown reality. The first few open leads were small and we were able to cross where there were small bridges made by ice rubble. The bridges rocked and moved as we crossed them; it was very disconcerting. It was like trying to cross the width of a swimming pool over small blocks of ice bobbing on the surface. However, the blocks were quite deep underwater, so they formed stable platforms.

Where the lead was wider, there was nothing to be done but follow the bank until we found a narrowing. It was sometimes also possible to find a "floater", a detached block of ice we could pull towards us with our ski sticks and use as a natural raft, often with the help of a rope. Even where there was no natural floater, it could be possible to carve one out with our ice axes. In the remainder of our journey we often had to improvise in this way.

Before the expedition, like every other Arctic traveller, we had at length discussed methods of crossing leads. Paul believed it was pointless to take additional means of support — sleds that could double as boats, as Swee and Armin had, or even lilos from the co-op in Resolute, as had been my flippant solution. Marine solutions rarely worked, and certainly not mine. Every time I suggested it, Paul's face was a picture.

"Don't push it, H. The lilo would flip over and we would all end up in the water and die. We'll just have to find a way across."

Borge Ousland had devised a dry suit, similar to what he had worn when he was a deep-sea diver, to enable him to swim across leads. This idea was a revolutionary innovation; it might well make Arctic journeys much easier. Paul was concerned by the possibility that water might enter through a hole in the suit, so he remained happy with the traditional answers.

There was another, extremely simple strategy. A lead near the end of the day would bring our day's travel to a halt, but we would hope, often with success, that the lead would refreeze overnight. On the first occasion this happened, it was already −24°C, but luck was with us, the temperature did fall overnight. Paul took the lead first, very carefully and very tentatively testing the ice as he went. For about twenty minutes he searched for a suitable bridge. The water was frozen but still looked very black, which indicated it might not take our weight. Paul tied a rope to his chest and started to make his way across. He was bold and decisive. We were silent and uneasy, hanging on to the other end of the rope far too tightly. As he glided warily across he bounced up and down on the ice as it literally moved with him. It was very rubbery and an unexpected vision of walking on a bouncy castle flashed before me.

We had taken to checking our GPS each morning to make sure we had not drifted. Our fear now was that we would drift east off our longitude taking us into the Lomonosov Ridge. There, the currents were extremely strong and we would not be able to travel back fast enough to compensate. We would thus be pulled steadily further towards Greenland. Our other fear was drifting back south. Matty had recently taken a group on a last degree trip to the North Pole. They had around ten days to cover the sixty miles, but the southerly drift was so bad they never reached the Pole.

The first time we encountered drift, we were surprised to find it was one mile in the right direction — north — but we knew that drifting was predominantly an enemy, not a friend. Geoff told me the worst story of this kind, of the *Jeanette*, and of her captain, George W. De Long, who had set out in 1879 with a crew of thirty-three to find the mythical polar sea beyond the Bering Strait. Trapped in the ice, the ship had drifted for eighteen months, covering over 2000 miles. Eventually, De Long abandoned ship, and the crew pulled the three lifeboats towards Siberia. But even now, they drifted north-west faster than they could escape, since they could only make roughly a mile a day under their own steam. After five days, the ship's master and De Long consulted, and found they had progressed five miles south, but drifted twenty-five north. They were forced to keep this demoralizing fact from the men to preserve their sanity, and although they did reach open water, only one boatload eventually survived.

My diary entries now became much more detailed and fluid. In the first fortnight I had only been able to write a paragraph at most, and it took some time to unfreeze the ink in our pens by putting them next to the stove for several minutes. When I eventually returned, I left my diary behind on the plane between Resolute and Iqaluit. It was handed back to me, but I felt momentary panic at losing such private thoughts so painstakingly recorded. The chores, too — maintaining the equipment, sewing and so forth — started to require less effort.

We were the only people in hundreds of miles of Arctic wasteland, but it was difficult to actually be completely alone, though at times all of us needed those moments. It must have been especially hard for Mike and Fiona, a married couple never able to be alone together for so long. Later on they would ski together during the day, because the weather was warm enough to let them chat, but there was no chance for them truly to be on their own. The first day when it was just warm enough to spend twenty minutes alone while the others were in the tent, I walked a little way from the camp. It was −34°. I needed to keep moving and especially to imitate a windmill with my hands, but I had a desperate urge to hear the silence and have a few minutes to myself. The beauty and silence were absolutely breathtaking. I looked far ahead north to where I would be skiing the next day and the next. There were just miles of beautifully formed shapes glowing deep blue. The sun was still low on the horizon — a bright orange ball giving out a yellow sheen around it, covering the landscape with a rosy glow.

I always took time to listen. Back at home I would spend hours on end listening to the sounds of the countryside by the sea or in the woods. Sound had such beauty in its own right. Each country I visited had its own sounds, birds, the bustle of the night markets in Asia, the exploding noise of voices and cars in New

283

York. Even different parts of London had very distinctive sounds. Often on my days off in the theatre I would sit in a coffee house in Soho and shut my eyes. I was aware of certain music, certain conversations and even accents. In the afternoon I would cycle over to the City and sit in a pub over a pint. The noise, the music, the conversation and certainly the accents were completely different. It were as if I had moved abroad in half an hour.

But there was always sound. Wherever I went, however remote, there was always sound. I wondered now what the Arctic would sound like. I closed my eyes and for the first time in my life listened to absolutely nothing, not even wind. It was completely silent and utterly bewitching, although, disappointingly, I was almost deafened by my own blood rushing around my head and ringing in my ears. I was one of those people that needed silence. The previous year I had had just one row with my boisterous flatmates. "I must have silence," I bellowed to them. "Just one hour, that's all I ask, but please give me silence."

Now, in this silence, I had time to reflect. I felt utterly relaxed. I realized that part of my reason for being in the Arctic was escape, to surrender for a short space of time, not to have to make decisions, or conform. It struck me how simple my life was here — ski, haul, eat, sleep and survive.

In some strange way I missed the cold, missed the beautiful spiky sea urchin frost that formed everywhere. It was now melting, rapidly losing its spikes and petals and turning into a slush. I even almost missed the challenge of surviving in extreme temperatures. But I had become so reliant on wrapping myself in as many layers as possible that I was developing a phobia of removing any clothing. I was starting to sweat in my sleeping bag. As the down became sodden each night, the bag worked less well, which in turn made me colder and even more obsessed with wearing more layers. Paul gave me short shrift. "Tomorrow, Miss Hartley, you are going to remove a layer of your clothing and I can guarantee you will ski faster. You've got to deal with your fear of the cold." He was right. The fact was I was terrified of removing a layer, and having that feeling so like scalding myself on hot steam or putting my hand in boiling water. But Paul told me that being warm was an indulgence. During the day it was important to remain cold, and just learn to be used to it. Although I had to be very careful at stops, I would travel much more quickly. And by sweating less, I would not face the daily problem of putting on a completely stiff, frozen jacket. "If you sweat, the sweat freezes and you die!" he threatened me. Whether or not this was overdramatized for effect, I took his point.

Of course, Paul was right. As soon as I started to remove clothing, my pace accelerated to that of the others and I felt comfortable. The first few moments, I was scared, and skied like a madwoman to generate extra heat, but, gradually, I relaxed. Ice stopped forming on my clothes and I learned to be comfortable being cold. The breaks became a torment because my body temperature plummeted.

Paul was still not satisfied; he had always thought our use of face masks was unnecessary, using the fur round the hood of his coat to protect his face from wind and cold.

"Let your face breathe, woman, let it feel the elements."

"Paul, I need to look after my skin, I'm not a tough male explorer like you, I'm a woman."

"True, and an unmarried one at that. OK, face mask back on, you need all the help you can get." Paul expressed more than once his concern that I was not yet engaged.

It was an interesting difference. Geoff would have refused to let me show my face outside the tent without my face mask. Indeed, I did get a hard white tip to my nose — frostnip — as a result of not sleeping with my mask on properly. In the end, I did not look in Fiona's small mirror until three days before our arrival, and by then I was quite shocked at the weathered, rugged face that looked back at me.

As before, food obsessed me as much as heat. I became like an animal, hungry all the time except for a brief period after breakfast and dinner, living for the next snack. I daydreamed endlessly about cafés, coffee bars, muffin houses, you name it, I had been there in my mind. No one else seemed to have this problem and one night I was even caught rifling through the food bags when I thought everyone was asleep. Paul told me I needed to learn self-discipline. He never allowed himself to fantasize about food. He told me I had hand-to-mouth syndrome, I had to be putting something in my mouth at all times, food, cigarettes, alcohol or my nails.

Fortunately, I discovered that neither Mike nor Fiona was fond of sewing. At last I had a bartering tool; I was soon repairing their gloves in exchange for salami. Aziz had also put some jerky — dried raw beef — in the resupply. I would not dream of eating it in London, but out here, it was our treat each time we reached a new degree of latitude. We devoured it like savage dogs.

Each day Mike saved his daily ration of salami, chopping it up in the evening and putting it beside the stove until it was warm and the fat was literally dripping. To have that nightly pleasure, so revolting in the city and so ambrosial out in the cold, I copied him. This meant I did not have my fat quota during the day. As time passed, I realized that by reducing my daily rations my moods were being affected. I spent one complete day crying for no reason and had to be consoled by Mike when he noticed the damning evidence of tears frozen all over my face. From my mother's diabetes, I had some understanding of how important blood sugar was, and once I started eating my fat during the day and a chocolate or energy bar every hour, I no longer felt hungry or weak, and my mood improved dramatically.

As I came to know Paul better, I tried to break through his tough French Canadian façade, until teasing him became an enjoyable pastime, and one he bore very graciously. All day on 31 March I racked my brain for an April Fool's joke to play on him. Finally I settled on blacking out the fingers on my hand as if they were frostbitten. I hoped Fiona might have some black make-up in her vanity pack, but all that was available was the charcoal on the stove. Maybe I could collect enough to cover at least the fingertips. As Paul was packing up early on the 1st, I started to scrape off the charcoal with my knife and spread it on to my fingers.

"I'm sure you wouldn't dream of it but I don't even want to sniff a possibility of any April Fool's gags from you, Miss Hartley," he said, as if reading my mind. I turned round with a black smudge on my nose. Quickly I stuffed the stove back into the box. I liked and respected Paul enormously, but the abrasive manner in which he periodically criticized my slow pace was always something difficult for me, simply because my experiences in the Antarctic had made me so concerned not to hold the party up.

Mike and Fiona were, of course, already my friends. When they were ahead of me, they would write me messages in the snow. "Hello and smile Cath!" with a big smiley face and "Keep on trucking". They were always unfailingly sensitive and kind to me; in an uncanny way they could always tell if I was down or sad. All three of my companions were perceptive in this way and showed their care for me by many small gestures. A comforting touch on the arm or a helping hand unloading the sled at the end of the day would be greatly therapeutic.

Fiona herself remained unfailingly optimistic. Where I continued to be analytical, endlessly ruminating over my life-choices, she never deviated from the dinner parties she would be giving on her return, what dress she would buy for the Farmers' Ball and the piano lessons she would be taking. Initially, these thoughts seemed frivolous to me, as I was frustrated that I could not discuss what I fondly thought of as deeper issues. But as time went on, she began to change my perception of my own life. She showed me the possibility of fulfilment in areas that I had not thought about for many years. She taught me how to be happy and find joy in the very simple and ordinary things in life and how to resist the urge to bang on about useless, indulgent, and, yes, what I now began to accept, meaningless issues. I have nothing but praise for her.

I have to say, though, that one day after she had been leading, it was Fiona who was the poetic one. She talked about the shapes she saw carved in the ice — frogs, a bird and a vulture. I unwisely admitted that all I had seen that day carved in the ice was a huge phallus.

We also managed to share a tent with remarkably few problems, although when we had rare rest days because of storms the space seemed very small. But my companions were extraordinarily noisy sleepers. As Fiona became more tired, her snoring became worse. I moved sleeping positions to have my head next to Mike, but, unfortunately, he had a periodic sinus problem which made him snort and croak. Fiona did suggest that if she snored I could stop her by making kissing noises. This worked, but I still asked Aziz for earplugs in the second resupply. By now, though, I felt in desperate need of a bath. My skin was covered in a rash and flaking everywhere. The hairs on my legs were so long they could be plaited and my white bra had turned a yellow-beige colour. I felt utterly disgusting.

As in the Antarctic I was drawn into their faith in a very gentle way. They had brought a small book of prayers and messages with them. Each night they read one quietly to themselves, one after the other, and then put the book away. Paul and I both noticed this ritual and always respected this as a moment of silence. Before too long I was curious and asked if I might read the book, too. I found the words beautiful, I enjoyed reading them and they gave me much comfort and reassurance. Mike and Fiona took enormous strength from their church at home, who every Sunday remembered us in their prayers. They believed this prayer was keeping them strong and bringing us all the luck and good fortune we had so far received on this trip. Again, I found it hard not to become intoxicated by their faith; it was hard not to believe, too.

From my obsession with danger and adventure, I knew I, too, was fascinated by what lay beyond our everyday world. When I had done my access course for university, we were asked to do a research project on anything we liked. Avoiding the suggested subjects of the works of Jane Austen or propaganda in WWII, I had chosen to do a study of new religious movements, the Moonies and Scientology in particular, pin-pointing the question of brainwashing — much to my tutor's concern. As I reflected daily on the spiritual life, and for the first time really considered belief, not

290

scepticism, I wondered whether my own approach had been inherited from my father.

My father had been fascinated by death; he kept a small book in which he recorded funny stories associated with death. When I was still living at home he applied to be a mortician's assistant at our local hospital. The main duty involved tying labels on to the end of the corpses' toes before shutting them into the freezer. He was turned down; I can imagine the pathologist must have thought him quite mad. Even I thought it an odd career move at the time. Instead my father settled for a tour around our local undertakers on the pretext that he had some schoolchildren interested in looking at a career in the embalming industry.

I remember him recounting with joy the tale of Auntie Jenny's funeral, with his characteristic dry humour. Shortly after my mother and father married, my great-aunt Jenny died. The funeral was the first time my mum met my father's huge extended family of Lancashire women. Unfortunately the undertaker had not performed the embalming procedures correctly. As she was being carried up the aisle there was a loud bang and Auntie Jenny unfortunately burst. Fluid seeped out of the coffin and on to the pallbearers' shoulders. My father left the funeral hysterical; he thought it the funniest experience of his life.

Years later, at my father's own funeral in 1991, when I was soberly drinking tea with my relatives, I opened the door to the undertaker and was struck, for the first time in my life, by lust at first sight. He was young,

291

blond and all in black. Knowing it would have appealed to my father's sense of humour, my sympathetic mother and various kind friends put £100 into a jam-jar as a bet for me to ask him out. I must admit I did feel mortified that my father's funeral had turned into a tasteless charade of me trying to pull the undertaker, but I knew he would have loved it. The undertaker declined politely, but I solemnly inscribed the story into my father's book of death stories.

Now past halfway, we started to strategize our arrival. I was always cautious, but even I had developed a streak of competitiveness. I wanted to finish in fifty-five days, because Mr Five Hats had taken fifty-six. Paul was cautious, too, for different reasons. He warned us that no matter how close we were, too much open water could still defeat us. At least, however, it looked as if we would reach the second resupply without further problems.

Before my mum left home we spoke to her and gave her a list of food that we had all been fantasizing about. I ordered her homemade chocolate biscuit cake; Fiona caramel shortbread from Marks and Spencer; Paul Walker's shortbread, and Mike and Paul half a bottle of Scottish malt whisky. It amused me how specific everyone was about their craving. Paul also asked my mother if she would bring in a bottle of champagne to celebrate our arrival. Resolute was a "dry" town; it worried me that my mother might be thrown in jail as a smuggler.

The thought of seeing my mum and all the food was more than I could bear. Greg from First Air called at

8a.m. to tell us all was well with the resupply. We all made final preparations, finishing off our diaries, writing letters home and trying to reduce any weight possible, even the excess toothpaste from the tube. To prepare for my mum's arrival I tidied the tent, straightening all the smelly socks hanging out to dry and clearing the floor of crumbs, as if I was getting my flat ready in London before she came to stay. I also succeeded in ringing her and reminded her to take her insulin and enough food for so long a journey.

Now we had to make a crucial decision as to how much food and fuel we should take for our last leg of the journey. At this stage in Antarctica, as we were travelling over solid ground, we could accurately predict, mishaps excepted, how long the remainder of the journey would take. In the Arctic, nothing was fixed — literally. We had no idea what lay in store for us. A wide lead might take days to cross. Negative drift could lose us days, too. But, of course, taking extra food and fuel as an insurance simply meant extra weight, and moving more slowly. However, the idea of less food made me extremely nervous.

We compromised. We took on twenty days of supplies, but extra chocolate and salami, for our remaining three degrees or 180 nautical miles. So we would have to average nine miles a day, not so hard in these warmer temperatures, and with the incentive of the nearing Pole.

This time we had found the perfect airstrip — a very old lead that had frozen thick. As we heard the engines, we ran outside and saw the pilots line up their approach immediately. The captain was called Muffet. It was his first ever landing on the Arctic Ocean. He was as excited as we were and took photos. Finally my mother got out, so well wrapped up she looked like a Michelin man. It was my turn to take care of my visitor while the others did the resupply. She was utterly overwhelmed. I showed her our tent and how we lived, and I pointed to the massive expanse of white landscape where we would be walking the next day. "The North Pole's that way," I explained unnecessarily. I showed her the ice formations and our skis. She was unable to speak, and too stunned to take it all in.

Twenty minutes later she set off again. The four of us waited until the plane had taken off into the distance, waving madly knowing my mum was waving madly back. It was one of the most special moments of my life and meant an enormous amount that she could have a little taste of what had become so important to me. She told me later that what had amused her was my asking if she would like to go to the toilet and showing where it was. When we had rest days, we designated a toilet spot, but, of course, it was just another lump of ice to her. I felt flat after she had gone but was kept busy by reading all the letters and messages she had brought over and over again and, of course, by eating.

My journey to the South Pole had been eventful — a cross between melodrama, soap opera and farce. In comparison, nothing happened on the way to the North Pole. No despair, no brushes with death, no frostbite, no personality clashes since we were already "bonded". The combination of our South Pole experience and

Paul's ruthless efficiency had turned our expedition into a professional one. Indeed, we were so successful that the *Daily Telegraph*, which had agreed to keep a weekly diary of Mike and Fiona's experiences, soon gave up printing the copy for lack of news.

There were not even any close encounters with polar bears. I had kept in mind that my climber friends in England had begged me not to be eaten by one, on the grounds they would be unable to keep a straight face at my memorial service. One day, Paul told me he had seen bear tracks; it took me a while to work out that this was a way of encouraging me to move more quickly. That evening, bent on revenge, I carved paw prints around Paul's tent with the last one going inside and, when he left our tent to go to his, giggled hysterically like an idiot schoolgirl. "Oh, Catharine really, as if I would fall for that one!" he said witheringly. I had even drawn the wrong number of pads on each paw, he told me. I felt rather stupid. Exhaustion was starting to make me silly.

The North Pole was, overall, a greater mental than physical challenge for me. The isolation, the fact of being with just three other people twenty-four hours a day, the need to be so controlled with all our emotions were all difficult for me. I had to struggle to believe not in the physical possibility of keeping going, but that there was a point in what I was doing. Occasionally I felt as if I were observing myself walking along, head down, nose running and, of course, freezing cold. At moments such as this, I just wondered what I was doing and why.

So what problems did we have? Above all, just that the constant physical effort took its toll on our bodies — the pains in Mike's back, the sores on Fiona's thighs and, ignominiously, a corn on my foot. From two weeks in, Mike had become worried about his back. He periodically feared he would have to give up, and one night between the resupplies I noticed an intense conversation between him and Fiona at the end of the day. Fiona was tearful that evening; I rightly surmised that Mike had been thinking he was afraid of holding us up and was considering leaving on the resupply plane.

On some occasions, we took weight from Mike's sled, but I myself was never strong enough to keep up my pace with the addition of any of his. Fiona, however, was a devoted wife for the remainder of the journey, helping him in every way not to put unnecessary strain on his back, while Mike took over much of the navigation. I understood how important it was for them to complete the journey together, and later learned that she had offered to go with him should he have to give up. I was absolutely blown away by her devotion to him. No wonder I am not married, I thought.

Fiona's own thigh sores returned early on. I knew she was worried about this after her ordeal in Antarctica. To combat them, she used hand warmers — two pieces of metal that, pressed together, gave off a chemical reaction and produced heat for a limited period. I sewed a pocket in Fiona's thermal trousers exactly where the cold injury was and every morning

296

and night she inserted a hand warmer there. With these and extra trousers, we kept the problem at bay.

But my problems were even more undignified. A month before I set off for Canada I saw a chiropodist about the toe problems I had had in Antarctica. Had the pain begun earlier there I might well have been forced to give up. I therefore spent £300 on an array of gels, pads, toe products and a surgical blade, since I had no time for the corrective surgery that was recommended. As early as the eleventh day of my North Pole walk, my problem returned.

It was a huge embarrassment. It was no more than a corn, but it turned my toe into a mass of blood and raw skin. Every step I took, stabbing pains went through my entire foot. My heels blistered badly, too. At times I had to ski with my right foot and walk with my left. Using the scalpel, I would remove growths from my toes, and Paul suggested with rather savage eyes that I burn the corn out with a red-hot screwdriver, although I chose the softer option of corn-removing ointment.

There were times when I thought my corn might cause me to give up. The shame of the newspaper headlines would have been unbearable. At other moments, I was amused, knowing that back in Nottingham, Mike and Fiona's congregation were saying prayers for something as small as the health of my toe. Eventually, the cure was simple — anti-inflammatory pills, Ibuprofen, combined with taping my feet every morning, every night and every break. It was unimaginably tedious to have to remove my boots and socks so many times a day.

The morning after the resupply was another crazed imitation of the aftermath of a London party. We had eaten and drunk so much that Mike had to get up five times for the loo, and I could not stop giggling from the effect of so much glucose in my bloodstream caused by a mountain of sugar and Easter eggs. We found the floor a mess, covered in pee, food and drink stains. Worse, Mike had packed a Walkman for the last leg of the journey. There would have been no point in having it any earlier. It would have been too cold for the machinery to work. But somehow the Walkman had not arrived. Mike checked his resupply bag five times at least, but to no avail. He was inconsolable.

Hardly anything irritated Paul, but he could not stand my silk sleeping bag liner. It was a physical and psychological luxury for me; it provided warmth and a protective layer between my body and the plastic vapour barrier liner. Paul thought it was useless and unnecessary and in a fit of petulance had ordered I send it out in the first resupply. I missed it, but I accepted I did not need it. Even after it had gone, Paul carried on telling me how much he had disapproved of it. At our second resupply, Paul had his thick sleeping bag replaced by a thinner one. As he unpacked it that night, I heard a bellow of rage. Aziz had clearly thought the silk liner had gone to Resolute by mistake, and had sent it back washed and pressed, inside Paul's new bag. Silently, I took it back. One day, I abandoned my travel book and my spare clothes in answer to Paul's criticism of my speed. He wanted the liner to go again, too, but at the last moment he relented and carried it for me for a day. The silk liner was later to come into its own.

We had sent away other things, too, as the weather became more summery. Our huge sleeping bivouac bags were gone, now we had just the vapour barrier liner, and a sleeping bag. Instead of sitting on the bivouac bags in the evenings, Fiona and I would carve chairs out of blocks of ice. Paul told me I had to be brave, and I still found it hard to lose more equipment that kept us warm. But once done, it was not as bad as I had imagined.

Each morning we would still turn our vapour barrier liners inside out and dry them little by little at the stove. They were generally covered in sweat and moisture and they would still have frozen solid left to themselves. When it was sunny, we could now dry our sleeping bags by spreading them over the sleds, allowing the moisture to vaporize in the current of cold air. This was a process called "subliming" and fluffed the bag out to its fullest, where in the early days it had resembled clumps of wet goose down.

Our closest call did not come until 29 April when we were only seventy-odd miles away from the Pole. I had been leading. Paul was initially reluctant, but was convinced by the fact that, as in the Antarctic, it increased my pace, perhaps because I was scared of holding the others up, more likely because I was simply enjoying myself. Moreover, the navigation kept my mind occupied and away from the pain in my feet. My session was ended by a wide, flowing and uncrossable lead. To add insult to injury, Paul misjudged the ice while looking for a crossing point and his sled fell into the water. Fortunately, we managed to pull it out before it dragged him in with it, since its weight would have made it sink instantly, before he could free himself from the harness. Only the previous day, he had made clear he thought I was a terrible driver and liable to tip my sled into the water at any time. I tried not to feel smug.

This first lead gave us problems enough. At one moment, we saw a gap narrow enough to cross, but by the time we reached it, it had opened up. Fortunately, we found a "floater" nearby, which we dug clear with a spade and dragged back to the gap, which was still widening. Using ice screws to attach a rope, we managed to use the floater to scramble across. The next lead came so soon after that we were able to drag across and then use the same block of ice.

Paul was annoyed by the many leads. Without the luck of finding the floater, we would have been stopped completely. And a day's travel that stayed broken ended when we reached a lead we could not possibly have crossed. Mike climbed to the top of some ice and came down very pessimistic. He could not see anywhere to cross for miles. It was only −12°C, so we could not see how it would freeze overnight. It would take a temperature of −35°C to freeze a river like that over. We were only five days from the Pole, we had been lucky not to have experienced any negative drift even, yet this would be enough to end our chances of success. We made camp despondently, and then we prayed to Sedna.

Sedna is the Goddess of the Arctic. Her father found her a husband, who promised to keep her well, to hunt animals for fur coats and delicious food, and to build her a fine igloo to live in, its floor covered with skins. But Sedna's husband had deceived her. He treated her badly and she became very unhappy. She begged her father to take her away in his boat, but he refused. When she would not let go, he pushed her out and chopped her fingers off so she could not cling on to the side. She died in the ocean, which she now rules.

Polar travellers must pay homage to Sedna, and often make sacrifices to her in the hope of good weather and frozen leads. Paul had spent long enough in the Arctic to respect these beliefs, and the night before we had sacrificed a muesli bar. Paul felt this had been too small a gesture and knew that the time had now come to sacrifice my silk liner. For two days I had strapped it to my sled for this moment. I did not need to be told twice. Although I was unconvinced, I knew my duty. Solemnly, I skied over to the vast open lead and offered the liner to the ocean. It was quickly sucked down. I bet Sedna will be really chuffed with that, I thought sarcastically.

That night I had a really bad night's sleep. I was troubled by the nearness of the end. Some would have welcomed it, but for me, it brought on one of my old 4a.m. panics. I pondered on my city life and the great sacrifices I had made to engage in this insane journey. After two hours I managed to get back to sleep, having vowed to become conventional again on my return. The very next morning, I heard from Tina over the satellite phone that an Internet company called testsonthenet.com had pledged £25,000 for Oliver, my teddy bear. The money could go to Sense on condition I made it to the Pole. I was absolutely delighted. It was the perfect motivational answer. Even more amazing, the lead had frozen over without any drop in temperature. Even Paul could not understand it. It was as if Sedna had answered us. She must have really rated that silk liner, I thought incredulously. We crossed without trouble and entered a new world of flat ice without pressure ridges. The going became easy and the ground was stunning — hard snow that reflected everywhere and looked as if it had been sprinkled with diamonds and jewels.

The last few days were warm — around −15°C — and generally easy travelling except for dangerous leads. I wore only two layers of thermals and a jacket; I no longer used a face mask, although I needed my sunglasses on at all times against snow blindness. At night, we used only one stove, not three, and wore only one layer of clothing in the sleeping bags, and Mike even considered sleeping outside to get away from his wife's snores. We knew that only an uncrossable lead could stop us reaching the Pole.

I am not one for hugging. In this, I am like Geoff, in fact. Every New Year's Eve, when Big Ben chimes, and everyone kisses and hugs, I find the moment awkward and embarrassing. I have often sneaked off to the toilet to avoid the whole thing. On the last night, ludicrously, I found myself becoming anxious about the moment of arrival in the same way. The previous year, my friends had had enough of my midnight absences and agreed that when the clock chimed they would just wave to me and call "Happy New Year". They had kept their word. I asked if my polar colleagues would mind doing the equivalent. There was an incredulous silence. I could see them thinking that I was even more mad than they had previously thought.

"Catharine, I've never heard anything so ridiculous, but if it stresses you out that much then fine, we'll just wave," said Paul, in his blunt way.

"I think you need proper professional help," Mike added.

The top of the world was really how we imagined it. Flat and white with dramatic formations of snow, sparkling in the sun, atmospheric and awe-inspiring when overcast. I was now pretty tired and was falling over at every obstacle and block of ice, but the end was really in sight. On the penultimate day, Paul had been tense, but that night we knew we were only seventeen miles from the Pole, and we resolved that, even if it took fifteen hours or more, we would carry on travelling the next day till we arrived.

Even over a short distance, we knew that the problems of leads or pressure ridges might still stop us. Paul was therefore absolutely determined to arrive as soon as possible and did not want to stop for anything. We were all in agreement.

The others seemed really energized and wanting to go at top speed, but I felt worn down and was struggling after just one hour. I was simply too tired to keep up with the pace. I was so exhausted that I fell into a completely foul mood as I tried desperately to keep up and I ate chocolate bar after chocolate bar. When I eventually managed to catch up with Fiona, I found her in an equally bad mood.

For some reason, Fiona's sled kept overturning when being pulled over pressure ridges. This was tedious in the extreme as she had to ski backwards over piles of rubble to right it, only to have it flip over again moments later. In addition, several times as she was descending ridges, the sled had crashed down behind her and smacked her in the back of the legs. In a strange way also, perhaps we were both dreading the end, sad that it was the last of our charmed days on the ice.

Halfway through the day the other three had a conference ahead of me and when I caught up, they took some of my load and divided it between them. The sting to my pride did not improve my mood, so it was not until the imagined Russian icebreaker that my spirits lifted. Although that proved to be the Arctic equivalent of a mirage, we were close enough to the end and I was able to focus on the idea of arriving.

By the time we were only about a mile away, Paul's navigational corrections involved weaving around so much that our trail was quite comic and Fiona and I started to giggle. But the absence of any fixed point to aim at, let alone the large dome that housed the base at the South Pole, meant that it was very hard for the feeling of nearing our goal to sink in. I spent the whole of the last South Pole day elated, watching the buildings grow larger, whereas this time, as we walked, everything was as it had been the previous hour, the previous day, week, month. At least the moment of attaching the flags to our sleds — there was also a Canadian flag to go on Paul's — brought some small sense of ceremony to the journey.

Suddenly we could see Paul muttering to himself incredulously. We heard him say "This is insane!" It appeared that the GPS had broken, as it was not giving a reading at all. Only last night we had read from David Hempleman-Adams's book that the same thing had happened to him. He and Rune wondered melodramatically whether the sudden outbreak of war had shut down all the satellites, then went through the day's routine to work out if they had done anything different. They realized they had donned radio microphones, which were now interfering with the GPS. As we were not wearing microphones, our problem could not be the same.

Paul skied around, seemingly at random, and then, to our relief, the readings came back. At first they were still confused and would not give a proper longitude, so he continued to cast around erratically. Head down, he tried to find that anonymous patch of ice that was actually the North Pole. We followed him, bumping into one another and finding it more and more hilarious and less and less that it was about to be a moment of solemnity.

When we finally reached the Pole, therefore, we felt relief as well as happiness, and at first, it was very hard to believe the journey was over. It was not until Paul planted his ski stick in the ice and announced our arrival aloud that I really realized we had succeeded.

And then we did lose control. After so many days of responsibility and tension, Paul was in tears, his emotions showing at last after so much brisk, almost superhuman efficiency. And of course, by hugging him, I went back on all my inhibited warnings to my companions.

CHAPTER
FIFTEEN

The Wanderer Returns

We had travelled to the Pole, as we had hoped, "in style", and with a very different ethos from the bearded explorers before us. Our plentiful supplies of fuel had kept us warm and our speed and efficiency had given us time and mental space to enjoy being in the Arctic. As we read the final day of the Hempleman-Adams diary while waiting for the plane, we reflected that, in some small way, we hoped we were changing fashions in polar travel.

We had set up camp where we stood, exhausted but exhilarated. Outside we flew the British and Canadian flags on two ski poles. The first thing we did was to warm the batteries and call our families on the satellite phone. My mum had been waiting up for my call. She was just overjoyed. It must have been so hard for her to endure another expedition, to know she might never see her daughter again. Her calm acceptance and support had been so important for me.

Then we called First Air and found they had taken advantage of a rare window in the weather to have reached Eureka already. They would be leaving shortly to pick us up. As the hour became more reasonable in

Britain, Mike and Fiona began to ring a long list of friends. I called Geoff, but only reached his answerphone. Then I tried Jo at my flat, but I only obtained the call waiting message. When I lived there, the golden rule had always been to pick up each new call; they were clearly slacking in my absence and I did not succeed in speaking to her either.

After a nap, we packed up our camp. We still had to find an airstrip, but we had already noted a very good possible spot about four miles south. We checked our position on the GPS and discovered that we had already drifted six miles from the Pole in only six hours. It was strange skiing south after two months of struggling north. We simply turned around and followed our tracks back. After two hours, we found our candidate runway, still in one piece, and not melted. So we pitched camp again. Then Paul and I went off to prepare the airstrip and to allow Mike and Fiona some time to themselves for the first time in two months. I wondered at how it must feel to have shared two experiences of such magnitude within one's love relationship. It must have created a wonderful bond between the two of them.

After the runway was prepared, I had a few moments alone with the Arctic myself. I left Paul and Fiona chattering away in the tent, but I saw Mike on top of a pressure ridge, so it was clear he had had the same thought. We left each other alone. This place is so beautiful, I thought. There were other places that had had a similar effect on me, all where the beauty was entirely natural and nothing was man-made — the red desert in Australia with its silver eucalyptus trees and mist of spinifex grass, or the cobalt sea and coral reef in the Solomon Islands — but I did not think I had ever been anywhere so magnificent.

But now I could allow myself to think of my home by the sea and of the gentler beauty there. I looked forward to returning to my favourite spot overlooking Bosham Church, one that I had visited since the age of six to think. I would ponder for hours about my future, my life or whatever was concerning me at the time. I visited it on every important occasion, and went there just before leaving for this journey. I wondered what my thoughts would be when I next returned.

It is so strange how the euphoria of success goes together with a terrible anticlimax. I had been expecting it and it came on top of that pressure ridge. Perhaps it was the case before my first polar journey that I might have expected to enter some kind of permanent ecstatic state after fulfilling a dream I had had so long, the sort of transcendent state of new religious movements. The reality was different. I remember hearing an Olympic medallist speaking. He was trying to describe the feeling of standing on the podium with a gold medal hearing his national anthem being played. But he did also say that the euphoria wore off frighteningly fast, and his ambition returned. So the key, he said, was to make sure there was a new goal immediately to replace the one just achieved.

It had taken me years to achieve my South Pole dream. On my return, the new goal of the North Pole had enabled me to focus on the immediate and avoid wider questions. Now it was all over. My dreams had come true. Many people had helped me — family, friends, sponsors, the other Plebs and the polar professionals — but I knew that it was still essentially the achievement of one person, myself. And I had just learned that dreams are really attainable, given ruthless perseverance. Now I had no more dreams, and that felt very strange. What on earth was I going to do from here? Suddenly I felt crushingly sad that it was all over, and also desperately concerned about my return. Bills, debts, work, responsibilities, relationships, future — all these would face me again. My time of escapism had gone, the real world — the cliché was completely appropriate — was returning. It frightened me.

I was entirely lost in my thoughts when the plane came in. By the time I recovered, it had already touched down and Mike, Fiona and Paul were busily packing. The plane brought in numerous sponsors' flags for Mike and Fiona, so we took some time taking photos, pretending we were at the Pole itself. But to my dismay, the Manugistics banner had not been flown in. As I boarded, I turned round and gave one last look at the Arctic.

We did not have a smooth getaway. The plane was too heavy and the runway too short. It took five attempts before we succeeded in taking off. Each attempt was aborted when it was thought we would crash into a pressure ridge. Paul was looking very stony-faced. On the fifth attempt we managed to take off. Once in the air, I felt quite numb. We all munched hungrily on sandwiches Aziz had made for us and read our many congratulatory e-mails. I asked Fiona if she thought she would find returning difficult, but, as ever, she was simply looking forward to seeing her friends, having a party, redecorating their new home, taking piano lessons and returning to work. She did not anticipate any problems at all. How I envied her optimism.

Apart from Borge Ousland, we were the only group to make it all the way to the Pole that year, although we did not know this until we were back in England. From Russia, Bettina Aller had been rescued after she was stalked by a polar bear, and Pen and Ben evacuated after forty-seven days. Dave Mill's solo trip had ended when he ran out of time. And Hyoichi Kohno? Just days from arriving at his pick-up point on Ward Hunt Island, he fell through the ice and sadly was killed.

Once in Resolute, Aziz put us up in rooms with Jacuzzis and Nick cooked us the most wonderful stew and dumplings. We spent four days there. We needed this time to ease ourselves gently back into the real world. I met an American woman there, my age, single. She had had enough of life and was "on the run". She had already spent one winter at Resolute working at Aziz's, and was preparing for her second. I wondered if I should join her.

If the wooden tables themselves in Aziz's dining room resembled those in my favourite haunt, Gastro's in Clapham, the conversations were nothing like, and were quite extraordinary. There was a large group from *National Geographic*, on a scientific expedition with huskies. To my amusement, their leader was putting nappies on the husky puppies. Next to our table were some polar bear hunters. In Arctic Canada that sport is considered as normal as football is in England.

Aziz had been watching me. Somehow he knew I was nervous about returning. We were to return to Iqaluit before getting the plane back to Ottawa, but the first plane had mercifully been cancelled, so we had an extra day with him. When I was packed and waiting very quietly in the dining room, Aziz came and sat down next to me. "There's someone here that would pay you for that," he said, pointing to the air ticket I was clutching. "He wants to get out today and would pay you more than it's worth. You can stay the summer here. I'll give you a job, and we'll find you a nice pilot to marry, if you want." He paused. "I know you don't want to go, Catharine." "Give me a few minutes," I replied.

It was an enticing prospect. I could spend the summer here, maybe even the winter. Then I could travel round Canada. I had always wanted to go to the Rockies. But there was the danger of drifting. I would be travelling to escape, pure and simple. On my travels in the past I had met many who were doing just that, some for years. Some were happy with this, but others not, knowing they could not indefinitely defer that moment of returning to their fate. Indeed, I remembered Arctic Tree Surgeon telling me that he had once returned from an expedition, gone through the arrival gate at Gatwick and realized he could not face walking out of the terminal into reality. Instead, he had gone into an airport travel agent, and bought a flight straight out again. I realized my staying would be foolish. I had been so brave on the expeditions and now it was time to be brave again. I must go back and face the real question of what on earth I was going to do with the rest of my life. I should not return to Resolute till I was at peace with myself.

Iqaluit was the next step back to the rest of the world. Paul and Matty's back garden was starting to melt and the iced-up streets were now turning to dust and gravel. It was so odd to find that the thaw had not revealed any green, and now I realized it was a colour I could simply not live without. I used the three days there to explore my real passion — that for local culture. After visiting the museum, I set about meeting the local people to have a brief insight into life in a High Arctic town. As always in new places, I went to the hairdresser's. It is the same everywhere. The hairdresser's is the perfect place to meet the locals, chat and get a real flavour of a place. I always book an appointment even if it is simply to have my hair washed. So I have had my hair done all over the world. I have sat on sacking in a longhouse in Borneo for a local Iban woman with tattoos and traditional long ears weighed down by heavy earrings, and I've had a gaudy hairdresser in the Bronx also with tattoos and extremely long and brightly painted nails. The conversation was fascinating everywhere.

My hairdresser in Iqaluit had spent her life out in canoes on the open water, fishing and hunting caribou. Sitting next to me was Darren, a Canadian man who ran the local air traffic control. He was desperate to return to the city. Head office was refusing to transfer him but by coincidence was making an inspection of the control tower that very afternoon. So Darren had spent the morning having six rings put through his ear and a stud in his nose and was now having his hair dyed purple. In this way he hoped he would be regarded as a madman and transferred, or at least sacked.

It was difficult to say goodbye to Paul. I wanted to avoid it, of course. And what on earth could I say to express my gratitude? He had not only believed in me and assured the success of the expedition itself but had given me all this time to reflect on my life. Three months before, he had been openly nervous about meeting us, now he was crying as we left.

Ottawa was so green, just so, so green. The markets were mesmerizing with all the fruit, vegetables and clothing. It was an extraordinary array of colour for my eyes to get used to. I could not get over seeing colour again. I left Mike and Fiona alone for the day. I had been the gooseberry long enough.

Mike managed to get us an upgrade, and I had forgotten my shameful entrance into Canada until the customs officer who had refused me entry recognized me. "Hey! Aren't you the one . . .?" Before he had finished I fled into the toilet. A few minutes later Fiona came in laughing to retrieve me. The customs man had asked if I really had been ill on my entry to Canada, and Mike had replied: "No, she was just completely and utterly ratted." As we entered the plane, the first class stewardess said to us, "Now, we have decided to upgrade you, but with that a certain standard of behaviour is expected. I'm sure you understand." I swear she gave me a wink.

We arrived at Heathrow very early on a Monday morning; again my family and friends were there to meet me. Ying later told me that I had looked quite different from when I came back from the South Pole. Now I appeared fit and ruddy-cheeked, like a "real explorer". But I was nervous. I knew it would not be the same as the last time, and I was more preoccupied with how I would take up the threads of my life.

Within four days I was back at work at the BBC, Jane, my boss, supportive as ever. But it was hopeless. I was unable to do my job properly. It was an impossible transition to go from the absolute peace and serenity of the Arctic to the madness, stress and long hours of filming a children's drama. Shortly after finishing I was offered a massive promotion and asked to become a production manager. It took me just three minutes to decide to turn it down. The thought of another challenge and more pressure terrified me. Instead, I took a job that involved making tea, buying people their lunches and booking a few cabs for a lovely children's programme. Strangely, this was all I could manage and all I have wanted to attempt since my return.

I had been quietly wondering if Arctic Tree Surgeon would be at the airport. I had not heard a word from him and did not even know if he had succeeded in his own expedition. He was not at the airport; he did not call or even send a card. I resisted for about a week, then I rang him. Well, I did see him again. I weakened when he told me he had intended to send me dried spring flowers from his garden on my resupply. Although he had forgotten, I melted anyway. However, I noticed early on, and accepted, that he was reluctant to get too close. I hoped this might change over time, but it did not. I always knew that many people in the world of adventure, mountaineering and exploration had chosen this way of life because intimacy and society sit badly on them. After all, there is something of that in myself.

Ironically though, a disastrous romance, financial ruin and having things to worry about did keep me occupied after my return. Fiona, who was so happy and content while away and was so looking forward to returning to her many friends, her great job and beautiful home, fell into a terrible depression. She recovered, but it was a reaction she completely failed to anticipate.

The next person I wanted to see was Geoff. Just a few days after my return I was driving up the M6 to visit him. On the pretext of seeing someone else, of course. I was greeted by a different man. Hugging Geoff, you remember, was like putting my arms round a tree, but this time I was enveloped in a huge, bear-like embrace. We stayed up the entire night eating chocolate brownies and talking about the Arctic. I was enchanted to be able to share my unique experience with a man who was, after all, my hero.

There was a period of great novelty. There was no stress, no trying to find a sponsor, no tearing around London forcing marketing directors to see me. No challenges at all, in fact. I had the novelty of reading books, watching TV, going to the pub, seeing friends, things that I had not been able to do literally for five years. I worked nine to five, and I socialized in the evenings. I was happy to live at a slow pace. Inevitably the pleasure wore off. I was unable to take my place at university because of huge debts and so carried on working at the BBC. I was struck by how little I could cope with; even paying a bill was difficult and any decisions were impossible.

For a while, I went back to the chardonnay and tequila days, smoking and partying to fill the void. One day, I met a man who had been partying solidly for forty-eight hours; we were now in the pub drinking schnapps. In the course of an interesting conversation on how to achieve "elation", I explained to him that I lived for excitement and adrenalin highs, and always feared the moments of "come down" afterwards. The rock climbing, adventure travelling or natural beauties of the past had always been enough up till now, but I worried where it would end and whether I would need more and more extreme challenges. Would I eventually find I had to live in war zones, say? When I asked how he got his excitement, he paused, and then replied thoughtfully: "Snort another line of coke, I guess."

It was a sobering moment. I could see how I might use binges as a substitute for real experience. I was drifting again, a rudderless ship. After much thought, I gradually realized that the answer was neither to run away, nor to pretend a pastoral dream like growing basil from a cottage could ever satisfy me, but to turn my drive to the next challenge. I had mistakenly thought that success would bring me contentment; I now understood that what it had given me was not happiness, or status, or glamorous opportunities, but abilities — wonderful tools for life. It was still up to me to use these tools as I decided.

I went on a holiday in Australia. I saw David again and had the benefit of his advice as well as the pleasure of his company. I realized that there was no way I could "follow" walking to the Poles, and any new challenge I should take up would have to be a complete change. Going to university would, indeed, give me a focus, especially as I have always struggled with academic matters, even though I know my feet will always itch to travel. In the last few months, my challenge has been to write this book. When it appears, I shall be delivering a copy in person to my old English teacher at school. It is not as if just by going to the Poles I will suddenly "be brilliant" at anything I turn my hand to; it simply means I have the courage to attempt anything I have a mind to.

In one way or another, we were all changed by our Polar adventures. Steve did marry, and now hopes to recreate Scott's expedition. Grahame had been a partner in a consulting firm that had also financially assisted his Antarctic trip; he resigned and moved into the area of, loosely speaking, life coaching. Veijo and Victor clearly both fancied somewhere warmer, so Veijo departed for a four-month cycle ride around Australia, and Victor is planning to guide a trip to Kilimanjaro. Fiona and Mike turned the initial flatness of being back in England into a mixture of charity work, lecturing and starting to guide "in style" themselves. Justin set up a business called Inner Limits based on adventure sports, whose first major project is a South Pole race, and which also combines exploring human potential and environmental awareness. Indeed, Nikki went on to achieve her dream of being an actress and Jo returned to her beloved Edinburgh to start a new life.

But of all of us, the most intrepid was Oliver the Bear. Since his return from the North Pole he has dived down to the Titanic, climbed Mount Cotopaxi in Ecuador, the world's highest active volcano, and run several road races and marathons. In all, he has now raised well over £100,000 for charity, not even counting his efforts with me.

When I returned to Bosham, the wooden jetty where I had played as a child had now all but disintegrated. Instead of sitting on it to think, I sat beside a rotting wooden post. I tried to take in the magnitude of my eighteen years' adult life, but I knew it would take time and much reflection to digest all the changes I had been through. But I did understand deeply that I had come a long way.

As I was finishing this manuscript, Caroline Hamilton and Ann Daniels, accompanied by Pom Oliver for the first part of the journey — all from the British Women's South Pole expedition — were reaching the North Pole a year after me. They were the first team entirely of women to do so, and they had done it unguided. It was an enormously impressive achievement. For one year Fiona and I had been the only women in the world to have man-hauled to both poles. It was, admittedly, with initial reluctance that I now had to let go of this record a year later. People would of course now be comparing the two expeditions and no doubt mine and Fiona's achievement would pale into insignificance. For a fleeting moment, an unexpected flash of competitiveness struck and I considered that I must do something to beat this — perhaps cross the continent solo and unsupported. Then I realized this was more in the nature of an irrational death-wish. I must never forget why I did the expedition. My trips were a personal journey, a search for the ultimate adventure, to test and challenge my abilities to the absolute limit but ultimately a search for respect, belief in myself and an ability to function confidently in everyday life. And that I have undoubtedly achieved.

The polar community, and, to give him all credit, Mr Five Hats in particular, was very generous in its comments on what I had achieved. But I see the nature of my success is personal, not heroic. I even think that the correct meaning of the word "hero" has changed in the modern world. The explorers of the past were true heroes — Columbus, who discovered a new continent not knowing what he would find, Francis Drake, who sailed round the world, and yes, Scott or Shackleton, who had nothing to rely on beyond their own resources.

Today, we have support for almost any eventuality. With our satellite telephones we can ring anybody, anywhere in the world. GPS means we are never lost.

Aeroplanes and helicopters can evacuate us from just about everywhere. The true heroes of today, for me, are those whose achievements are almost unintentional. They are ordinary people who have behaved courageously or selflessly in situations not of their choosing — the Paddington rail disaster that happened between my two journeys, "September 11", of course, or even something as small as saving a child from running in front of a car.

Fiona and I received a "People of Britain" award for our achievement. I had not ever imagined we would be recognized in this way. My mother sobbed through the whole ceremony. It was a wonderful pleasure to see the pride on her face, but I felt humble and out of place beside people I regarded as real heroes, beside people who had truly done something for others.

I am, therefore, pathologically against being called an "explorer" myself. I was merely an "extreme tourist" and I always want to remember that. At least the fact I raised and continue to raise money for charity can mask the self-indulgence and privilege of my journey. And my polar travels were not made for fame or recognition, they were my own personal journey to come to terms with myself, to succeed at something and leave my old scatty character behind. I had not been able to find myself through my job, or yet in having a life partner and family. I had needed to do so through adventure.

I can see how far I have come if I go and visit Geoff, who continues to guide and is planning to travel solo to the North Pole to crown his career. He has accepted me into his life now. I do not need to pretend I am in the area on a pretext. I know that if we were ever to be on the ice again, we would fall into our old roles. He would look after me, maybe save my life as he did when he pulled me from the lip of the crevasse. But in the town, or the English countryside, I can feel I am his peer, someone whose company he enjoys, and even someone who can go with him to a party or a social function and bring him out of himself. Not until this year did I ask him about his wounding words about me in Antarctica; he had the grace to be embarrassed, but he stayed completely silent. It is very special to me to have won the respect and affection of a person who was on so high a pedestal for me when I met him.

The changes in me have been subtle, not sudden. I am no longer shy, but my contentment and confidence are quiet ones, not qualities I flaunt. I do not feel any need to prove myself any more, and I know this makes me calmer and more pleasant to be around. It is not just the loud ones that can succeed, quiet people can do it too.

Whatever field I turn to next, I will always have the knowledge that I managed to achieve with Fiona, something that no other woman in the world had yet done, and this allows me to believe that any dream can be made reality, if I am determined enough. After all, dreams may be just fun yet they can make life quite extraordinary. My life is perfect, I might say, because I accept it as it is. And while my character is still far from exemplary, were I to write a list of the personality traits I hate in myself today it would be blank, a piece of paper as white and empty as the polar landscapes that so inspired me.

Sponsors & Supporters

Enormous thanks to everyone below for taking the huge gamble in supporting me in my journeys.

South Pole

Club Direct Travel Insurance
Berghaus
Mr Hugh Perkins, Barclays Bank, Chichester
Olympus
The Mackintosh Foundation
The Really Useful Group Ltd
Damart
Rachel and Jon Hardy at Contact
Ski
Asda, Clapham Junction
Bollé
Bert Harkins Racing
Rab Carrington

Helen Allen
Anna and Jonathan
Delph and Cliff Archer
Nikki Ashley and her many friends
Mrs Sue Ashley and all her friends in Tarporley
Rita Aspinall
Olga Baldwin

Christopher Banner
Xandra Barry
Ann Beal
Paul and Sandra Belcher
Neil Bellers
Anne and Jonathan Bental
Anna and Peter Blencowe
Charlie and Vicki Blencowe
Rupert and Lucy Blencowe
Julien Boast
Mr and Mrs Body
Lucy and Ian Brewster
Malcolm and Betty Brown
James Burstow
Christie
Caroline Caley
Kay and Sarah Chadwick
Sandra and David Cheeseman
The Chichester Singers
Margaret Chidell
The wonderful residents of Chidham
Chidham Parish Council
Roger Childe
Jilly Cooper
Lois Cope

325

Geoffrey Cotton
Harold and Dorothy Couch
Michelle Davies
Frank Derry
Richard Deverell
Jenny Doland
John and Kim Dutton
Julia and David Dutton
Jean Field
Mr and Mrs Foulds
Henry and Barbara Fox
Kate and Barry Goodchild
Pamela and Victor Gough
Joanna Hall — Lifestyle
  Management
Mary Hartley
Oliver and Louise Hartley
John and Maggie Haynes
Jerry Johns
Alyson Johnson
Cathy and Johnny Jonas
Christopher Jonas
Richard and Tina Jonas
Jean and Ian Graham Jones
Jess King
Dawne Lemon
Gillian Lipscomb
Gilly Longton
Ali Malone
Marylebone Mountaineering
  Club
Madelaine Mason
Fergus Meiklejohn
Stephen McCrum
Rebecca and Tim Neal
Nutbourne Stores

Helen O'Connell
The Old House at Home
Denise Parkinson
Andy Philipson
Pinewood Nursing Home
Portsmouth Baroque
Juliet and Tony Probert
Jenny and Christopher Rayner
Esther Ross
S. J. Rowitt-Johns
Giles Sarson and Jane Edden
Jean Sell
Caroline and Robin Sherlock
Nigel Shilton
Anthony and Wendy Shore
Vanessa and Noel Simon
Phil "Budge" Smith — it's all
  your fault
Maureen and Terry Staples
Julian Steel
Philip and Liz Stephens
Dianne Taylor
The Three Peak Ramblers
Alan Thresher
Mrs Tolhurst
John and Sorrel Trumper
Mandi Upward
Lynne and Andrew Wallace
Lynn and Angela Wallice
Stephen Wass
Jerry Watkins
Catherine Wigley
Donald White
Barbara Yeatman
Gillian Yeatman
Robin and Raphina Yeld

North Pole

Manugistics UK Ltd
Smirnoff Ice, UDV
Berghaus

Tara Creegan
Danielle from Acorn Estate
Agents
Mrs Anita Harris, Barclays
  Bank, Chichester

Hettie Hope
Damien Martin Hair Designs
Glenn Morris
Sirion Penfold
Mark Rennie
Georgia Veats from Sense
Mark Winfield
Don & Jennifer Worley from
  testsonthenet.com